CW00376049

HAILWOOD to VINCENT

The story of the BSA A65 and A50 motorcycle

1962-1973

Volume II - The Racers

Peter Crawford

Dedication

To Chris Vincent, *The King of Drift* (20th January 1935 – 18th February 2021). He was hard on the track, but generous off it, a legend and inspiration to a generation of sidecar racers, future British Sidecar World Champions among them. Thanks for the memories.

The story of the BSA A65 and A50

Motorcycle 1962-1973

Volume II - The Racers

WIDELINE

Copyright © 2021 Peter Crawford

All rights reserved. No part of this publication may be reproduced, distributed, or transmitted in any form or by any means, including photocopying, recording, or other electronic or mechanical methods, without the the prior written permission of the publisher, except in the case of brief quotations embodied in critical reviews and certain other noncommercial uses permitted by copyright law.

Peter Crawford asserts his right to be identified as the author of this work in accordance with the Copyright, Designs and Patents Act 1988.

Published & designed by **WIDELINE**

www.wideline.co.uk

A catalogue record for this book is available from the British Library

ISBN 978-1-8381336-2-7

Printed in the Czech Republic via Akcent Media Limited

CONTENTS

Foreword

I'm tickled pink to have been asked to write this foreword, since you could say my involvement with these bikes goes way back to when my dear mother first took me to see the TT in 1949. Ernie Lyons, Freddie Frith, John Lockett, these were the sorts of name which stuck in my mind and an ambition was born to race around the TT course one day. I had no idea of how I was going to achieve it, nor the part BSA would play, but life is full of twists and turns and fate would have it that the day I found myself at BSA two Peter Browns applied for the same job, as assistant to Bert Perrigo. I later found out that my namesake got it and I was sent down to Len Crisp, a great big bloke, with bushy eyebrows, who looked at me and said: *"You don't look like a clerk, what are you doing here?* After a discussion of my background I was accepted as a development road tester as fortuitously there was a vacancy occurring at the end of the week. I had met Chris Vincent previously, and he was sort of chief road tester, so I joined him doing hundreds of thousands of miles, rushing around like lunatics and we remained good mates ever since.

In terms of competition, after trials riding and scrambles with very moderate results, at the behest of my wife I had a go at sidecar racing on the grass. This seemed to be my *thing* for a while and I was a member of the team that won the British Championships in 1964, using A10 engines on petrol. Well, Clive Bennett was sort of between me and Bert Perrigo in the management and one day around then he says: *"Peter, you've had your fun and games, I want you to come off the road now and take over twin development"* and was fortunate that Graham Sanders, who was a meticulous fitter, was in the same boat. Initially we prepared engines for Tom Kirby's Terry Vinicombe, Mac Hobson and Mike Hailwood's successful production racer, for Silverstone. But we also prepared Vincent's engine for the Race of the Year at Mallory Park, after which Peter Chapman, his entrant, asked me to accept I suppose what you'd call a donation. This I refused but asked if he would consider assisting with entry fees for road racing. He agreed on condition that I won the first five events he selected for me. Gosh! But thus began a long and successful association and my sidecar road racing career began.

But BSA was a funny old place. One never received acknowledgement for what one did nor expected praise, though I received support from people at all levels throughout the factory to help develop my engines. I had the opportunity to demonstrate this to the hierarchy, an A65 engine producing 85hp and Bob Heath borrowed one of these for a solo, doing quite well as I remember. However the emphasis was centred around the triples, in both Triumph and BSA guises so whilst there was no objection to twins competing in the sidecar classes, solo-wise it was not I suppose in-line with Company policy. Nevertheless, because of BSAs I was able to achieve my ambition of competing in the TT and I would never have been able to do it without them.

I was at BSAs for 14 years and if any of you have not read Peter Crawford's first book *Thunderbolts and Lightning* I earnestly encourage you to do so. Having been in the middle of it all for so long I still learnt an awful lot from the immense research that went into it and there were certainly things included that I didn't know myself. As such I thoroughly recommend this one on the racing side of things too, as I am sure you will find it equally as enjoyable to read, as it was for me to have taken part in those events all those years ago.

Peter Brown
Earlswood - July 2021

Introduction & Acknowledgements

A list of classic competition machines from the golden age of the British motorcycle industry is unlikely to include the BSA A65/50. Which is odd. It won seven British National Sidecar titles, a TT, the American AMA title and plenty of club and district sidecar, flat track and production race titles besides. Sadly those production championships were all before any ACU sanctioned National championship existed, while the final British and American titles both coincided with the collapse of the parent company.

The development of the A65/50 also overlapped initially the BSA Group's evolution of the C15 through to the B50 and subsequently the launch of the Trident/Rocket Three. These factors, combined with BSA's long time focus on off-road competition, conspired against the machine's more active development as a racer, in a classic case of *'what could have been?'* As indicated above, there were still plenty of successes along the way however, which this book covers. What it doesn't cover is the evolution of the A65/A50 in detail, since this is covered in the companion volume *Thunderbolts and Lightning,* covering the road machines. As with Volume I the story is told, as much as possible, through the words and recollections of those directly involved and as such I am indebted to:

Steve Abbott, Dave Abrahams, Dave Aldana, Dave Ashton, Ray Beach, Roy Bevis, Mick Boddice, Mike Bowers, Steve Brown, John Cart, John Cooper, Mel Cranmer, Denis Curtis, Martin Davenport, Clive Davies, Frank Dean, Dave Degens, Norm De Witt, Stuart Digby, Don Emde, Eunice & Hugh Evans, Laurie Evans, Kevin Fletcher, Alistair Frame, Vince French, John Gleed, Dick Greasley, Rod Gould, Randy Hall, Norman Hanks, Roy Hanks, Reg & Irena Hardy, Steve & Lester Harris, Gary Heap, Bob Heath, Dick Herzberg, Frank Hodgson, Bill & Gordon Hogg, Ray Hole, Chris Hopes, George Hopwood, Graham Horne, Mick Horspole, Alex Jorgensen, Ray Knight, Pete Krukowski, Bill Lindsay, Chris Lodge, Malcolm Lucas, Michael Martin, Les, Dave & Ron Mason, Dick Mann, Brian Mee, Gerry Millward, Jody Nicholas, Tony Price, Ted Reading, Jim Rice, Nigel Rollason, Terry Rudd, Martin Russell, Bryan Rust, Malcolm Scott, Peter Seager-Thomas, Colin Seeley, Larry Simons, Pat Slinn, Dave Smith, Ron Smith, Tony Smith, Malcolm Stanley, Ian Thomson, Andrew Thorburn, Rollo Turner/Panther Publishing, Chris Vincent, Ken Vogl, Clive Wall, Mick Ward, Colin Washbourne, Derek Whalley, Derek Wood and Eddie Wright.

In terms of photographs and images I'd like to thank many of the above, who have assisted with contributions from their personal archives, along with Dave Friedman/The Don Emde Collection, Chris Sammons/Darley Archive, the generous Bill Snelling of FoTTofinders, the Cooper family, Tom Clark, Chris Killip, Mike Richards, Jayne Skyman at the Mortons Media archive, Herl photography, Dan Mahoney, Mirko Herzog at the Technischesmuseum Austria, Bill Riley, Mark Upham at British Only Austria for access to the Peter Howdle archive, the ever helpful Steve Foden at the BSA Owners Club for many original images taken on behalf of BSA's Reg Dancer and David Lloyd, the VMCC archive, David Brown at MCA, Bill Millburn, Nigel Clarke, Ian Gittins, George Spence/Coventry VOC, Dominique Bresson, Lee Dove, David Cutmore, Derek Jarvis, James Callis, Jim Todd, John Hartell, Ann Sheridan, Phil Ridley, Barry Gollings, Mike Carling, John Churchill, Bill Allen, John

Lancaster, Spencer Oliver, Ron Aitchie, Ian Waugh, Bryan Hands, Les Hurt, Martin Clarke and James Stensel at Bonhams. In regards to photos and images, as with volume I, I make no excuses for using these irrespective of quality, since events covered in this book took place over 50 years ago as did the vast majority of the photography. In cases where the hard copy images have come through third parties, or carried photographer details, every effort has been made to contact the original photographer or current copyright holder.

In terms of quoted material, apologies for those who may recognise some from *Thunderbolts and Lightning*, but a degree of duplication has proved unavoidable to ensure completeness for those reading this book in isolation. I'd also like to thank for permissions to quote from Ed Youngblood, Gregory Pearson, Mick Duckworth, Caroline Smoogen - for permission to quote from the unpublished second volume of her father Roland Pike's biography, Octopus Publishing for permission to quote from *Sidecar Championship* by George O'Dell, Jacqui Harris at the Bauer Archives, Tim Hartley at www.mortonsarchive.com for permission to quote from both their current and legacy publications, Mark Hoyer at *Cycle World* and Liza Miller at Re-cycle Motorcycle Garage for use of additional Jim Rice podcast content. I'd also like to thank Nick Jeffery and Pat Crawford for proofing and suggestions.

I am particularly grateful to 1968 British sidecar champion Peter Brown. Peter worked extensively on A65/50 engine development at BSA, in both Small Heath and later at Umberslade Hall and shared with me his memories, photos and test documents extensively over a five year period. It was as a result of this, just before Christmas 2020 when COVID restrictions briefly allowed, that I called in on Chris Vincent. He was due to sign a few copies of Volume I, but I also wanted to say that although his name would appear in the title of this volume would he mind me asking Peter to write the foreword? *"Brownie? Yeah, actually he knows more than I've ever forgotten. He could build a good engine. For the unit twins, he was the chap."* As such I'm glad he has been able to oblige.

Peter Crawford
July 2021

Chapter 1

Testing the water - 1962/3

John Harris at the 1962 ISDT in Austria. The A50 proved far more capable than anticipated though it was largely mothballed subsequently. With the C15/B40 to hand for off-road sport the A50 was surplus to requirements

The A65 and A50 were mildly tuned machines built by a company which didn't go road racing. They were also launched at a time of stagnating UK sales. The potential of the American market hadn't yet been fully understood and the new unit twin A65 complemented rather than replaced BSA's A10, and in a junior role at that. It was true that production of the 500cc A7 was curtailed with the launch of the A50, but the Gold Star single remained available in the States for another two years as BSA's performance 500. As such there were no great sporting aspirations for the new unit twins.

When it came to competition BSA were firmly entrenched in off-road sport, which was reflected in the management of the *'Comp Shop'*, as the Competition Department was universally known. In 1962 the current incumbent was Brian Martin, a skilled trials rider whose background mirrored that of his predecessors Dennis Hardwicke and Bert Perrigo, who had similar off-road expertise. Martin also had two problems, both of which would impact on the future competition aspirations of the A65/50. The first was entirely positive, as with the enlargement of the 250cc C15 into the 350cc B40 it looked like BSA had a potential, off-road, Gold Star replacement on their hands. The second problem was far more difficult to deal with. As while BSA was often touted as *'The largest motorcycle manufacturer in the world'* it scarcely had a Competition Department at all.

Graham Horne, Arthur Crawford and Jeff Smith *were* the Competition Department in 1962. Staffing would increase over the 1960s but initially all work on the twins was carried out elsewhere

Graham Horne: Initially when I joined the Comp Shop there was just the workshop foreman Arthur Crawford and myself. BSA had had a big cut back and got rid of works riders so there was just Smithy left. Jeff Smith. They'd had such a big cut back. The Taft brothers were still with them, but they didn't have a big rider line up. It built up again with Banksy (John Banks) and Dave Nichol, Keith Hickman and John Lewis, once Smithy was World Champion it all built up again. So '64-65 it started to gather momentum and Smithy was my boss. But I was the only road racer amongst them and originally the workshop was just part of a row of old buildings. You had the Comp Shop, Engine Development, Experimental, etc. Though later on, towards when it all finished, you had road racing and the off-road side all under one roof. So obviously when the two Shops were brought together there was a bit more of a road racing focus, but obviously with a bias, as they were all sidecar racers.

But I think back then BSA were more than happy with the results they were getting from the motocross and of course trials. I was road racing mad and I remember one of the guys hearing Brian Martin say – this was before BSA went back road racing – it was *MCN*, a Wednesday, in the summer and he said *"I'm fed up with all this road racing."* But, of course, as it all developed he had to take an interest in it. It was his job and he was very good to me. A lovely man. I rode the 500-miler '64, on my own bike. I rode it to work again on the Monday and I used to keep it in the Comp Shop. Well Brian Martin said; *"That bike is not to move until you've put a new tyre on it!"* Because it was down to the canvas, as that's how we'd finished. And the first year I'd ridden the Manx Brian gave me a works 350 Gold Star engine. I mean they were surplus by then, they were finished with them, but it was still a works engine and I didn't get it on merit, but as I was a good lad. I did the hours, worked hard and worked long, so he gave me this works 350 engine. But getting back, '62-63, there was just the three of us in the Comp Shop. Arthur Crawford, Smithy and me.

Next door it wasn't very different in Engine Development either, though ironically here there was a greater history of road racing involvement.

Graham Horne and light-weight 350 Gold Star, featuring the Comp Shop engine. Oddly, later, Horne only infrequently raced an A65, preferring the 250 class instead, winning the Midland Championship on a DMW before moving on to a Yamaha TD1

Ray Beach: I used to be a paperboy and deliver down what they called the Radleys. American style prefabs. And one of the guys who lived there was a bloke called Cyril Halliburn. He worked at BSA and was in fact in charge of the Gold Star shop. He said: *"What are you gonna do when you leave school?"* And when I said: *"Be an electrician"* he said: *"Rubbish. Electricians are two a penny. You're going to come to the BSA and be an apprentice. Get your dad to come and see me."* The next thing I knew I'd started, at 15, 1952-3. You did 6 months' probation and when you'd done your time, they'd decided if they were going to take you on. You had to go in with your parents. You had to put your fingers on this seal and say: *"This is my word and deed"* to promise to see your six years out. I started in the drawing office, then piston inspection and main inspection and the next thing was they said: *"You're going into Engine Development."* It seems Cyril Halliburn had got onto Rolland Pike and said to take me on, as Pike was in charge of all engine types and I was put on the twins. A7 and A10. Anyhow Chris Vincent was in the Experimental bike shop doing road testing and he asked me one day: *"How heavy are you? Do you want to be my passenger for grass track racing?"* We went up to this farm in Knowle, which was a well-known track, but his Gold Star engine was coughing and banging and missing so I said: *"This is rubbish, you'll never win anything with that. Get a twin, get some torque."* He said he'd not got one, so I said to the boss: *"I want to buy an engine"* and Pikey says: *"I'll see what I can find."* And on this A10 I got for him Chris won everything.

But the company was going through a real rough patch financially in the late '50s, and they got rid of a hell of a lot of people out of Engine Development. There were some real good people there. There were some real good machinists, we'd got shapers and lathe operators and all sorts in there. And when all those people went there were only three 'adults' left, as the rest of us were apprentices.

3

Racing the pre-unit twins

While Triumph and Norton toyed with full-on racing versions of their pre-unit designs - with the T100 Grand Prix and Domiracer respectively – BSA never really campaigned theirs actively in the UK. This was not entirely surprising given the dominance of their Gold Star single and BSA's historical preoccupation with off-road sport, where the singles excelled.

This is not to say that they were not raced however. They were used more extensively on the club racing scene than is acknowledged, with Pete *PK* Davies being a prime example. While he is now better known for racing a Laverda Jota during the 1970s he started on an A10, winning Midland Championships in the early 1960s before either the advent of a National production racing championship or the unit twins.

Mississippi rider Bill Tucker on a typical late '50s American competition A10

Due to their engine characteristics the 650cc A10 and 500cc A7 engines were also ubiquitous as sidecar machines on the road, with many finding their way on to the track. This was most notably in the hands of Chris Vincent, who used them in both grass track and road racing, taking an A7 to victory at the Isle of Man TT in 1962 and winning the ACU stars (the forerunner to the British points-based title) in both 1961 and 1963. The factory also wheeled out solo examples for the annual 500-miler too – the UK's premier two rider production race - though not with the same enthusiasm or level of preparation put in by other factories. Triumph and Royal Enfield in particular hired in top professional riders on specially prepared and tuned machines. BSA did not and it was much the same with the Clubman TT, where BSA had little interest in the twins given the Gold Star's domination.

> **Roland Pike:** In 1952 BSA had hoped to provide a challenge in the 500cc Clubmans with an all alloy twin engine which would be promoted as a *Gold Star Twin* if successful. However the regulations prevented their use as it was not yet a production model. A few standard A7 500cc twins were built to Clubmans specifications, they pushed out 36-38bhp which was about the same as the production Manx Norton, but in fact they were unreliable and had a peaky performance. Also, they did not handle as well as the single.[1]

They may have been lagging behind the singles but the twins were more popular and affordable in America where they were selling in increasing numbers and where competition disciplines were also different. As such Pike was tasked with producing machines to promote these road models and did so with great success.

> **Roland Pike:** I was sent back to America in 1953 for Daytona, during this visit I listened carefully to what the Dealers, their riders, Tommy McDermott, Warren Sherwood, Gene Thiessen and Al Gunter had to say and went back to the factory and explained to them that BSA had to produce a bike entirely for the American competition market. As a result I was given the go ahead to produce a prototype.

An A7 racer prepared in Birmingham for Daytona, with a Gold Star version to the rear. The A7s were incredibly successful machines but BSA very quickly lost interest in their development for competition

The twin engine in the meantime had been developed to give more power and reliability using an alloy head and a hot cam, the power was available from about 5,250rpm to 7,250rpm, but it was not so tractable as the single, although it gave more power and was 2mph faster on the timing strip. Running side by side the single would reach the end of the timing strip first, although finishing the measured mile at a lower speed.

We went to Daytona in 1954 with eight rigid frame lightweight racers, four with singles and four twins. Alf Childs wanted an extra bike for Bobby Hill, all we had available was a 500cc twin in a Clubman type spring frame, ironically this was the winning machine! We collected five of the first eight places, the best BSA ever did at Daytona. The AMA at this time were very strict with compression ratios, the maximum allowed was 8:1, we were allowed 1mm over-size pistons, so naturally all these bikes had the extra few cc capacity (508cc) and it did give a wee bit more power. Later on the AMA allowed up to 9:1 compression ratio, which was more helpful to the twins than the singles (but) by 1958 the factory was not giving much support to the American racers.[2]

That tailing off coincided with a general downturn in BSA's racing programme and increased focus on the newer C15/B40 as the way forward in off-road competition. As such any future road racing involvement with the twins would be down to the potential of the new unit models, which were then in the early stages of development.

There was David Harris, who was a scrambler and did quite well. Bob Trigg who went to work for Yamaha and ended up with a big office in Belgium. There was Paul Taft who was also well known in the scrambling world, me, Alan Sandilands who was one of the senior people and Reg Wilkes, who did the Gold Stars. So when Pikey went – he fell out over the MC1 racer project – and just before I went to the army for National Service, they brought in Colin Washbourne. But all the main adults had left and in the end it was about three blokes and all us apprentices running Engine Development!

Colin Washbourne: BSA was a hot bed of activity in the 1950s, but then it all fell away. My gaffer - this was 1961 – Bill Johnson, was not unfortunately a well man, and a very difficult person to get on with. BSA kept him on, but he should never have been in the position he was really and when Pikey left there was nothing much new coming on stream. The Gold Star was finished and Reg Wilkes was doing all the development on the 250. Ray Beach and myself, as apprentices, were doing all the twins work in Engine Development and I assembled the first A50, straight off the drawing board.

Ray Beach: In June 1961 I went back to BSA and they said; *"We're just going to bring this unit construction A50/A65 out. See what you can do with the 650 version."* So I did, though all the initial development was down to just me and one apprentice called Eddie Graham. I never got into the model names as for me it was just a case of testing the engine and improving it as best I could. As Bill Johnson, Roland Pike's replacement, would go off with the results to see Bert Perrigo, as they'd decide if they thought any improvement was worth doing or not. If you made a big improvement, they pushed it in to production, but on Harris' bike it took ages working out and testing where to put the siamesed pipe. This was about torque of course.

The reason the pipe was about torque was that it was for a bike that John Harris would ride in the 1962 ISDT, in September, at Garmisch Partenkirchen in Germany. The A50 seemed a uniquely unsuitable bike for off-road competition but it ran faultlessly, picked up a gold medal for cleaning all five days of the event and helped the British team to second overall behind the victorious Czechs. It was an interesting aside, and a fairly typical way for BSA to test the water, since the rolling chassis was a Gold Star parts-bin special. But as had been the case with the A7/10 the real push for performance development came from the United States.

Studio shot of what would ultimately be a far more important off-road competition A50 than the ISDT bike

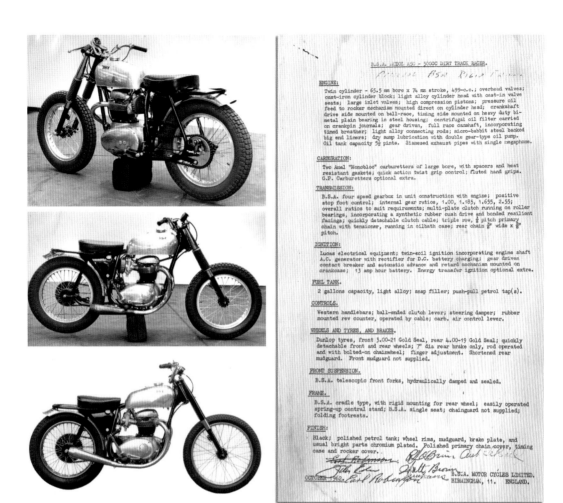

The October 1962 communiqué outlining the specification for an AMA compliant A50 flat tracker, as requested by BSA's American wing, along with slightly different mock-up photos for the homologation machine

The July before Harris' ISDT result a Gold Star tuned by Al Gunter had won the Ascot ½-mile, taking BSA's only AMA National win of the 1962 American season. Matchless also managed a win with Dick Mann, while Triumph won a couple too. The other eleven races were a Harley-Davidson whitewash but it hadn't always been like this. BSA had won big time a few years previously, with twins as well as singles and those Gold Star singles were now becoming out of date. The Americans were hoping that the A50 would be the answer – since 500cc was the maximum capacity allowed at the time for AMA sanctioned flat track and road racing events – so for homologation purposes they required a *'factory'* specification, on paper at least, with photographic evidence that such machines actually existed. As such a flat track A50 was put together at Small Heath though it is not clear whether the machine was ever shipped. Probably not, since no real performance tuning had been carried out in Birmingham by this point and the American importers were already well ahead of the game.

Though better known now as a Harley-Davidson tuner Tom Sifton had done great things with BSA engines for Everett Brashear in 1958, leading to an impressive 4th place in the

National Championship. As such he was asked to produce a cam-shaft for the new engines, though BSA tested the water cautiously and with as little fanfare as possible. Gold Stars were wheeled out by the BSA runners in the first National of 1963 at Daytona, for only middling results. But in the Novice class new boy Ed Moran took a Herb Neas tuned A50 to the win. It was a promising result, particularly as Sifton's analysis was that they were running the wrong cam, the item installed having only been tested on an A65. His assessment was probably correct, as his ideas for an improved exhaust system very closely adhered to what the BSA factory also discovered later - that essentially the unit twins ran best with shorter, stubbier, mega-phones than the longer tapers most favoured by other manufacturers.

The cam and pipe design issues were speculation at this point. But what was clear was as the twin-carb cylinder-head used by Moran was a one-off special BSA had to make a similar factory part available and soon. As such both A65 and A50 twin-carb cylinder- heads were introduced in 1964, albeit only in the States initially.

Ed Moran and Tom Sifton's views (below) on his bike's performance

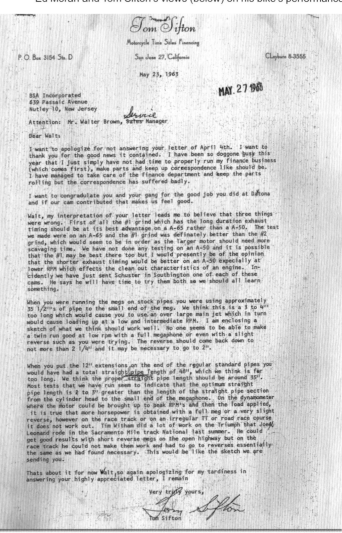

The Vincent phenomenon - 1964

Chris Vincent on his A7 at Cadwell Park. Formidable in 1963, once on his A65 he was unbeatable in 1964

While the new engines clearly had potential, as complete machines it would be hard to think of models less suited to racing than the original A50 and A65 Star twins. Bulbous, under-braked and uninspiring to look at this all changed in 1964, for American buyers at least. Competition versions called the Spitfire Hornet (A65) and Cyclone (A50) were released and while BSA's Comp Shop were preoccupied with helping Jeff Smith defeat Rolf Tibblin in the 1964 World Motocross Championship, there was interest in Engine Development. Since staff there already had some familiarity with performance tuning BSA's earlier twins.

Ray Beach: We built a 500 short-stroke, with a special one-piece crankshaft. It used to run up to 8,000 rpm, machined from solid, with a Torrrington bearing in place of the plain bearing and an end-feed. But of course, the management rejected it as they were against anything revolutionary, or new, so I bought it and had it in my road bike. Then Vincent wanted it and said: *"We're going to go road racing"*. He borrowed a frame off Johnny Warren, a farmer. A Featherbed frame and we grafted the twin into it. And he did quite well. In fact, he did very well. The first time we went to Oulton Park Bill Boddice came up and said: *"What the hell are you going to do on that?"* But he started doing so well that in the end they used to make him the scratch man in the handicap races. They used to let everyone else go and he'd be held back. But he'd invariably catch them all, and break race or lap records. But I wasn't passenger-ing. At Mallory he got me to have a go, but hanging off the back with chains whirring about? No way! So, I just did his engines.

As mentioned, there was a hiatus for Beach, caused by National Service, so Colin Washbourne took over at BSA and was himself quickly roped into Chris Vincent's A10/7 racing activities.

Colin Washbourne: The 1962 TT, I built that engine. It wasn't standard, but it was all parts you could get over the counter. Just well put together and tuned. The Achilles heel was the crankshaft, the plain bush, as Chris used to rev those things. I told him he didn't need to rev it so high and he did nurse it in the end, at the TT, when he knew he was winning. But we took it to Belgium and it blew up. I was in the chair at the time and a conrod broke. The cap broke. As I was passenger with him at the time - as well as being mechanic and dogsbody - to save money like, 'cos we were privateers don't forget. There was no help from BSA at all, except we could get parts. But that changed after the TT win.

Chris Vincent: Roland Pike, he was such a genuine chap. Really ace. These Steve Lancefields, Pettys, Bearts and the like they thought they had these secrets, but Pikey he'd talk to me all the time. You could ask him anything. The first one he helped me with was my Gold Star, but the engine was faster than the chassis and by '57 I'd gone to a twin. At places like High Wycombe it was 90mph down the straight and by the time I'd gone road racing I was running five A7 engines. Of course when they blew up they destroyed themselves completely, they were just scrap. If I brought one back to the factory they'd be lucky to get a crankshaft out really, but Pikey would help me out. I've got the old receipts here: *"Engine with carb and magneto 24 quid."* Usually it was fiddles like that he'd help with. This one says: *"Rigid obsolete frame 3 quid"* but it was a Daytona frame, a 531 tube sifbronze welded rig. Never made them like that for production. I'd see these things down in the surplus store and the gaffer would say: *"I'll see what I can do for you!"* But when I won the TT they announced it over the speakers at BSA and the whole factory came to a standstill. That's what I was told anyway. I got telegrams from all the Directors and afterwards old Bert Perrigo says to me: *"We're going to cut you loose. We're going to pay your wages, you can have anything you want. We're going to leave you here in this workshop and you can do what you want, we'll just pay your wages."* You couldn't have a better deal and they never pestered me with a single-carb A65. But as soon as they got a twin-carb running Ray got it to pump out 65hp. They came to see me and said: *"This has got to come to an end. It's not doing us any good you running the old A10/7 when the A65s are out. We want to do your engines for you."*

A youthful Vincent in conversation with future team mate Tommy Robb - a story for later years

Well if there was ever an offer that at first you thought was wonderful, this was it. But it wasn't. Bert says to me: *"There's a bit in the budget for you. If you see Brian Martin he'll give you some."* A waste of time that was, as while they were thick they weren't barmy. I never saw a penny and when I was running A7s I had five 500cc and three 650cc engines. All prepared by me and my mates, all of them more or less to a different specification. But then BSA did me *one* engine. *One bleeding engine.* And worse than that they only had one cylinder-head. They only had one in the whole place. So after every race we had to take it off and take it back to the factory!

The A65 engine

A much modified engine from George O'Dell's early 1970s racing outfit. Early race engines were very standard however

The most remarkable feature of the A65/50 was probably the fact that it didn't have any. In a period defined by Edward Turner's seminal, vertical push-rod twin, the A65/50 was briefly the newest example, indeed the first Unit 650. But that was it. It did have a few advantages over its peers however. It was physically smaller, being more compact and shorter in height, with its greatest asset being a very rigid top-end. This lacked the myriad joint faces, exterior plumbing and gaskets of its main adversaries, which were of course ideal attributes for a sidecar racing motor. It also had an extremely good combustion chamber, which matched with its unique – in A65 form – short-stroke motor allowed for big valves and high compression ratios, without recourse to pistons with Himalayan-profile crowns. The A50 was hindered by having the same crankshaft as the A65 however, which meant reducing the bore drastically to achieve 500cc. This condemned it to traditional long-stroke dimensions and hindered its future development as a real competition engine.

If the engine had a generic weakness it was the plain timing-side bearing, which was probably carried over from the A7/10 range as BSA never envisaged the units as competition engines. They had the Gold Star and B40 for that as BSA didn't *do* road racing. Luckily though, when Small Heath introduced the twin-carburetor models they also phased in the perfect, 68-473, *Spitfire* camshaft. This cam was soon fitted to all 654cc and twin-carb 500cc models and while these appeared in numerous different guises – Lightning, Hornet, Wasp, Cyclone, Firebird, etc – the only real difference between any of them, between 1964 and 1972, were piston compression ratios. As, with the exception of a close ratio gearbox, BSA never offered any race/performance engine parts for the twins.

The same engine showing a remote Lucas magneto fitted to the rear. Americans similarly mistrusted the standard points, but preferred a front mounted Hunt mag instead

Ray Beach: It's true. Chris was the first out on an A65 and the only one out. Well we'd only got this one twin-carb cylinder-head, so I used to borrow it of a weekend and put it on his sidecar. If we'd ever blown it up I'd have been in a right mess, as it really was the only one we had.

Going Racing

They needn't have worried. A test engine was installed in Vincent's outfit for the season opening meeting at Mallory Park on Sunday 22nd March 1964, though in truth it was not high on his list of priorities. Vincent was running a BMW in Grand Prix by now, as well as a variety of solos, so the engine had not even been run in the bike before. Vincent thought the power might be a bit more than his existing A10; "*According to the figures taken on the brake. Call it 60-plus bhp at a peak of 7,250rpm*" but that was probably speculation.

While still working on the A65 in the paddock he found time to go out on the Hannah Honda CR93 in the first round of the British 125cc Championship, to beat similarly mounted Derek Minter and Billy Ivy. In fact, he won relatively easily, and in a style which would become familiar to anyone who witnessed his sidecar victories over subsequent years. Starting badly, he carved his way through the field to be fifth after three laps and two laps

Chris Vincent with what looks like John Robinson in the chair. Robinson would go on to win World Championships with Fritz Scheidegger in 1965 and 1966, on the quality of BMW machinery which was never available to Vincent

later he was gone. It was then on to the experimental A65 outfit, which had never been taken round a race track before, to break the lap record at an average speed of 78.56 mph, with a fastest lap of 80.20mph. Established stars Pip Harris, Bill Boddice and Colin Seeley must have wondered what had hit them. None even got close to the new BSA so it was no surprise that Chris Vincent appeared emblazoned across the front cover of the following Wednesday's *Motor Cycle News* under the headlines: *"Two records for Vincent."*

The following Sunday Vincent won again at Snetterton. He then won four races at the Mallory Park Race of the Year meeting on 12th April and the British championship round at Brands on the 19th. Before winning again at Snetterton on 26th, where he also broke Mike Hailwood's 125cc lap record for good measure.

The Season opener 1964. No one knew what to expect of the new A65 but their worst fears were very soon confirmed

The dominance of Vincent's BSA justified a huge write-up and technical analysis in the April 29th edition of *Motor Cycle News*, which also featured a boxed summary of his first six finishes of the season. OK, he'd had two DNFs due to water in the electrics, but out of his six race finishes he'd taken six wins with a lap record at every circuit.

Built to win races not beauty contests. A studio shot of the early Vincent A65 *kneeler*. Like many, Vincent started with a cut down Featherbed Norton frame, but was soon experimenting with every aspect of the machine's design. Though not as gifted an engineer as others he was an innovator in many areas. Though in truth it was his riding style which got him his victories. Crowds were wowed and adversaries in awe of his ability to drift his outfit at will, during the period when engine power first started to seriously outstrip tyre adhesion

Chris Vincent was instrumental in testing many early A65 upgrades, either officially or in his spare time on the race track. There weren't many solo machines which could wheelie up Cadwell Park's famous *'mountain'* in 1964, let alone a sidecar. Winning at the Louth & District International meeting, 13th September, 1964

At this point Vincent was off to France for his main focus of the season, the World Championship. He left his 654cc BSA outfit behind and was more concerned about his BMW since he was due to race the following Whit Monday at Brands Hatch too, where only 500cc machines were eligible. He returned to be confronted with an un-tested A50 engine however, rather than a BMW.

Ray Beach: Vincent had got a BMW on the continent but was not doing very good. So, Bert Perrigo came to me one day and said: *"How much power are you getting out of that A50 now?"* It was about 50bhp, so he said: *"I'm gonna get his outfit sent down here, so you and his mechanic - who was Colin Washbourne by now - graft the A50 in and I'll send him a telegram and say we're taking it down to Brands Hatch"*. We worked all night, grafted it in, then put it all in the back of the ambulance which Chris had converted as a transporter and took it down to Brands Hatch. When he arrives he says: *"What's this? An A50. Is it any good?"* I told him 50hp, so he goes out in practice but comes back moaning about the clutch slipping and this being wrong and that being wrong. But I did some adjustments and of course he went out and saw off most of the works BMWs. On an A50. Anyway, this lot at Brands Hatch said: *"That's a 650."* He had to strip it but of course it was just a 500. It was down to the kneeler outfit - the way he could get round the corners on that thing was unbelievable - and of course those good, reliable, engines. Once he had those, the A65 and A50 all reliable and sorted, he was away.

Away he was, as while Pip Harris' Rennsport BMW had beaten the sleep-deprived Vincent for the victory at Brands Hatch, the 500cc BSA had in turn beaten the similarly exotic machines of Fritz Scheidegger and Colin Seeley, Scheidegger's having just won the French Grand Prix. It demonstrated that not only could a 650 BSA engine beat the German unit, but the 500cc version too. There then followed a pattern of monotonously predictable results, of Vincent winning on his 250 Aermacchi and 125 Honda - over a *Who's Who* of British solo motorcycle sport including Billy Ivy, Derek Minter, Alan Shepherd and Tommy Robb – but in turn having mixed results on his BMW in comparison to those on his A65. This was with one notable exception for the A65, the non-championship invitation race at Mallory Park on July 12th. Where a new BSA employee directly benefited.

Norman Hanks: I went to BSA in 1964 as a Development Tester. It was mileage, a perfect occupation for a 19 year-old and with my father's connections with Clive Bennett and people like that I went straight in on the 650s. Which put a few people's noses out, as in them days you had to work your way up. The Bantams to the C15s and so on. But with the 650 riders there was always someone in hospital and Peter Brown had already moved from road testing into Development by then. Chris had just stopped using the A10 so at Mallory lent me his old engine. You picked your place out of a bag and he came up to me after and said: *"What you got then chap?"* As he called everyone chap. He was never very talkative. I said: *"21. I'm right at the back."* So, he says: *"OK. You better have this then"*. It was 2 or something like that, which he'd pulled out, so I thought; *"I'll take that!"* This A10 engine was as good as it got really, as he'd won all those races on it the year before. So, I was in the lead going round and round, but kept looking back at the hairpin, seeing him getting closer and closer and he passed me with a lap and a half to go. But then out of the hairpin a big flame came out of that siamesed pipe he used to use and he stopped. A push-rod had jumped out, or bent, or something, so I won. On his engine. And it was a televised meeting too!

Everyone knew when the Hanks team were around. Race transport circa 1964

It spoke volumes that Vincent could voluntarily take a back-row position like that and this confidence was repeated on 3rd August when he turned up on his BSA A50 rather than BMW, to win the British Championship at Oulton Park. A one-off, 500cc event until 1966, when a points system was introduced.

He then won at Brands Hatch on 16th August, Cadwell Park on 13th September and Brands Hatch again on the 20th. The big news here being that for the first time all season he *failed* to win, in a race in which his A65 reached the finish.

> *"Fireworks in the sidecar races came right at the finish of the four-lap handicap just as Chris Vincent seemed all set to zoom over everybody and take his second win of the meeting. From the scratch mark he had flashed into third after three laps and was all set for the kill when 100yards from the line his famous 650 BSA burst apart in a great sheet of flame, sending its shattered internals all over the track!"*[3]

Ray Beach: That A65 he had, he did a whole season on and it lasted well. With just taking the head off and grinding the valves in now and again. The bottom end I just left alone, running ordinary bushes on the timing-side, but he was in this scratch race, the handicap race, down at Brands and they let him off last of course. He was passing people left, right and centre as they were coming down to the finish and as he approached the line the bloody thing blew itself to smithereens. I remember Fred Hanks coming over saying: *"Does this piston belong to you?"* holding up this piece of alloy, as there were bits of this and that all over the place. But they were fundamentally a good engine already by '64, as we did loads of races that year without even touching it.

As the season came to a close Vincent won again at Oulton Park on Saturday 3rd October, but things proved more challenging the following Sunday, further south, at Brands Hatch when Vincent crashed his 125.

Chris Vincent: That Honda was the best bike I ever had. Bill Hannah gave it to me and said Bill Smith would supply any spares, but it never needed anything. I rode it two years round Europe and England and I only fell off it that once. Fell off leading Billy Ivy at Brands, last race of the year. I threw it away. I was leading the championship and chucked it away as I think it was double points or something that day.

As a result Vincent needed hospitalisation, but a doctor's inspection approved a delayed departure to the hospital until he'd completed the sidecar race. He duly won it, then retired to the ambulance, having secured £100 and the Brands Hatch shield.

It was a fitting end to a hugely successful debut season for the A65 and one which was wildly beyond reasonable expectation. Prior to March no one had even raced a unit twin in the UK. But by October it had won the ACU Star, broken the lap record at every circuit at which it had competed and had arguably won every race in which it had crossed the line – since as pointed out by Ray Beach at Brands on 20th September, the engine never reached it! The A50 showed some promise also, as it had actually won the British Championship at Oulton Park. These were astounding achievements but intriguing too, since Vincent's results on the BSA were far better than those on his BMW. There were mitigating circumstances here - Vincent's BMW was not as good nor as new as those of the Germans against which he competed in Grands Prix - but the layman was not to know this and BSA themselves presumably didn't care. All the buying and racing public saw were the headlines. Vincent could be beaten on a BMW, while he was invisible on an A65. Unwittingly BSA had a winner on their hands, but there was one factor which conspired against the A65 in 1965. A World Title to better Vincent's British equivalent.

While the threat of closure had hung over the Comp Shop at the end of '63, Jeff Smith had soldiered on in motocross, on a new 420cc B40 derivative, and in 1964 it all came good. Smith won the World Title and received huge publicity off the back of increased TV coverage. BSA Chairman Harry Sturgeon was fully behind the motocross effort and directed that every effort should be made to both retain the World Title in 1965 and make customer, production, versions of Smith's bike available to the general public. It was great news for BSA but as highlighted by Graham Horne, given the Comp Shop's meager resources it came at the expense of investment in the A65/50. It wasn't all doom and gloom however. The blue touch paper had been lit and while Vincent's was the sole A65 on the British grid in 1964 this would change in 1965. The A65L Lightning was launched in the UK too, meaning that the British public would have access to the previously *"export-only"* twin-carburetor cylinder-head, for both leisure and sporting purposes.

A young Brian Martin among a sea of Comp Shop Gold Stars. Once he was Department Manager it would be his responsibility to oversee the replacement of the pre-unit single motors with the new unit singles and manage development of the C15 and B40 derivatives. It left little room for the A65 and A50 in his plans

Chapter 3

Hailwood's Hutch - 1965

Tony Smith *'Mr A65'* for much of the 1960s, riding under the Dick Rainbow, Tom Kirby and then official BSA banners

The combination of the US market 68-473 camshaft and twin-carburetor cylinder-head did not initially create a deluge of Vincent-clones. Sidecar teams were almost exclusively self-funding and the prospect of buying and cannibalising a brand-new Lightning from a dealer's showroom wasn't really on. It was different if you had a sponsor however, so it came as no surprise when *MCN* reported in February that: *"Tom Kirby is coming into sidecar sponsorship with Terry Vinicombe. Another plan Tom has is to enter a couple of lively A65 twins in the Thruxton 500 Production race."*[4] Those engines weren't quite ready at the beginning of the season as the official Dispatch Records indicated:

"23/3/65 A65 Lightning. Engine only on loan. Tuned for racing. To Mr T W Kirby of Hornchurch Essex. 23/4/65 Engine 3818D to Tom Kirby. 11/5/65 A50DC 593. A50 engine only, plus pair of megaphones. To T Kirby"[5]

The delay was due to BSA preparing a limited run, UK-only, homologation-special early in 1965. 200 Lightning Clubman models, to meet ACU PR (production racing) eligibility rules. The machines were subsequently prioritised for those dealers intending to race them, with Ware dealership Dick Rainbow Motorcycles right at the head of the queue.

Tony Smith; I took delivery of the very first one and I was so keen to do well that we bought one for racing and one for the road. It was the only way to do the job properly. I literally lived on it. Dick bought the race bike and I bought the road bike. I went to the factory on the Wednesday to collect the race bike, as I had an entry at Brands for the opening race of the season, March 1965. They said they'd have one ready, but it wasn't, so Fred Green - the Sales Manager - promised they'd deliver it Friday. Dick said: *"You better have your bosses there, my boy's gonna win"*. I hadn't even sat on the bike! Not only that but I hadn't raced for six months and it was raining. Can you imagine, a brand-new bike, unknown in the wet, Brands Hatch on the long circuit? Anyway, they dropped the flag and I disappeared. I never looked back and apparently at the end of the race there was no one else in sight. I thought; *"This bike's pretty damn good!"* and that season I had a hard time not to win.

That first victory for Tony Smith and the Lightning Clubman was on 21ˢᵗ March at the Brands Hatch REDeX Trophy meeting, where Dave Degens won the unlimited and 350 races, Derek Minter the 500 and 250 races, and Billy Ivy the 125cc event. This was no club race and Smith took the production race victory from established performers. It was a sensational start for the new solo model and Chris Vincent backed it up with win number two in the sidecars.

Tony Smith looking more suited for a road ride than a race, prior to his first Brands Hatch outing of 1965

He'd won at Mallory on the 7ᵗʰ too and then did the same at Snetterton on 21ˢᵗ before *MCN* came up with one of its better headlines at Mallory Park's Sidecar Race of the Year - *'Mods to Rockers'*. Pathé News covered the 'Victory-from-the-jaws-of-defeat' story too, which initially saw Vincent cruise across the line, qualifying for the final with a dead engine. Two BSA Engine Development staff then frantically tried to track down the problem.

Peter Brown: It had gone onto one and it sounded naughty. I thought what the effing hell was that? It wasn't the plug out or something like that. So I said to Graham Sanders: *"That's serious, the only thing we can do, ever so quick, is take the rocker cover off and have a look."* So, we did and there was an exhaust rocker busted. *"Oh Shit!"* 'cos I bet we'd got everything in our spares but a rocker. We could have built a whole engine, but we didn't have a rocker. Well I spotted a brand new A65 sitting on its stand, adjacent to the hospitality suite. We couldn't find anyone to ask but I says: *"Come on we'll have a bloody*

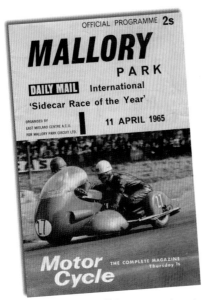

Sidecars were hugely popular in the 1960s, with a number of sidecar-only meetings being held. Such as Mallory Park's 11ᵗʰ April 1965 event

rocker out of that." We whipped the tank off, ripped the rocker cover off, it was all quite easy. But we were getting a bit of a shuffle on and we knackered a rocker shaft and two rockers out of this thing. Well we put this into Chris's bike, stuffed it all in, and of course he went and won the Race of the Year on it.

Chris Vincent: I went to the grid to see if they'd hold the start of the race until the job was finished. But by the time I'd got out there they were holding up the *"one minute to go"* board and my chances of starting seemed to be slipping away fast. Then there was a bit of a delay and I could see my BSA being rushed on to the track. But there hadn't been time even to start the engine. So, there I was on the third row of the grid with a cold engine not knowing whether it was even going to start or not. Not surprisingly the bike didn't start cleanly, in fact it was dead sluggish.

To confound matters Vincent missed a gear at the hairpin and fishing round for one on the run down to the Devil's Elbow he'd convinced himself he'd broken his chain there was so little connection. He only got it back into gear once he'd come to a virtual standstill, following which there was a textbook last-to-first battle, as he clawed his way back through the field. He took Terry Vinicombe on the inside going into the Esses, taking to the grass when both drivers went for the same bit of tarmac, then passed Colin Seeley starting the fifth lap. He then slowly chipped away at Fritz Scheidegger's lead.

Chris Vincent: I just couldn't seem to close the gap so I had to go over my normal limits. To take a few calculated risks, in other words. I stuck my neck out, having a real go and came out of the Devil's Elbow faster than he did and slipped by before we got to Gerards. Then we started lapping riders and I'm a bit of a specialist at that and I think I gained some ground as a result. But I was horrified when my pit signalled that we'd got five laps to go. I thought the race was nearly over! Those last five laps were really nerve-racking. In the lead and plenty of time to think of what could go wrong and listen to the noises. I wasn't worried about Fritz, the agony was making sure that I finished and the bike would be capable of doing a lap of honor.

It did both, just, winning by four seconds in the end, with Vincent picking up £500 (£10K in 2021 values) for his efforts. Even if the owner of the rockers never knew it.

> **Peter Brown:** We then took the rocker out of his engine, put it back in this road bike and left a note stuffed into the handlebars saying: *"To whomever it may concern. You may be pleased to know, or not, that your exhaust rocker shaft has just won the Race of the Year. If you wish to have a chat please get in touch with Peter Brown. BSA Development"*. But I never heard a bleeding thing. I think that it was a bike loaned to the Industries Association, or a Sales bike, run by one of our sales people, thus I reckon they wouldn't want anyone to know it had been fiddled with?

1965 then continued much as '64, with Vincent winning again over the Easter weekend. With victory at the King of Brands meeting on the Friday, the Snetterton Race of Aces on the Sunday, and at Mallory Park again on the Tuesday. Tuesday being another public holiday in those days. Tellingly Vincent had only made 4th at Oulton on the Monday, when the 500cc limit saw him back on his BMW and behind the continental triumvirate of Scheidegger, Deubel and Camathias. But it was results on the Saturday, the only day of the five day holiday weekend when Vincent *wasn't* racing, which were actually the most interesting.

Early incarnations of the Vincent outfit. Various specifications were quoted over the years, but as it was under constant development there was never a definitive set-up

Peter Brown on his *croucher* outfit, built around a chassis salvaged from Bill Boddice's front garden. It had originally housed an experimental 4-cylinder Ariel Arrow-based engine and suited Brown's purposes since a knee injury made a full kneeler-type chassis uncomfortable. It never hampered his speed

Peter Brown: I went to see Bert Perrigo. I was very polite in those days and said: *"Since I've built this engine for Chris and since I'm going to start road racing, if you could see your way clear to giving me some help I'd be very appreciative"*. This was the year after my Grass-track Championship win, so it obviously helped my machinations with Mr Perrigo. *"What do you want?'* he says: *"An engine? Well I tell you what, you can have an engine, but you can't work on it in work time. You can stay over, and work on it unpaid."* So I did, and proceeded to build a replica of Chris' engine, poked it in to this thing and eventually it became an outfit. I was entered by Peter Chapman, Chris Vincent's sponsor and in the years to come he negotiated the money side of things which was useful, going through a third party, as the people who organised the meetings were miserable bastards. But anyway, around that time Mallory, Brands, Silverstone, *the conglomerate*, was running *'Stars of the Future'* events. So, Chapman says: *"I've entered you in all of them. Now, you've got to win 'em!"* Well I thought: *"Hell, I'd never raced on the road. Thanks a lot!"* Whatever, the first I won and the second. Then we went to Mallory Park and for the first time I was affected by *'swill'*, fuel starvation. But I won that too, even though every time I went round Gerards I was on one cylinder. Actually, I was a bit overawed at the end of 1965 'cos Chapman was on about getting me entries for this and that Grand Prix in 1966. And I thought *'I don't think I'm ready for this?'*

This was obviously all in the future at the start of '65, but showed the trajectory Brown was on and the impact the results of Chris Vincent's A65 were having. As while Vincent was the sole competitor campaigning a BSA twin at the start of the season, by April, eight top runners had them, or at least had them in preparation. And all had some form of factory connection. Vincent was nominally a BSA Development Tester; Terry Vinicombe was sponsored by top BSA agent Tom Kirby and had his engines prepared in the factory as a result; Peter Brown was in Engine Development; while the Hanks family, of father Fred and son Roy ran a motorcycle dealership in Birmingham and had eldest son Norman then as a Road Tester at BSA; Bill Boddice was in the auto trade also and his son Mick was an apprentice in the BSA Comp Shop. It would give rise to the *Birmingham Mafia* myth which was only stoked by results on 16th May, at Snetterton, where the last named made all the news;

16th May 1965 marked a big day for the Boddice family

"First win for a ginger-haired 17-year-old who is going to be a great rider. The spotlight was turned on young Mick Boddice who tore away from a top line field including his father Bill, in the big sidecar event. And Mick's passenger 18-year-old Dave Loach had never been in a racing sidecar before. The two teenage tearaways went into the lead on lap three."[6]

The status quo was reestablished with Vincent winning the pre-TT Derby Cup Races, at Mallory on May 23rd, though it was Mick's dad Bill catching the headlines at the TT. Mick Woollett, reporting for *Motor Cycling*, noted that while Boddice's engine was his own, it was prepared in the BSA factory and had a second gearbox fitted behind the empty case normally housing the four-speeder. *MCN* similarly reported that Bill Boddice: *"On the semi-works BSA with 6 speeds."* In both cases the remarks were erroneous for the *semi-works* comments, not the gear box observations, about which the factory was far from pleased.

(handwritten race results)

1965.

4th 1300cc   Snetterton   March 28th   B.S.A.
6th 1200cc   Mallory Park   April 20th   Norton
2nd S/Car Invit No2. "   "   "   "
6th H'Cap.   Brands Hatch   May 9th   B.S.A.
1st 1300cc   Snetterton   " 16th   "
4th 1200cc   Brands Hatch   June 27th   "
2nd " H'Cap.   "   "   "
2nd S/Car.   Castle Combe   July 10th   Norton
1st " A.   "   "   "
1st 1300cc Consol No2. Mallory Park   Aug 22nd   B.S.A.

A young Mick Boddice beat Tom Kirby-sponsored Terry Vinicombe on to the track with an A65 in 1965, as his hand-written race results show. Both Mick and his father Bill Boddice alternated between an A65 and Bill's older Norton sidecar until they both had their own A65/A50 outfits sorted.

By the mid-60s Bill was entering the twilight of his racing but son Mick would go on to have a racing career spanning over 30 years including 9 TT wins

Mick Boddice was one of the first competitors to trade in his pudding basin helmet for a *'jet'* type. And that in turn for a full-face helmet later on. His outfits were also considerably better turned out than many of his rivals. **Mick Boddice:** We do take the mick out of Norman (Hanks) on presentation. He's the same now with his pushbikes. I always thought: *"If you want someone to sponsor you, you want to look clean and tidy"*

Mick Boddice: When I started Dad was still on a Norton. But when I got the job at the factory he said: *"Have a word with Brian Martin and see if you can get an engine?"* So, I got him an engine, and the first thing he did was cut the bloody gearbox off it. To stick a 6-speed Schafleitner behind it. You can imagine it didn't go down very well back at work; *"We gave him an engine and now he's cut it up and he's using all the wrong parts on it!"*

It wasn't an entirely surprising move though. Chris Vincent thought the same type of 6-speed gearbox, purchased with his 1962 TT winnings, was worth 10hp and made his A7 the competitive force it subsequently became. An advantage he probably wished he had on 6th June, when the BBC covered the Brands Hatch Evening News International Sidecar meeting. As he could only manage 3rd on his 4-speed A50, though easily beating TT winner Max Deubel when back on his A65. Saturday 12th then saw Bemsee's Silverstone sidecar event won by the ever-improving Peter Brown and while Vincent was absent from the Brands *Golden Sash* meeting on the 27th - taking 2nd place at the Dutch TT – it got tongues wagging. Since Owen Greenwood scored a first victory on his four-wheeled, car-based, *'Mini'*. A machine which would spoil BSA's party many times in the year to come. Mick Boddice then took a second win on July 10th, to prove his first was no fluke, this time at Castle Combe. After which it was the Lightning Clubman solo back in the news again.

Whither Tony Smith?

Mentions of BSA's new A65 production racer had been few and far between after Tony Smith's initial Brands Hatch win, but subsequently there had been mitigating circumstance. On Saturday 24th April he'd come 2nd to Dave Nixon's Triumph at the Snetterton meeting run by the Bantam Racing Club, on what *Motor Cycling* reported was *"a very sick machine"*. It had set the fastest lap at *"a shattering 86.95mph"* however

Tony Smith leads Chris Hopes at the Spring BFR Snetterton meeting. Hope's would be a regular adversary in production racing events

and *Motor Cycle News* also chose to comment on Smith, rather than the winners. Noting: *"Tony Smith did the quickest laps in each production race on the BSA Lightning but had magneto trouble* (sic) *on the last lap in the first race in which he was holding a considerable lead."*[7] He'd also come second at the British Formula Club's meeting at the same circuit, which augured well for the rest of the season. But soon after, following an accident, he was in hospital with a suspected broken neck. Irrespective Dick Rainbow Motorcycles bought two more Lightning Clubman models and had a new recruit on one soon after. Mick Andrew's dad happened to own the chemist shop over the road from Rainbow's dealership and on July 18th both he and Smith were back at Norfolk's fast, open, Snetterton circuit.

> *"Riding BSA Lightnings from the Ware, Hertfordshire, stable of Richard Rainbow, Andrew and team-mate Tony Smith won three of the four big machine races with another Lightning rider, Robert Lovell taking the other event. Andrew and Lovell shared the fastest lap time only ⅖[th] of a second outside Bill Penny's record on a Triumph."*[8]

The final race had actually been a clean sweep of Andrew, Lovell and Smith and it acted as a good warm up for the prestigious Thruxton 500, run at Castle Combe on a one-off basis, a month later. Among a field dominated by Triumph's recently released *Thruxton* Bonnevilles four A65s acquitted themselves remarkably well, with the two Rainbow machines scoring 2nd with the Smith/Ling partnership and 4th with Andrew/Gardiner. In comparison the more fancied Eddie Dow entry of Rod Gould and Ron Langston only made about an hour, while the Sid Mizen/John Holder partnership, on the Southampton dealer Alec Bennett's machine, made only a further hour before a seizure. Those track-side, including the *Motor Cycling's* Pete Kelly clearly saw that both bikes had big-end problems and reported that *"the second hour decimated the field"*. The A65's survival rate was better than achieved by the Norton or Triumph entries however, particularly as these included thinly disguised full factory machines, which should have overcome the teething problems the A65s were experiencing in what was the engine's first distance event.

Clubman and Spitfire - The Production Racers

Machine Frame 5922, engine 2999DC was earmarked for *"Richard Rainbow, Ware, Herts"* on 2/3/65 as the first Lightning Clubman dispatched to a UK dealer. As Tony Smith said it wasn't actually ready the following day, but it won first time out regardless. It was probably also a good 'un, as road tested and possibly dyno-ed before being handed over. But the Clubman was far from remarkable. Internally it was identical to the Lightning, as it was cosmetically to the UK road model. US Lightnings were red but the 1965 UK Lightning was gold as was the Clubman. The Clubman was produced purely to promote sales of the road model, so just 200 were made to meet ACU race homologation rules. Indeed the only differences between the Clubman and road going Lightning were largely cosmetic, the main ones being rear-set foot rests, ace-bars combined with a different top yoke, hump-back seat and a slightly altered 2 into 1 exhaust system to give better ground clearance. There was also nominally a 500cc Cyclone Clubman version too, though only one genuine dealer model may have been made, with one or two more for exhibition purposes. As a 500 it struggled to match the performance of Triumph's T100, Velocette's 500 or even BSA's own Gold Star.

In 1966 the Lightning Clubman was superseded by the Spitfire MkII (the MkI being an earlier US off-road model) with there being no Cyclone Clubman equivalent. The Spitfire was a standard series production model however, of which more than 7,000 were made between 1966 and 1968. It didn't have the Clubman's close ratio gearbox as it was intended for the road, but the MkII formed the basis for all future Production Racers, as being in a higher state of tune than subsequent Spitfire models. This specification included 10.5 compression ratio pistons and Amal GP carburetors and, while troublesome on the road, they were the definitive items for the track.

The ACU homologation numbers required for Production racing were actually dropped to 100 machines in 1966 but contrary to stories leaked to the press BSA were never tempted to produce another bespoke machine - as both Triumph and Velocette did with their Thruxton variants and Norton with its later Norvil models. Road racing was never BSA's *thing* so A65 racers were always at a disadvantage.

Out on his own. Tony Smith averaged 71.19mph in the wet to take the Lightning Clubman to its first victory at Brands Hatch, three days after taking delivery. The only concession to *'lightening'* was removal of the tank badges

John Chubb in striped jumper, John Gleed with hand to mouth and Ron Langston in leathers, discuss the finer points of the Dow Clubman with an unidentified well wisher

John Gleed: I remember making a solid head gasket for that bike out of a piece of copper, with a hacksaw and file, buggering about because we knew the head gaskets were suspect as they were. They were composite and of course after a short while BSA started making them solid too. But there were none available for the bikes being prepared for that race and what happened to the bike was that there was a problem with the oiling. The return feed-pipe hole wasn't big enough and it allowed oil to back-up in the crankcase, which then got very hot. It rattled the bottom end out which is why Rod Gould never got a ride. I remember it as Tony Smith came up to me - I didn't know him from Adam at the time - and started talking about the oil feed. I mentioned we had the same problem and he said: *"We had to drill out the hole in the top of the return pipe, to allow more oil to come back into the oil tank, to keep the temperature down."* And of course his bike went very well, so we did that afterwards too.

Smith was back on that well-sorted Clubman on Sunday, August 1st, winning the all-comers race at the BRC Snetterton event, and while only 2nd behind Peter Butler's Triumph in the production race he set a new production machine lap record in the process. Smith then won again the next weekend at Cadwell Park.

With that level of competitiveness the BSA factory may already have been looking for more direct involvement, when fate undoubtedly dealt them a lucky hand.

OFFICIAL PROGRAMME 1s.
SOUTHAMPTON & DISTRICT M.C.C.
Motor Cycle INTERNATIONAL
500 mile race
Castle Combe Circuit, Chippenham, Wilts.
24th July, 1965
Motor Cycle THE COMPLETE MAGAZINE

Hailwood's *Hutch*

At the time Mike Hailwood was winning all before him. He had claimed his third 500cc World Title for MV Agusta in 1964 and had won every race so far in 1965. While Hailwood is revered virtually as a deity today he was still not the finished article in 1965 and scepticism abounded. That his success was down to money and his father, *'Stan the wallet'*.

> **Tom Kirby**: This upset Mike no end. He was frustrated with the lack of equal competition which would put the others in with a chance to beat him, if they could. His tarnished public image badly needed restoring. It worried Mike to the extent that he approached me on the subject, asking my advice. *"What do you think I should do 'Uncle'?"* I said that there was only one thing he could do: *"Get a bike for the production race at Silverstone and blow them all off! Nobody can say it was the bike if you win on a standard road machine, identical to everyone else's."* Mike was amused at first, but the more he thought about it the more he liked the idea. *'I'll do it'* he said. And how.[9]

With Kirby's BSA contacts Hailwood was contracted for the *Hutch* - as the Hutchinson 100 was universally known - on 14th August. It wasn't disclosed how much he got paid - possibly not much. BSA weren't over generous to their road racers - and they saved on machine preparation either way. BSA were far more scrupulous than others when it came to eligibility so, like the A65 engine generically, the most surprising feature of Hailwood's machine was that it didn't have any. It was entirely road legal with standard pistons and camshaft, though probably fitted with the '66 cylinder-head then being prepared for the export models. Which had bigger inlet valves than the Clubman.

Practice times for Silverstone indicated that the Triumph and BSA twins were quite evenly matched. It came as no surprise however that Percy Tait's highly developed factory Bonneville had a speed advantage over everyone else

For those in attendance, and there were thousands, the 1965 Hutchinson 100 was largely memorable for the horrendous weather in which it took place. It didn't seem to worry Hailwood though, who pulled away to win. One of the newly made Cyclone Clubman models - possibly the *only* Cyclone Clubman ever made - also came home in 3rd place in the 500cc class. However two privately entered A65s had actually, briefly, led the race. Smith's Dick Rainbow machine and that of future World Champion Rod Gould.

Rod Gould: The first bike I raced was a 350 Gold Star which I bought from Eddie Dow. It was about the fastest 350 Gold Star out there and I could give Manx Nortons a good run for their money. Eddie was very good to me after that, when I was a sort of semi-professional, as I worked for him when I wasn't racing and in the evenings I could use the workshop to work on my race bikes. Though the people who built the A65 were John Chubb and John Gleed. The first race we were entered in was the Thruxton 500 and I did the road testing on it, ran it in and everything else and while I practiced Ron Langston went off in the first hour so I didn't actually get to ride. But I raced it again later in the production race at Silverstone. A friend of mine, the journalist Bruce Cox, was on the inside of the corner at Woodcote and next to him was Mike Hailwood, who was also with a friend. I was coming round on this A65, wide open, and it was weaving all over the place, and Bruce said Mike's mouth fell open and he said: *"Faaarkin'ell...! Just look at this!"* It *was* incredible, as I didn't really know much about setting a bike up back then. So, it was a case of wide open and hang on hard. That was in practice. It was alright

Rain master: Along with Hailwood's A65 win the 1965 *Hutch* was largely memorable for the appalling conditions. Rain, poor visibility and a saturated track were the order of the day and while they did for the hopes of budding hot-shots, Tony Smith and Rod Gould, their short-lived field-leading performances enhanced their growing reputations

in the race as I was used to it by then, 'got a great start, led the field away until half way round, when I ran wide on a corner and Percy Tait and Mike Hailwood passed me. I sort of got back in mid-field, got through them again and if I hadn't been so young and the blood gone to my head I think I could have been a bit closer to them by the end.

He was still fourth behind Percy Tait, who was pipped for second place by Phil Read. But whichever way you looked at it, it was a big day for BSA. Hailwood took the win and was duly feted in the press. *'Hailwood's Hutch'* ran one headline *'Mike kills that MV myth'* was another. BSA themselves perhaps lost the initiative by not pushing Hailwood's win enough in the press, but what wasn't lost was the opportunity seen by BSA Sales Manager John Hickson. He was equally impressed by the recent performances of youngster Tony Smith. His second place at the Thruxton 500 was noteworthy, but what really caught Hickson's eye was Smith's little publicised achievement at the Hutchinson 100 itself, since Gould wasn't the only one to have pushed Hailwood that day.

Hailwood's Lightning

Production racers went on to become increasingly non-standard as the 1960s progressed. 4LS brakes then discs appeared, alongside five-speed gearboxes and very *'non-production'*, one-off, special, engine internals. Things were simpler in '65 and Hailwood's Lightning was a case in point, as those working on its engine and chassis well knew.

Peter Brown: I had instructions from Clive Bennett that Mike Hailwood was going to ride an A65. *'Would you build the engine?'* So, I did, and we went down, with Clive in tow of course, to Silverstone. 'Would have been the Thursday as then we had another day messing about, when Clive says: *"Oh, we've made another frame for you as well. It's got a so and so head angle. We can change that tonight and you can try it tomorrow."* Hailwood just says: *"Well if you want to. But this is OK, it doesn't worry me."* He just got on the bike, rode it as it was and blew them all off. And with a virtually standard engine. Nobody believed us but there was hardly anything in those early engines that wasn't standard. We always used production camshafts and pistons. We didn't have anything else. It's just that the design of the engine lent itself to development.

Mike Bowers: The bike that Hailwood won the Hutchinson 100 on was actually my 'going-home' bike. They *did* do a special bike for Hailwood, but Hailwood didn't like the bicycle. He liked the engine, but he just didn't like the bicycle. So, he rode several, differently set-up. My old knackered going-home bike was well fettled, fork-wise, suspension-wise and everything else-wise, as I was into that sort of stuff, and the chassis did everything he wanted it to do. Being a motocross-er mine was slightly different in that it had got different length dampers and stuff on it, which jacked it up slightly at the back, and that's probably where stories about a different head-angle came from. Mike liked the chassis, so they pinched basically most of it and Hailwood won of course - beating Percy Tait, which the Triumph people weren't best pleased about - and afterwards Norman Hanks took it over and crashed it. So, what he says is true, as I never did get my going-home bike back!

An iconic image from BSA press department. It's a pity that they didn't do more to publicise the victory

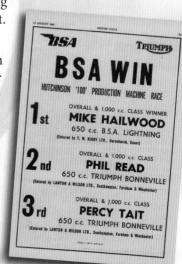

Publicity for Hailwood's win was actually pretty scant. BSA simply circulated photos to the press and expected them to get on with it

Tony Smith: When it came around to the Hutchinson 100 this was like *the* big race of the year. Hailwood was the cat's whiskers and they were going to give him the best bike they could. So we figured that we had to do something different, to try to close the gap. And what we did was exactly what the factory had done to his one. Which was increase the inlet valve size, to the size of those going in the '66 bikes. But we'd never seen in his bike of course and the problem was we didn't have the right valve

Smith at the 500-miler on a still very standard machine

springs for it. So, it was actually 1,000rpm down on what it would rev to before. But I was blessed, as in the race it rained, which virtually eliminated the deficit of the speed it lost. So I managed to stay ahead of Hailwood for a while, though the writing was on the wall. He wasn't bad was he? Probably the best the world has ever seen. So, it was inevitable and at Chapel Curve I aquaplaned off the circuit and on to the grass, stood it up and had to jump off. But what I'd done impressed the factory sufficiently for them to give me a call. A month later I was working there. I walked in that first morning and asked what to do. The foreman just said: *'Build us a race bike.'* I was like a kid in a sweet shop. It was the best job in the world! I asked John Hickson, why he wanted me, and he said: *"Because your bloody bike was beating the factory one!"* and I inherited that bike after. It was good, but in the space of 12 months it was transformed. If Hailwood had the same bike a year later, he'd have been even further away!

Indeed, but that may have been because it wasn't quite the same bike after all.

Norman Hanks: The bike that Mike Hailwood rode, I actually broke my leg on that and wrote it off. It had GP carbs and was a pig to start, but they then made a production run – what was the Spitfire - and nobody could start them. They wouldn't tick over either, so they gave me his old bike to take out on test and find out why everyone was moaning. But I could not start this thing! I had to push it down the road in the morning but as it had such a high first gear - it had a close ratio gearbox - that it meant I had to run at about 20mph. After about a week I said: *"I can't deal with this bike any more. Give it to someone else!"* But they'd made arrangements for me to take it to Amal's, so me and another tester went off and I hit a car head on down George Road. I broke my femur and the bike was written off, but of course they had to resurrect it after, as it was Hailwood's Silverstone winner wasn't it.

It was 2nd place at the 500-miler for Smith but a good result nonetheless. Enough to convince BSA that he was who they needed to continue on the solo A65 in UK competition

Jody Nicholas at Marlboro, Maryland. The best result for a BSA twin, before they went flat tracking with the A65

Flattering to deceive

And the Hutch would have been it for the solos, in terms of big performances, were it not for matters on the other side of the water. It's popularly believed that official interest by the BSA Group in the Daytona races started with factory machines prepared for 1966. It was actually in October 1964 when discussion first took place however with the American wing of BSA setting out their needs. Following Ed Moran's 1963 Novice win it had been back to Gold Stars for the majority and this was a problem for a company for whom their Hornet and Cyclone replacements had yet to really take off. As such three 'official' A50 engines were prepared at Small Heath and shipped to America in early 1965 and while they made no early season showing finally, on September 5th, they made their mark. At the Marlboro road races in Maryland. By now fitted with a new type of Joe Hunt magneto, Jody Nicholas picked up a hard fought third place after a lousy start. But that would be it for the season.

Jody Nicholas: Herb Neas built Ed Moran's bikes and Moran was a spectacular rider for his grade. He won a couple of important races, but they weren't as long of course as the Expert races and those Expert race results were disappointing. Because, as compared to the Triumphs and fast Harleys, the bikes weren't particularly quick. Malboro was the only time an A50 got on the podium of an AMA National up to then, and that was as it handled well. Mainly I still did Gold Stars, as the A50s weren't very fast and were not very reliable either. Herb Neas prepared all those Gold Stars too, that I raced from 1961 right up to 1966, and the couple of years when we rode the A50, Dick Mann and I told 'em -

Dick was my team mate - we told the people at BSA that if we couldn't ride our Gold Stars then we weren't going to ride our BSAs at all. Dick told BSA: *"We're wasting our time on these twins. They don't go and they're unreliable – we better have our Gold Stars back"*. So, in 1965 we got our Gold Stars back and started getting good placings. They pulled the Gold Stars out from under a table somewhere and dusted them off pretty quick but it was disappointing after I was reading about Chris Vincent and all those other guys in England managing to win races with their sidecars, when we couldn't win as a solo over here.

A modified version of the early Joe Hunt magneto cover. The later version, while much smaller, had an exposed mag and was more vulnerable to crash damage

It must have been, particularly as those Vincent victories continued to rack up, though there were other interesting results too. Terry Vinicombe picked up a 3rd at the Brands Sidecar Trophy meeting where Roy Hanks took 6th on his dad's A65. A machine which was harder to come by than Boddice's, even though Fred Hanks was a Birmingham bike dealer too.

Norman Hanks: It was obvious that the A65 was the best to have as a sidecar engine, but he could *not* get an engine. You couldn't buy an A65 engine for trying and to be fair to BSA they probably didn't have any sitting in the spares department fully assembled back then. They wanted any engines they'd got for production, so, as he was friends with Aston Autos, who *were* BSA dealers, they ordered every single part to build up an A65 engine. Which Ray Beach then did and I used to go to Ray's, as he showed me what he'd done so, when I got mine, I could do the same too.

Fred Hanks leading through the Cadwell Park greenery. Fred Hanks, like Bill Boddice, never moved on from a *sitter* outfit which was de rigueur for the previous generation

Norman Hanks would soon have that engine up and running but in the meantime Vincent hit a blip and a significant one at that. Mallory Park's Sidecar Gold Cup, on 22nd August, was predicted to be a Birmingham benefit and so it proved to be. But the win went to Longbridge and Austin-Morris, rather than Armoury Road and BSA. Vincent and his BSA twin could be beaten, even if it had taken a season and a half and a machine with four wheels, a 50% bigger engine and a steering wheel to achieve it. Owen Greenwood's Mini had finally arrived on the scene. Whether it affected Vincent psychologically is hard to say but his downturn in form continued at Castle Combe on 4th September, since it was Peter Brown who won both the scratch races and the final too. At Snetterton the following day Vincent was 2nd again, this time to Pip Harris's BMW, though there were perhaps some ironic smiles since Greenwood was forced to retire with a broken fan belt. Probably a first for a British *'sidecar'*?

Down but not out, Vincent travelled back to Cadwell Park two weeks later to entertain a 20,000-strong crowd. The media were whispering, so a big result was due, and he delivered it, beating Greenwood in the 1300cc event then winning emphatically in the final open race too, having swapped paint for six laps with the man who would be World Champion the following year, Swiss rider Fritz Scheidegger. Vincent then won again on Saturday 2nd October at Oulton Park and at the Brands Hatch Race of the South, on Sunday 10th October. This was a hollow victory however following the death of the other popular Swiss driver, 41-year-old Florian Camathias. So the 31st October meeting made a more fitting end to the season, since it confirmed Vincent as the National champion again. It was also another exhibition piece, captured for posterity by Pathé News, at a rain lashed Mallory Park. Vincent's iconic green and black outfit chased home by Terry Vinicombe's, with Bill Boddice 5th and Roy Hanks in 6th. That meant four A65s in the top six, which would become the expectation in the seasons to come.

Vinicombe and Flaxman. A formidable pairing which proved that you didn't need to come from Birmingham to make a BSA go fast. Though admittedly their engine was prepared there

Peter Brown's first excursion on to tarmac was in 1965, on a chassis purchased for £40 from under an apple tree in Bill Boddice's front garden and an engine built from bits provided by BSA's Bert Perrigo

Proddy title closer

Tony Smith had not been idle during all this sidecar racing activity, as with a final victory at Snetterton, on Saturday October 16th, he secured the BRC Production Championship for 1965. This and the National title Vincent had taken were obviously the headline news, but as victories by others demonstrated – from Hailwood to Boddice – the A65 was unquestionably a competitive unit in anyone's hands. As such other competitors on both two and three wheels started to look at the option, including at least one future factory star.

Bob Heath: I'd got mates with motorcycles and we often went up to Bridgnorth. Not just riding but racing on the road and ending up in coffee bars. Then we went to see some road racing at Oulton, Mallory and Darley Moor and realised that we could actually race a road bike in the production class. Four of us joined different motorcycle clubs and I joined Darley Moor. I'd seen a BSA Lightning Clubman at the Blackpool Show and I finally found one - BRW 298C - at the Coventry Motor Mart. Norman Vanhouse, the local BSA Rep. was there when I collected it and years later, at a TT function, he told me he'd thought: *"That lad won't last long"*. I remember the first meeting it was at Perton, an airfield circuit near Wolverhampton. I finished sixth and at the time the people who were going well were Peter Davies and his mate Ray Hole on A10s. We used to watch 'em coming through the top corner, with sparks flying from those BSAs, and that's what I wanted to do.

Chapter 4

Cooper too - 1966

Neat and compact, East and West Coast importers both modified one of the 1966 machines supplied. The rear disc brake above identifies this bike as one of these. In the background is a Gold Star. Although out of production for several years it remained the preferred option for BSA riders in most sporting disciplines

It wasn't only Bob Heath who saw the potential of the unit twins in 1965. BSA saw enough promise in the A50's brief US outings to start work on AMA rule-compliant 500s to race in '66. Their commitment went only so far however as while they incorporated some American feedback sadly, as would be demonstrated in future years, this never went far enough, even if bringing in an experienced ex-road racer to oversee preparation.

Pat Slinn: Sometime during 1964 the Comp Shop was moved and there was now enough room in this department for all the factory competition machines to be under one roof. Alan Shepherd was appointed under Brian Martin to look after the road racing side of things, which then concentrated exclusively on the A65/50 machines. One of his first jobs was to oversee the development, building, preparation and testing of 500cc A50 machines, for the Daytona 200 mile race. BSA Incorporated in the US had sent over a couple of their people to help with the preparation, and to advise on the specification for these bikes.

The handling of BSA's twins would soon be called into question but as no such doubts had been raised at this point the frames for the Daytona machines were similar to the production models. Though manufactured from manganese molybdenum tubing their design's only other major departure from standard was the straightening of the rear mainframe loops. On the bikes for Daytona these went directly down, from the nose of the seat to the swinging arm pivot point, to give the bell-mouths of the non-standard 1³⁄₁₆ Amal Grand Prix carburetors unobstructed access to clean, cold, air. The front forks, suspension and brakes were otherwise almost standard BSA, with the front end effectively that of the MkII Spitfire. Within the engine Nimonic 'tulip' valves were fitted, with the inlets having a reduced stem diameter and lighter springs. While above, the rockers were lightened and polished, with the Thackeray washers, which normally took up any side-play, being replaced by shims. The crank assembly was re-balanced to 54° but otherwise preparation consisted of generic polishing and lightening, which could have been carried out by any good home-tuner. The machines were finished off with plain white fairings and aluminium Gold Star-pattern tanks, in dark polychromatic red. They couldn't be mistaken for anything other than BSAs however, due to the huge Star transfers on either side of the tank.

> *"Four special 500cc BSA twins are now on their way to America for the AMA national races at Daytona, on March 18, 19 and 20. They were tested at MIRA, the Motor Industry test track, near Nuneaton, Warwickshire, last week. The BSA racers have special racing frames, of Reynolds 531 tubing, modified steering with hydraulic dampers, oil cooling radiators in the fairing, and 190mm racing brakes front and rear. The Triumph factory is also sending special machines to fight off the 450 Honda threat. Technician Clive Bennett will accompany the BSAs, which develop about 55hp."*[10]

They didn't have 190mm brakes at the rear and the claim of 55hp was slightly exaggerated too, as the dynos indicated 53 (actually 53.25 average from the three engines tested - ED260, 259 and 256). These figures equated to not uncompetitive top speeds at MIRA of 125.7mph, 125.7mph and 124.8mph respectively, but what was perhaps missed was the temperature at which these readings were recorded. 30-33ºF. In British money that meant bouncing around zero, when temperatures on 20th March in Florida were over 79ºF/26ºC. Vastly different conditions.

On arrival one A50 was modified by BSA East Coast and one by BSA West Coast, through the fitting of Airheart disc brakes at the rear and the early type Joe Hunt magneto conversion, as on Nicholas' 1965 Marlboro machine. One machine was also fitted with double front discs, making it perhaps unique at the time in having a full disc set-up.

The planning and investment were all to no avail however and the results must have made for abysmal reading back at Small Heath.

The special American Airheart rear disc set-up which would become standard in 1967

Don Vesco (frame/engine 260 – West Coast modified bike) was the best performer, finishing 53rd completing just 18 laps, while Bobby Winter (frame/engine 102 from 1965) was next best in 55th, completing 16. Top line riders, Dick Mann (frame/engine 261), Eddie Moran (probably on another 1965 machine frame/engine 101) and Jody Nicholas (frame/engine 259 – the East Coast modified bike) made a pitiful 17 laps between them.

Winter snapped a primary chain, Vesco broke a crank, while the remainder were reported as retiring with that old chestnut *'ignition trouble'*. Crankshaft flex was cited, causing the alternator rotor to give the stator coils a hard time, but how crankshaft flex caused failure of the two modified machines, running magnetos – the drive for which came off the timing side idler pinion – remains a mystery. Two bikes weren't used. Frame/engine 256 was earmarked for Dan Haaby who opted, in retrospect wisely, for a Suzuki, while frame/engine 262 was a spare. A third bike (frame/engine 263) was dropped by Howard Utsey in the 100-mile Amateur support race. All in all it was a horribly poor showing made worse by the fact that Buddy Elmore's Triumph was running exactly the same ignition system which BSA claimed caused all their problems. And won. The differing fortunes of the two marques also highlighted an issue which was to blight all of BSA's Daytona attempts with the twin. Triumph 500s were campaigned up and down the country, week in week out, to the point where Triumph test rider Percy Tait's formidable open class racer was able to take second place behind Giacomo Agostini's MV Agusta at the 1969 Belgium Grand Prix. In the UK privateer Hugh Evans was the sole racer to campaign an A50 and he did not really start that until 1967.

Torello Tacchi from Chicago took 2nd place in the AMA Amateur race at Loudon in 1966 but the AMA Pro class was where BSA needed to win

An official American request for an A50 of 75 x 59mm bore and stroke. That it never happened was a great shame

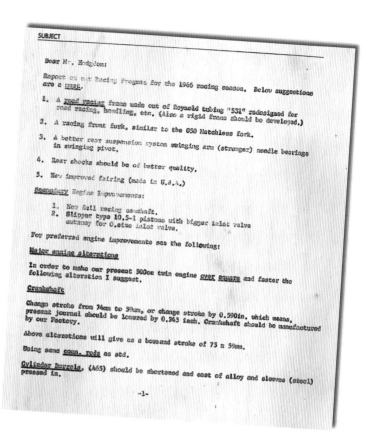

SUBJECT

Dear Mr. Hodgdon:

Report on our Racing Program for the 1966 racing season. Below suggestions are a must.

1. A road racing frame made out of Reynold tubing "531" redesigned for road racing, handling, etc. (Also a rigid frame should be developed.)

2. A racing front fork, similar to the G50 Matchless fork.

3. A better rear suspension system swinging arm (stronger) needle bearings in swinging pivot.

4. Rear shocks should be of better quality.

5. New improved fairing (made in U.S.A.)

Secondary Engine Improvements:

1. New full racing camshaft.
2. Slipper type 10.5-1 pistons with bigger inlet valve cutaway for O.size inlet valve.

For preferred engine improvements see the following:

Major engine alterations

In order to make our present 500cc twin engine over square and faster the following alteration I suggest.

Crankshaft

Change stroke from 74mm to 59mm, or change stroke by 0.590in. which means, present journal should be lowered by 0.245 inch. Crankshaft should be manufactured by our factory.

Above alterations will give us a bore and stroke of 75 x 59mm.

Using same conn. rods as std.

Cylinder Barrels, (A65) should be shortened and cast of alloy and sleeves (steel) pressed in.

-1-

Tony Smith: I barely raced the 500 in this country. At the time I don't think I had raced it until we built them for Daytona. So, it was all just a bit unfortunate really, as the bikes needed much more development. There was also no depth of knowledge of solo racing in the BSA factory at the time and that was the other half of the problem. The 500 was OK, but was basically *wrong* in design. What it was, was a smaller bore version of the 650 engine. When it should have been the other way round. We should have had a shorter stroke A65 as a 500.

Had Smith seen correspondence from BSA America? Probably not, but if he had it would have made him smile, as they had made exactly the same request. To alter the bore and stroke to 75 x 59. i.e an A65 top end on a short stroke crank. Had it transpired it would have led to a vastly different A50 motor, but sadly that was never to be.

The sidecar with four wheels

In the UK the three-wheelers had actually kicked off the 1966 season before their American counterparts with a fairly consistent early season pattern emerging. Vincent picking up ninety percent of the wins followed by a lengthening tail of A65s, all in the hands of Birmingham connected racers. With the A50s the wins were fewer, with the continental Grand Prix stars more often than not picking up the money. Of the British runners, the Triumphs of the Horspole brothers and Nigel Mead were the most likely to appear in the minor places, while the BMWs were invariably those of Pip

For all his innovation Vincent's sidecar outfit was entirely conventional when compared to the *Mini*, the *Scitsu*, the *Mogvin* and many other *Cyclecars* which would follow

A blur of speed. Colin Seeley leads Chris Vincent in a typical Brands Hatch battle. Vincent rarely lost out

Harris or Colin Seeley. As the season progressed however the major fly in the ointment was the Greenwood *Mini*. As, while Vincent won the opening Mallory Park Birmingham Cup and Snetterton East Anglian Cup events, Greenwood got his own back at the Mallory Park Sidecar Race of the Year. Though Vincent won again, at the same circuit, the following weekend. It was a BBC televised event, with Vincent possibly hamming it up for the cameras by winning from virtually last off the line. That form continued into the Easter weekend with Vincent winning the Good Friday King of Brands race and the Snetterton Race of Aces, where four Rennsport BMWs and several World Champions were left in his wake. It was to the cheers of a partisan crowd as in 1966, in the run up to the football World Cup, there was more than cash and championship points at stake when racing against the Germans! Vincent was then largely absent in the run up to the TT fortnight, which was postponed in 1966 due to a seamen's strike. Tony Smith was also absent, but he was already booked on a ferry heading in an entirely different direction.

Spreading their wings

Smith was heading for Imola, in June, for the first round of the FIM Coupe d'Endurance. This was the predecessor of the World Endurance Championship and this type of racing, covering races of up to 24hrs duration, was gaining increasing popularity. BSA could see the benefit of the publicity it could generate and it wasn't a bad first stab either. Smith qualified his A65 on pole and he and co-rider Peter Butler were leading until they had to stop to replace a split fuel tank. A blown cylinder-head gasket then followed but they were still credited with 3rd in class, 8th overall. Though the Italian result was possibly even better.

> **Tony Smith:** There was nothing organized in those days at all so anything we did was off my own back. It was a bit like when I came in and they said; *"Here's a workshop, build yourself a racer"*. After that it was: *"Go racing!"* And the thing was I was still only a very naive kid back then. I was in my early 20s and hadn't travelled but it was still very much left down to my own initiative as to what to do and where to go. I had nobody to guide me or

A gun for hire

During the '60s none of the British factories had teams or sponsored riders for international events. This only started in the early 1970s, so big names were contracted in on an ad hoc basis for the *Hutch*, 500-miler and later the Production TT. These were the three big events where the manufacturers could show off the prowess of their top of the range performance roadsters and in this BSA were at a disadvantage having a Competition Department directed towards off-road sport. As such BSA's 1965 and 1966 rider selections reflected Tom Kirby's influence since all – Hailwood, Cooper and Ivy - had close connections to his independent racing activities. Subsequently while the names of Mick Andrew and John Blanchard were mentioned in the press, it was Dave Croxford, Dave Degens, Paul Smart, Pat Mahoney and Steve Spencer who were brought in to ride the twins. Only Degens and Spencer had real production experience however – Spencer bizarrely as he was a road tester for Triumph – and while the others were up and coming 'names', BSA staff with road racing experience might have come up with different ones if consulted. Tony Smith was certainly never asked for a list of production racing possibles and the small amounts of money offered by BSA always made their machines second string priorities for the riders concerned. They were add-ons to more lucrative rides in the 500 and 350 classes in particular, so more astute management might have selected more motivated runners. Peter Butler and Dave Potter would have been obvious choices. They were both committed to the production formula and at the very top of their game, and while Butler did appear in '66 on an A65 alongside Tony Smith, the factory never followed up on the interest.

John Cooper at the anti-clockwise 1966 *Hutch*. With the small amount of cash offered by BSA victory alone was evidently enough motivation for *Cooperman,* which he demonstrated to win over a quality field

even to discuss things with and in that race we were actually higher, as the results were fiddled. George Collis was undoubtedly the winner, but even after he'd been interviewed as the winner the organisers managed to find an Italian machine to name as the victor!

The following Saturday, June 11th, Smith's ex-teammate Mick Andrew took a 3rd place on the Rainbow Lightning, but focus now was on the first of the two big National production events, the 500-miler at Brands Hatch. The *Hutch* and the 500-miler were the primary focus for all the factories, as they generated huge crowds, the biggest interest and the best publicity and as ever the 1966 500-miler was a battle of attrition. Unfortunately BSA's big names, Cooper and Ivy, fared no better than the club runners in a race won by the Triumph of Dave Degens for the second year running. He was paired this time with Rex Butcher and with Phil Read and Percy Tait as runners up on another factory Bonneville it was a good day for Triumph all round. It had started well for BSA however with Ivy and Cooper 5th after the first hour, followed by the Gould/Landrebe Eddie Dow machine. Both were soon out however, Ivy hurling his works Spitfire into the scenery at Dingle Dell shortly after taking over from Cooper, while Gould and New Zealander Landrebe's Eddie Dow bike ran its main bearings soon after, as in '65. Club entrants Moore and Stanton had their Lightning up to 5th by the

Billy Ivy helps John Cooper with the fueling but it was all to no avail. Ivy would soon have the works Spitfire in the undergrowth for a team DNF

second hour but all the other A65 runners had their own share of difficulties. The works Smith/Butler bike was reported as going out with engine trouble, while Ron Chandler pushed his Parks Motorcycles entered machine into the pits having dropped it. Then, at the 5-hour mark, the machine he shared with Roger Hunter was in again for a rear tyre. *Motor Cycling* correctly identified this as a works machine too, but with it out the 6th place Melvin Rice/Colin Burton machine was the only Birmingham twin to really feature, winning the accolade of the highest placed, genuinely private entry in the field.

Hugh Evans on a Rainbow A65. He was better known for his A50 however and was a bit of an endurance specialist, later picking up factory supported rides with Norton, Honda and BMW

Putting their disappointment behind them the pairing of Tony Smith and Peter Butler were back on the continent again by early July, trying to improve on their Imola performance at the Barcelona 24hr race. Held at the tricky, twisty, Montjuic Park circuit, they managed a highly creditable 4th place finish and while the race report recorded seven replacement light bulbs being needed during the night and Smith recounting only six, the point was clear!

> **Tony Smith:** The gearing was too low and we were red lining everywhere. Bulbs blew, stays broke, mudguards fell off. It was terrible. We daren't tell the works we'd cocked up the gearing, so I thought: *'Break the engine!'* But it wouldn't! We strapped a torch to the bars but still finished fourth or fifth in the end and my hands were so swollen there was no gaps between my fingers!

> **George Hopwood:** It vibrated like hell so half way through Peter Butler's hands were swollen so much with the vibration that we had to cut his wedding ring through with a hacksaw, to give his fingers some chance of getting some blood! I rode one of Tony Smith's bikes later at Cadwell Park and thought it vibrated a bit, but maybe that was normal?

It was perhaps on the highly tuned factory bike at the time. It was not as well developed as it would become, and as the Dick Rainbow machine shared by Rice and Burton had indicated at the 500-miler, private bikes were probably at the time as well developed. As such this same machine was the Rainbow Motorcycles choice for entry at Barcelona too, their rapid and previously reliable Lightning being tested over even greater distance and experiencing all the problems which that could entail.

The rise of Production Racing

Today everything is production racing. In WSBK, BSB, TT and Moto2 the engines raced are all road bike derivatives, but in the early 1960s it was a vastly different landscape. Grand Prix solo racing categories were across the classic 50cc to 500cc classes with National championships being in the same capacities. Sidecars were also 500cc but these classes were increasingly out of step with developments on the road. Pre-war, 500cc was the ceiling capacity for most solos, but subsequently 650cc had become the benchmark in Britain, with even bigger machines in the USA. Many manufacturers were also withdrawing from race machine production as they were unable to keep up with the technical advances pioneered by the large Japanese companies and smaller, but more racing orientated, Italian concerns.

As a result, on the domestic racing scene 'open' races started to be run at National level, where 500cc Grand Prix singles could be challenged by bikes developed from 650cc road going twins. This was frowned upon by the purists but at Club level there was even greater creativity. Classes aimed at making motorcycle racing more accessible were promoted, with races and championships exclusively for BSA Bantams and Triumph Tiger Cubs being prime examples. In terms of production racing however whilst Oulton Park had its *Clubman Trophy* meeting and the BMCRC (British Motor Cycle Racing Club) ran its annual Silverstone *Club Day* and *Silverstone 1000*, these were aimed at 'clubmen'. Amateurs. The Southampton & District Motor Cycle Club's Thruxton 500 increasingly attracted National level riders however, particularly once incorporated into the FIM Coupe d'Endurance championship. The 1965 Hutchinson 100 represented perhaps a watershed however since, for the first time since 1925 it featured a production race. It acknowledged pressure from manufacturers, racers and fans alike, with the growth of production racing from then on being exponential.

The Bantam Racing Club (BRC), British Formula Racing Club (BFRC) and Midland Motor Cycle Racing Club (MMCRC) were at the forefront, hosting production championships over a number of circuits. While tracks such as Darley Moor and Aintree promoted their own circuit-specific championships. Despite their popularity the ACU - the UK motorcycling racing governing body - would not sanction a national accredited series until the 1970s, so it was these Club Championships the production runners competed for most fiercely. Along with those run by The British Motorcycle Racing Club, known universally as 'Bemsee', the Southern 67 club, Racing 50 and many, many, more as the '60s progressed.

At National level races for 500cc-plus machines also became more common but as these were more likely to be 'open' than production events, they proved unfavorable to the A65 until the advent of the Kirby Metisse, Featherbed-framed and later factory 'Daytona' machines. By the end of the '60s however there were likely to be six or seven circuits a weekend hosting production races, with even more running open, unlimited, 750cc or 1000cc events in which A65 solos could compete.

Saturday 20th May
"SILVERSTONE 1000"
628-mile ROAD RACE for
PRODUCTION SOLOS
START 11.0 a.m.

ANOTHER BEMSEE MEETING

How it all started

Chris Lodge: We were all production racing at the time, so knew each other and the ride came about as I happened to phone Dick's business one day for….. I don't know what? Some spare parts or something. Anyway, Mick Andrew answered the phone and said: *"We need a rider for Barcelona?"* So, I said: *"Yeah, I'm coming!"* and that was that. I rode with Hugh Evans, as when Tony Smith moved out to the factory that sort of gave a place for me and space for Hugh too.

One of the problems with the BSAs was that when you put a lot of load on the gearbox the main-shaft bent a bit and caused the selectors to rub up against the gears. Well, Barcelona that first time, we went out did a couple of laps of practice and the gear was jumping out. Out of third. We pulled out all the bits the next day and the selectors were all burnt out. They were blue. Well Dick Rainbow brought a fair amount of stuff, so he could rebuild the gearbox, but because of that we got hardly any practice. I really didn't know the circuit well at speed, so went straight out into the race and on the fastest part of the circuit all the lights had gone out! So, we had a 35watts headlight bulb, doing 110mph round a series of fast curves at the top of the circuit. It was ludicrous. Then either Dave Degens or Rex Butcher came past, in company with another Bonneville and I found I had no trouble whatsoever staying with them. They'd just won the 500-miler but I hung on to them quite easily, as the handling of that bike it was lovely.

Chris Lodge on *'Fred'* one of the Rainbow A65 Clubman machines. This time fully faired. Normally they would run without fairings in distance events, to assist access since time lost on the circuit was always less than the time spent in the pits

A standard A65 wouldn't have been able to do that. It wouldn't have been as stable, and this bike was quick too. The ones we had were a bit special. I mean an ordinary A65 wasn't worth racing . '68 I rode an almost brand-new Spitfire, with all mod-cons. You know, twin GPs and that and I couldn't ride it properly it was so slow. But Rainbow had a lot of help from the factory you see and was almost like the unofficial works team. As if it hadn't been for that I don't think they would have gone that well.

Hugh Evans on the Rainbow Lightning he shared with Lodge. More normally seen on an A50 he cropped up less in the publicised race results due to less coverage of the 500 production class in the press

But even so those distance events really did punish bikes. It was always down to attrition and with Hugh that year we had a bit of a stop-start sort of race. Niggling problems. The bike stopped one time up at the top of the circuit and I was exhausted. I leant forward onto the tank and as I did so I saw the top of my boot had rubbed through the battery lead. So, borrowed a penknife off one of the spectators and screwed it all back together again. Same day the bike stopped again and, looking around, the fuel tap had come undone. So, I'm soaking with petrol from the waist downwards and suddenly there's all these Spanish guys round me with fags on! It must have looked ludicrous, me pushing and flapping my arms but I had to keep all these guys away or I would have gone up in flames. While another time the whole of the left-hand exhaust system departed. I pottered round on one cylinder, went past Dick at the paddock - who must have thought: *"Oh that's the end of that then!"* - but went 'round again, found it and hooked it over my shoulder so the bloody thing was dangling down my back. A whole exhaust system! That pleased old Dick as he said: *"I didn't believe you'd do that."* But then, I think it was early morning the second day, there was a sharp left-hand bend after the start line and as I came 'round there's a fella walking across the zebra crossing with a dog on a lead! I thought: *"If I go left I'll hit the railings over there and if I go the other way I'll hit him."* As I reckon he was ten-foot from the curb. Well, I passed between him and the curb and if he'd run we'd both have been dead. Tony Smith was behind me and saw it all.

That may have sounded like a comedy of errors, but it accurately reflected what endurance racing was like in the 1960s and resulted in a highly creditable 6th place against top line opposition. That was expected at Darley Moor too, on 30th July, but the threat largely failed to materialise. The big news here was that Bill Smith was out on one of the much anticipated Honda 450cc Black Bombers and while it was able to beat teenager Bob Heath's Lightning back into third place, its performance was not as earth shattering as feared.

The *Hutch*

At Darley Moor it seems there was still no substitute for cubes and two weeks later there was no substitute for a helpful rule book. America's AMA didn't like Overhead Valve (OHV) machines, but the Swiss' FIM didn't like Overhead Cam (OHC) engines either.

On Sunday, August 14th, John Cooper filled the large boots left by Mike Hailwood, at a *Hutch* run backwards round Brands Hatch. It was run anti-clockwise to negate the dominance of renowned Brands specialists, so it came as no surprise that *'King of Brands'* Derek Minter wasn't pleased. Mike Hailwood's reservations proved academic however as the CB450 Honda he had planned to enter ran foul of the FIM rules. As the ACU, bizarrely, were forced to declare that the Honda was not a true production machine. Cooper had no qualms about the circuit's anti-clockwise nature anyway, even though he manhandled a Spitfire woefully short of perfection. This was evident in the race but earlier, while practicing at Silverstone too.

Tony Smith: I remember testing at Silverstone for the *Hutch*. Cooper was in the team and Tom Kirby was involved in the early days, in the factory team too. I did a couple of engines for him actually that he used in Terry Vinicombe's bike and Tom was a lovely guy. A great guy who put more effort as a private dealer into British racing than anybody else I know. But this morning he was there I was like a second a lap quicker than Cooper. We went to lunch at the local pub and he was having his rum and cokes and come the afternoon I couldn't get within half a second of him!

50 years later Cooper might not have remembered the rum and cokes but he still remembered the handling.

Most famous for his victory on a BSA Rocket 3, over Agostini, at Mallory Park four years later, Cooper's victory at Brands Hatch in '66 failed to have the same impact. Mainly due to the obvious difficulties he faced with this unruly Spitfire, his bike proving a bigger challenge than the opposition

The Greenwood 'Mini'

The Mini as most remembered it. Clever, but not a sidecar

The 1960s were a period of constant development. On two wheels an explosion in the number of cylinders and gears ultimately backfired, resulting in Grand Prix races becoming predictable and legislation which inadvertently brought in the homogenous, two-stroke dominated paddocks of the 1970s. On three wheels there were parallels. The domination of unobtainable BMW engines in the 500cc GP category largely killed off British interest, with a knock-on for the category at National level too. Classes for road machine-derived engines were markedly more popular, but allowing increased and often unlimited capacities opened up new possibilities too. Car and later two-stroke speed boat engines started to appear on the scene and while never truly competitive in an orthodox sidecar chassis, innovation got round this hurdle too. Through careful reading of the rules Triumph racer Owen Greenwood developed his *Mini*. Through dint of its narrowly spaced pair of rear wheels this met the eligibility criteria, with the *Scitsu*, *Mogvin* and other imitators soon following. Even though they all faced one big disadvantage. All events were push start and as the driver and passengers of these machines were to all intents and purposes incarcerated, they needed 'pushers' so had to make back row starts. Their larger engines and increased braking compensated however and the *Mini* in particular was a real threat. A threat to the sport too, with repeated calls for it to be banned, as outside the spirit, if not the rules, of the game. Greenwood was often booed off the track, but there was a silver lining. The cyclecar (as they were universally known) threat probably accelerated development of conventional racing sidecars. This led to the universal adoption of lower, sleeker, faster, *kneelers*. The reduction of wheel sizes from 18", to 16", then Mini size wheels. The use of disc brakes before they were common on solos and much wider tyres. They also used leading-link, Earles-type steering, before even better systems were evolved. As a result it was no surprise that some of the finest sidecar builders and racers of the 1970s hailed from the UK.

The root of all evil: The Owen Greenwood Mini as many would prefer to have seen it. Four wheels took a lot of skill out of the equation, both to the detriment of the spectacle and Vincent's win rate. Ironically it made the charismatic BSA rider even more popular however, as now the fans could cheer him on, not just to beat the Germans, but the pesky *'cars'* too!

John Cooper: Coming up paddock and Clearways, getting the power on there, super. But It was wobbling all over the place going round Bottom Bend and up towards Druids. Apparently, the people in the paddock were frightened to death the bike was going to chuck me off. It was so bad, going down the bottom straight, towards the hairpin, that in the hotel the night before Alan Shepherd, the team manager, said: *"It's that bad at steering if you ride it tomorrow we'll give you £100"*. But I told him I never had any intention of *not* riding it. Anyway, I won the race, but in truth I was only able to, really, as Percy's Tait front brake adjuster kept coming undone, so he had to slow down along the straight to adjust it.

A win was a win however, though it was a case of déjà vu for Rod Gould, who brought the Eddie Dow entered Lightning Clubman home fourth again. It was also déjà vu for Tony Smith, as while challenging Percy Tait his Spitfire put a rod through the crankcase, ending his challenge for the second year in succession. BSA had beaten Triumph for the second year running however, in the biggest production race of the year, though oddly they achieved little more than criticism in the press. *Motor Cycling's*: *"John Cooper tames 'Spitfire' for Brands win"* piece being typical;

"Wrestling his works 654cc BSA Spitfire to victory in the Production-machine race, John Cooper netted one of the hardest-earned £15 of his career at the British Motor Cycle racing Club's International Hutchinson 100 at Brands Hatch on Sunday.....despite the rather alarming handing of the BSA Cooper got ahead three laps from home and stayed there to win from Tait, with the relatively inexperienced Andrew a close third."[11]

Gould at speed on his '65 Clubman in '66. The 2-into-1 exhaust gave more torque at the expense of top speed

It seemed unfair criticism. Cooper noted on the handling at the time: *"It was still good enough to win!"* which Gould proved the following weekend too. With a resounding victory at the big August bank holiday Cadwell Park meeting, ahead of the Triumphs of Steve Spencer and John Hedger. Tony Smith came 4th that day, but experienced a rash of mechanical issues subsequently causing him to pull out during a three-way dice for the win at Snetterton, on September 11th. He then crashed in practice at the same circuit two weeks later, but patched himself up to come 3rd in the race and was soon back on form next time out at the circuit, as noted by *MCN*:

> *"As always the production race sparked off the most interest and produced a repeat result in both events. Tony Smith rode his incredibly fast BSA Spitfire into first place both times followed by Peter Butler (Triumph T120). Smith was so fast that his rivals never really had much of a chance, despite his poor start in the final race."*[12]

It was a good way to end the season on the solos but as the production racing titles were only up for grabs at Club level the record books concentrated on the ACU sanctioned National Championships. In which there was one obvious omission. For the first time since 1963 Chris Vincent *wasn't* the British sidecar champion. On three wheels no one could match him, but Owen Greenwood had managed it with four. Following the June hiatus Vincent had beaten Greenwood at Castle Combe, but Greenwood repaid the favour at Mallory Park. There then followed a run of BSA wins, for Brown at Croft, then Vincent at Castle Combe, Cadwell and Cadwell again, the latter over the Rennsport BMWs of Max Deubel and Fritz Scheidegger. Greenwood beat Boddice at Snetterton towards the end of October, though neither he nor Vincent finished at Mallory Park on October 30th, where Brown took advantage, to take the Gold Cup win. It made no odds to Greenwood however, as through a new points scoring system – decided by each competitor's best six results – the title was already his. *"Mini Racer Deathblow?"* read the *Motor Cycling* headline within weeks - quoting FIM regulations banning such machines - but the ACU were indecisive and in the UK it was not to be. The Mini was legal and would be back in 1967, much to the purists' disdain.

Norman Hanks follows Peter Brown at Cascades, Oulton. Both were beaten by the 100cc bigger Norton of Charlie Freeman at the beginning of October, but it wouldn't be so easy in '67. By the end of the year Brown was working on a 750cc A65 engine of his own

Irish competitor Joe Coxon was typical of the many sidecar racers picking up on the A65 as *the* engine to use as the 1960s drifted towards the 1970s. A study of concentration in the Isle of Man paddock the A65 would have to wait until 1968 to really come into its own on the Island, with the launch of the 750cc capacity Sidecar TT

That bloody *Mini* again - 1967

Over the years two wheeled winners of the Grovewood Award - for most promising up and coming rider of the year - included Dave Croxford, Steve Parrish, Damon Hill, Keith Huewen and Phil Haslam. In 1967 it was Mick Boddice.
Mick Boddice: Grovewood owned Brands and a lot of the other big circuits and they gave a rider award and a car driver award each year. £250. Well I was going to buy Derek Minter's van with the money I won, so as he was the person handing it over, he says; *"Just sign the back and you can hand it back to me after it's over."*

"Watch out for this young man during 1967! Mick Boddice, with his BSAs, could be the star sidecar man of the year on British circuits. The top performer at the Mallory Park 'opener' Mick very nearly beat much more experienced BSA exponent Chris Vincent next time out at Snetterton".[13]

Mick Boddice: Yeah, Chris Vincent, he was alright. I beat him once at Snetterton actually. I out-braked him, this is the old Snetterton I'm talking about, and I out-braked him into the hairpin at the end. I can remember 'cos I never beat him again. I nearly beat him once at Castle Combe too, when we both broke the lap record. But that day I came close at Snetterton I was going to go over to see him afterwards, but the old man said; *"No you're not. Wait for him to come and see you."* So I did. Well eventually he comes over, looks my bike up and down and just says; *"Pedalling hard weren't you chap?"* and walks off.

It was a great start for Boddice but Vincent probably felt like walking off for most of the season, since by and large it was a re-run of '66. Following Snetterton, while quite clearly superior to any other sidecars on the grid, when faced by *cyclecars* the BSAs could struggle. Everyone did, though there were still plenty of victories. Vincent won from Brown at the Sidecar Race of the Year and the Post-TT International among others, while Brown and Vinicombe picked up wins too, as did new name Mac Hobson. He was sponsored by Newcastle dealer Cowies who had sufficient clout with the factory to secure especially prepared engines, as Tom Kirby had for Terry Vinicombe. It allowed Hobson to make northern circuits, both north and south of the border his own, with his biggest win in '67 being a treble at the August Bank Holiday, Croft, *'Battle of Britain'* meeting.

Due to a southern media bias it was sometimes perceived that these northern races were peripheral affairs, but a crowd of over 10,000 clearly dispelled that illusion and Hobson's wins did not come easily. He was as likely to come up against the cyclecars as others, with his hard fought victory over the Triumph-engined *Scitsu* of John Worthington on 5th August being as typical as Peter Brown's experience on 1st July. Here Brown finished 2nd at Cadwell Park, sandwiched between the *Mini* and the *Mogvin*, a similarly unconventional Vincent-engined three wheeler. The *Mini* had spawned imitators and two events at Brands Hatch perhaps captured the feelings they were generating.

The epitome of 1960s cool. Norman Hanks and Rose Arnold at the TT. In '67 they limped home 29th while Peter Brown (fiddling with number 14 behind) didn't get past lap one with passenger Dave Bean. **Peter Brown:** *"On the very first lap the front brake, which was a 190mm Gold Star brake, exploded out of Unions Mills and locked the front wheel and forks in a gentle right hand curve. I ended going up some old girl's drive, who proceeded to give us cups of tea and great big slices of fruit cake."* Both Hanks and Brown would do an awful lot better in subsequent years

Rise of the Birmingham Mafia

Roy Hanks, Cliff Mellor, Norman Hanks, Rose Arnold, Fred Hanks and Gerald Webb. By 1967 Norman Hanks in particular was starting to assert himself on the domestic scene. His Snetterton double on April 19th was an opening salvo. Note the three full fairings and lack of trade mark black and orange colour scheme. The Hanks' naked, *Tangerine Dream* paint-scheme machines would roll out only from 1969

During the 60s a myth arose of the *Birmingham Mafia*. A group of sidecar racing BSA employees and associates who, through access to special parts and working together, were able to dominate the domestic racing scene to the detriment of all others. Probably nothing could be further from the truth. Any parts they used were made themselves and while these undoubtedly benefited from their learning on the factory shop floor that learning certainly wasn't shared among them.

Norman Hanks: We were just in the right place at the right time, as the BSA A65 became the engine to have and with Brian Martin you couldn't ask for a better boss. It wasn't so much to do with the cc or that, it was just to do with the characteristics of the engine. And while the 654 was a good engine to begin with if you bored it out to its maximum it would be 670. You'd think that can't make a big difference but the difference in performance was incredible. So everyone found that out and bored the engines to the maximum, +60 I think it was. But inevitably within a few meetings they all cracked under the first barrel fin and we were always trying to catch up on what Browny and Vincent were doing on theirs. As soon as we got a whiff of something we'd think: *"We'll have a go at that"* and I think Browny fed Chris stuff a bit. So when we found they'd fitted A10 cranks to make them 740s or some-such we had to go out and find second-hand A10 cranks of course - which didn't last long, as we kept snapping them - but they made us as quick as them again. Then we'd think; *"We're not quite so quick again"* and we'd be breaking this and that, to catch up. As we were trying to keep our secrets from each other and were always looking over each others shoulders, trying to see what the others were doing.

Peter Brown: The Competition Shop was next door to us so Hanks and Boddice were always in and out, trying to see what I was up to. I used to get up to all sorts of nasty tricks to confuse them. We had a very, very good team, a bloke called George and his son in law. George came from the Ariel's and was an absolutely incredible welder. And his son was a very skilled sheet metal worker. They used to do jobs for me so I got them to make me some megaphones. Long, thin ones, then little stubby ones, then with reverse cones on. I'd leave them lying around as these things didn't make the slightest bit of difference to the performance.

Norman Hanks: Me and Michael Boddice always thought Peter didn't like us, as us being at BSAs, seeing what he was up to, he was a bit of a grump. But if you got him in the right mood he was great and we all enjoyed the racing, as we were all sort of even keel matched. So it had a lot to do with how you rode it and you had to accept that some people were better than others and that Chris was just better than all the rest. But with all us racing you could imagine what it was like back at work on a Monday morning.

As such while they never worked together, secrets could rarely be kept for long and the Birmingham boys were not averse to sharing some of that knowledge as a future World Champion outlined.

George O'Dell: Roy Hanks being a kinder sort of driver, offered to help me in any way he could, as long as he didn't have to reveal too many secrets. As with any other engine, it took me a year to become accustomed to all the problems that the BSA engine could throw up. With the Triumph we'd suffer from petrol swill going round right-hand corners which would cause an engine to cut out: then with the BSA came little troubles like misfires, very low oil pressure, oil scavenging problems. Roy was good enough to help me out each time.[14]

It put the lie to the rumours of a closed shop around A65 secrets, though as Norman Hanks said there was a pecking order in which these would filter out. The truth was that by 1967 there still weren't many tricks of the trade to be shared by the Birmingham drivers, as there were still very few trick parts to let out. The engine was just inherently sound, straight from the crate and as popular with the fans as the racers. In 1967 this popularity was nowhere better demonstrated than over the slew of Easter events.

Norman Hanks, Vincent and Brown at Mallory's Devil's Elbow. It was often a toss up between these three for who would get the win

The Easter King of Brands meeting saw five A65s in the top six - the order being Vincent, Nigel Mead (Triumph), Vinicombe, Mick Boddice, Brown, and Norman Hanks – but what was significant was Owen Greenwood's faltering Mini *"Being cheered to a standstill"* by a large and clearly unsympathetic crowd. It was not very sporting, but reflective of the feelings of the day and perhaps one of the reasons why the Brands' September meeting saw a change in format. Interest in the 500cc capacity was waning and offering just an unlimited capacity as an alternative was encouraging cyclecar and car-based opposition to the detriment of true sidecars. Brands therefore hosted a 750 and 1000 split, meaning one capacity too small for

The Mini trailing Vinicombe was visual poetry to the supporters of traditional sidecar racing

car-engined machines and another which would limit their capacity. It worked, with the 750 result being Vincent, Vinicombe, Norman Hanks, Harris (BMW) and Brown, while the 1000 race concluded Vincent, Vinicombe, Greenwood (Mini), Norman Hanks and Bill Boddice.

It was the sort of BSA dominance replicated at the final race of the season. Mallory Park's *Finale 67 Motorcycle Races*, which saw an A65 clean sweep of Peter Brown leading home Bill Boddice and Norman Hanks, after the Greenwood Mini faltered again. It was reported as possibly its last competitive meeting, since there were already rumblings within the ACU that cyclecars would soon be banned. Not least as while the BSAs, of Vincent and Brown in particular, had reeled off far more wins than anyone else, those made little difference to the National Championship standings. By dint of how the Championship was scored again, Owen Greenwood had secured the British Motorcycle Sidecar title once more. As some wag later noted: *"As a first for British Leyland!"*

1967 saw a successful Mallory Park try-out for new-boy Malcolm Lucas in the chair of Fred Hanks A65 *'sitter'* outfit.

For Lucas the BSA bug would stick, resulting in him campaigning a solo A65 and the ex-John Copper Rocket Three in a career featuring a TT 3rd place and a 2nd place in World F2 Championship among other highs.

His ability with the A65 was helped by the fact that he rode them as a Production Tester at BSA's Birmingham factory working Monday to Friday 9 to 5

A BSA publicity shot of the beautiful 1967 Daytona model. The beauty only went skin deep however. Porous cases being the biggest problem for BSA in their second year of full factory involvement in the States

If at first you don't succeed

The sidecars had been beaten by an overly flexible rule book and while the solos struggled with an overly strict one in America – being allowed 250cc less than their Harley-Davidson adversaries - they were back in early 1967 with bikes reflecting learning from UK short circuit experience. The frames were still clearly related to the road models but now incorporated a lot of significant changes. They were 1" longer, had a more substantial swinging arm and a full-width alloy oil tank. The Gold Star pattern fuel tank was replaced with a lower version, incorporating cut-outs to allow access to the spark plugs and a high, narrow, rear section, so that the carburetors could also be worked on with the tank still in place. Additionally a disc was fitted to the rear as per American preferences, a much more appropriate Fontana 4LS brake at the front and a Jakeman fairing.

As previously, time for testing and a largely un-tried engine were the biggest challenges, particularly as the A50 and A65 engines were dynamically quite distinct. They had completely different bore and stroke dimensions which meant that carrying learning over from the bigger A65 to the A50 was not as simple as it might have seemed. Though one update which would improve both types was introduced on the '67 Daytona models. Crankshafts where oil was fed far more directly to the big-ends than could be achieved by the road bike's bush arrangement. The engines also incorporated a lot of magnesium

BSAs FOR DAYTONA.

Inter-group rivalry on the American front between BSA
and Triumph is highlighted by the fleet of six specially
built 500 cc. BSA twins like the one illustrated here.
These machines have been air freighted to Daytona where
they are entering the annual 200 mile experts race, won
last year by a Triumph at a new record average speed of
over 96 m.p.h.

PRESS OFFICE, MOTOR CYCLE DIVISION OF BSA GROUP, BIRMINGHAM 11.
Tel: VICtoria 2381.

The 1967 A50 as prepared for Daytona. An undeniably attractive and purposeful looking motorcycle it was flawed primarily through a lack of testing. The long-stroke motor also worked against it as a serious competition machine

components as a spin off from BSA's off-road competition programme, with bench test figures for a typical engine being round 53bhp @ 8250rpm. This was both impressive and in excess of what rivals Triumph were claiming, but power on the dyno doesn't always deliver results on the track.

Peter Brown: Towards Christmas time '66 the instruction was that we were sending more bikes to Daytona which occurs as I expect you'll know in March or thereabouts. They'd got roller bearing cranks, the camshaft had got needle bearings, the idler shaft had got needle bearings, and Lucas had made some rather smart, separate, remote ignition blocks. These had the points inside, connected via Oldham couplings, to the drive. They came with special magnesium crankcases and me and Graham Sanders we had a hell of a game building them. As we had precise specifications to build them to as well. Roy Bevis worked on these engines too. Anyway, we did these engines, brake tested them and off they went to Daytona. And they sent Clive Bennett and me with them as well. Which was excellent. Except that it wasn't.

The crankcases were made out of what I can only describe as Gorgonzola cheese. I mean it. They were totally porous. The bearings fell out, they leaked oil and I was surrounded in Daytona, in a bloody great aircraft-hanger is what I remember of it, just me 'cos Clive Bennett didn't do any effing work, surrounded by this rubbish. I was gluing them together with all sorts of things. Trying to get them back together and for the life of me I can't remember whether one ever finished. Doubtful I would think?

Correct. It proved an even greater fiasco than '66, as while the fastest A50 - Dick Mann's - was timed at an impressive 133mph, all six BSAs failed to finish. None went beyond 29 of the 53 laps and to add insult to injury all six factory Triumphs finished, scoring a one-two, with Gary Nixon and Buddy Elmore. The A50s were once again wheeled away in ignominy leaving it to the British racers to provide the headlines. Here the *'PR Notes'* column in *Motor Cyclist Illustrated* was avidly read by production racing fans and where journalist and top production race competitor Ray Knight observed:

Don Twigg on the 1967 specification Daytona A50. Attention was taken to getting breathing right, from creating oil tank cut-outs to re-aligned frame tubes. It still didn't stop the bottom ends failing however

"As the season gets underway it is interesting to speculate on the form for 1967. Indications may be had by looking back at last year. In the beginning Peter Butler seemed to have the edge and chalked up several victories while John Hedger and Dave Dixon did not quite have enough horses to get to the front….. and Tony Smith was struggling against mechanical unreliability. What a difference there was towards the end of 1966. Tony had his BSA's troubles sorted out and scored four wins on the trot….If Tony Smith, no longer Kirby-sponsored, continues to be reliable as well as rapid, then he must be sure to feature prominently….This year is going to be a real cracker."[15]

Chris Lodge and Melvin Rice, both back on Triumphs, lead Hugh Evans (A50) and Kevin Moyes (A65) at Snetterton on March 18th. The Moyes machine would soon be in the hands of new boy Clive Wall and used to good effect

Tony Smith's '67 *proddy* racer with '68 brake. Parts like this would be legal by each August as by this time they were already being fitted to machines for shipment to the US, the Americans always getting the new parts first

And so it proved to be, with the potential of the A65 demonstrated by a new departure, run-outs by Smith's production racer against open class opposition. On March 26th he was 9th at the Daily Mail Master of Mallory meeting then 4th the next day at Oulton Park, behind John Hartle's Rickman Métisse and the Manx Nortons of Rex Butcher and Dan Shorey. As an added bonus Smith pipped Triumph's Percy Tait, which always went down well back at Small Heath, where resources put into road racing weren't really in the same league as at Meriden.

Ron Smith: At Triumph Doug Hele would do all sorts of things on the side without Bert Hopwood knowing. When we'd go over there to the Triumph factory, to take something or pick something up, in the 'Experimental' they'd be: *"Enemy's here!"* and if there was anything special on the bench they'd cover it up. They had loads of special parts, but our budget was so small we were always playing second fiddle to Triumph in that regard. If they wanted it, they got it. While our special parts list probably ran to one side of A4 paper! Against all these Triumphs it was just Tony, and maybe one other A65, and Hugh Evans out on his A50, in the 500s. So, it used to annoy them when Tony beat Percy and often he did. As our 650 was faster than theirs, even though with their 500 it was the other way around, as it had a lot more development than ours.

With the production racers we'd start by just pulling a production bike off the track, to get all the bits and pieces we needed, like cables, brackets and that. But it'd end up nothing like it came off the line. Everything was reasonably standard, but ground and polished, and you could get a good increase in power by just opening out the ports. Tony did his own of course, but everyone used to muck in on the others and none of the bikes we did were exactly the same. We mainly trusted the frames, though some got checked in the tool room and we'd then build the bike back up again, checking that everything was OK before taking them off to MIRA, The Motor Industry Research Association track, which was the main thing. This was to see that they handled, though Tony's frame was different of course, Reynolds, there was just the one like that. I'm not sure if he had that from the very beginning, but he definitely had it later on. It was made of 531 tubing and if you put an ordinary A65 frame by the side of it, it was vastly different. For example we were grinding all the silencers away on the Production bikes so had some big flats put on them, welded on. But Tony was still grinding them away. So what was done on that frame was the pillion foot rest loops, where they fastened on to the sub-frame, he cut those off and raised them up.

Then when Clive Bennett got Alan Shepherd in to look after the production and the Daytona bikes it was even better. As Alan was a hands-on sort of chap. When *Shep* was there he had us trying all sorts of back suspension units to get them perfect and he was always playing round with the forks. The damping on the standard production bikes wasn't much good. We used to put thicker oil in, but that was about it. But Alan had mates at Girling and they did him some special parts, turned up in the tool room, which were proper hydraulic dampers. Just like a rear damper, but on the front and we ran those from then on. They were proper *Shep* jobs. But it was just Tony, me and Mick Boddice - who was an apprentice at the time - in there working on the twins, as otherwise for parts it was just a case of Brian saying; *"Go up to the track and get your bits"*. We could take what we wanted off the production line, but there were very few special parts. There was a list of optional extras - close ratio gears and that - but when most people tried to get them through the shops they said they simply couldn't get them.

This would always be the case with the A65/50 as, while the factory machines progressed, even the few listed options were very hard to come by.

Ron Smith at the Thruxton 500-miler followed by Amal Technician Alan Lines

Clive Davies: My first race was at a BFRC Cadwell meet in early 1967. l finished three races mid-field or lower and it was quite an eye opener. l thought l was really motoring along but l was overtaken either side by two 250 Aermacchis. l'd bought the *Spit* on the strength of David Dixon's MkII road test in *Motor Cycle*. The fastest road bike tested at that time. But my MkIII was a huge disappointment. Vibrated very badly and top speed was probably about 110mph. At the time Tom Kirby was fielding a Spitfire production racer so I wrote to him asking if rear-sets, performance exhausts and things were available. He wrote a very courteous reply saying: *"No, BSA didn't make such things"* and that he'd actually tried to get them for his own customers without success. Owen Greenwood lived nearby and ran his own tuning business, so it was engine out and over to Owen's. He stripped the engine down, balanced the crankshaft, fitted 10:1 pistons, as per the MkII, did some porting work, lightened the rocker gear and fitted a close ratio gear cluster. He recommended keeping the Amal Concentrics, saying the MkII's GP's only gave an advantage at very fast circuits like the TT. His bill was about £40 and when l got the bike back the performance was amazing. Very little vibration and a top speed around 120mph, give or take. The next BFRC meeting at Snetterton was much more fun. Very fast and open, l could really motor though the 190mm brake wasn't particularly good nor the handling. You snaked round the corners, while the silencers ground out quite easily too. But over the next year or so l rode at circuits like Thruxton, Brands and Mallory, as there were plenty of clubs offering *proddy* races by then.

One such was Darley Moor where Norman Vanhouse's: *"He won't last long"* comment rung hollow as Bob Heath got a win just before the *Hutch*. A race where journalist Dave Dixon noted that there would be: *"John Cooper and Tony Smith on BSAs and a horde of Triumphs."*[16] Horde of Triumphs indeed, made worse by the fact that John Cooper was actually just for the TT. It was Dave Degens, Dave Croxford and Pat Mahoney this time as BSA's hired-hands, alongside staffer Tony Smith. In a field which featured just three BSA twins the press grudgingly acknowledged the A65s prodigious speed but again decided to dwell more on

Bob Heath (left) had more success at Darley Moor on 12th August than Pat Mahoney (right) at the 24th March *King of Brands* meeting on the Kirby A65. It was no luck for Mahoney at the *Hutch* either, though from 1967 onward he became a regular when BSA needed a hired rider for the top line National events

BSA's woes, and not overly accurately at that. Smith and Mahoney were reported as out with a thrown rod but the papers failed to point out that this occurred trying to retake a comfortable second place, with a few laps to go. A slipping clutch had forced them in to the pits and it was only as they were pushing to catch up that the con-rod let go, when the engine was pushed to excess. Such details were rarely covered in the press and it was similar with

A blurry Dave Croxford, for whom a clearly broken front mudguard stay only added to his problems

the other works machine of the two Daves, Degens and Croxford. When they went out they were in 3rd, only losing the place ten minutes from the end. It was a huge disappointment. 2nd and 3rd places had looked almost certain just a few laps from the flag and perhaps a bit more road racing nous and better preparation could have made all the difference.

Dave Degens: I'd won the Thruxton 500 on the two previous occasions, with Rex Butcher and Barry Lawton and then, the following year, Tom Kirby, who was running BSAs, approached us and actually offered us money! I was then to do it with Dave Croxford. The bike, apparently they said: *"It was 10hp more, it's quicker than a Triumph, it's this, it's that"*. But we went down on the Wednesday and poor Dave got launched off, as the rotor welded to the stator. We'd always take 1mm or even 2mm off a rotor when you raced, as you don't want the thing wasting energy, charging bloody batteries up anyway. It showed me how naive they were, though I don't know what was in Chris Vincent's outfit? I think that must have been a completely trick thing, his engine, as he was incredible.

Vincent's engine was still just 670cc and actually quite ordinary, which was unfortunately what the factory contracted road racers were finding in America too. June 18th was the first opportunity since Daytona to wheel out their recalcitrant A50s and Dick Mann declined the offer, wisely as it transpired, in favour of a Gold Star borrowed from an amateur competitor.

Dick Mann was in there in eighth place behind Elmore. Mann's workhorse BSA was not very swift, but it lasted the distance without conspicuous troubles and that is more than could be said for the BSA 'Works' bikes. Ron Grant coaxed one of these home in 12th place. Misfiring and sputtering all the way. Bobby Winters' BSA twin suffered a variety of misfortunes, not the least of which was a persistent misfire. Winters made a trip into the pits at the conclusion of nearly every lap and finally grew tired of the exercise. After his last lap, he rode right off to where his truck was parked and left his crew standing down in the pits wondering what had happened: *"They kept sayin' go out and try it again, so I rode back there where they couldn't send me out anymore."*[17]

Bob Heath: The reason I had a red band round my helmet from '67 was because I used to have a plain white helmet, with a transfer on it. A Union Jack or something. Then John Hartle was making his comeback and those were his colours. I didn't want anyone thinking I was trying to do a Hartle! So, I added the red band

Proddy TT

That pretty much put a nail in it for the road racing A50s in the States for '67, but back in the UK there was much anticipation for the solos on the Isle of Man, since it was hosting the inaugural Production TT. This was a big deal as the TT was a Grand Prix event which normally only hosted 50cc to 500cc solo classes. No other World Championship meeting ran such an event but it was reflective of the status production racing had now attained and its importance to the large British manufacturers in particular. None of whom had active interest in the GP classes. Following his previous year's Hutchinson victory John Cooper was tipped to do well, but hopes were dashed before his bike had even turned a wheel in anger.

> **Ron Smith:** I hadn't seen John Cooper at all until the TT and in practice we were trying out a new aluminum clutch. But there was some problem with the push rod and the clutch springs binding, so after an OK practice Cooper comes straight in and says: *"Don't touch it now. I want it pulled out next morning just like that."* So next morning I got the bike out, went to start it and as soon as I put my foot on the kick start it just went straight down. There was nothing there. It must have gripped fine when hot, with all the heat expansion and that, but there was no grip cold in the morning. No amount of fettling made any difference, but Cooper was alright about it. He just said: *"I don't mind, I got my 50 quid off Brian"* and that was it. But can you believe it. £50 was all he got to ride?

It was just pennies and it left just four A65s and two A50s among a field of sixty, over twenty of which were Triumphs. As such ever-consistent Tony Smith's 3rd place behind the factory Triumph of John Hartle and Paul Smart's fast Dunstall Norton was highly creditable. Particularly as it was Smith's first ever time round the TT circuit and the factory had experienced inherent problems on the A65s first visit, beyond those of the clutch.

Tony Smith: The night before the race Brian Martin said: *"Shep's withdrawn the team because of the handling problems"*. I said: *"What handling problems? I'll ride"*. The bike *was* diabolical, but I knew how to ride it and finished third. It was my first time round the Island and Brian was so thrilled, he sent me a £75 cheque!

To that 3rd a good 5th was added in the 500s, by a rider used to a third wheel.

Norman Hanks: Chris Vincent had showed them he could do it, by winning on a Honda. So we all thought we could have a go after that and being a Development Tester I thought I was the bees knees. I actually first rode a works BSA in the 500-miler at Brands with one of Tony Smith's mates, Melvin Rice. I did the first stint and because I had been riding these things day in day out I think after the hour I was in 5th place and had lapped Chris Vincent on his Suzuki Super Six. Which was good, as I knew he'd know it was me when I went past! Then they gave it to Melvin and we dropped down the field again, so I asked Brian Martin to let me have another go. They brought Melvin in early and, of course, within a lap and a half I'd thrown it into the trees at Stirlings! I was meant to ride the same works bike at the TT, the inaugural production race, but later Brian says: *"I've been thinking about the TT"* – and I'm limping about at the time, with all these stitches in my foot - *"I think it would be better if you rode your own bike. And don't ride in the 750 class. We've got enough in that. You've got some 500 barrels haven't you? Build your own engine with those and ride in the 500 class"*.

Norman Hanks in the 500 Production TT. Other than Hugh Evans' machine no A50 was ever raced at the TT or on the UK mainland after 1965. Indeed, Hanks' machine was actually a Lightning fitted with 500 barrels, so not a true A50 at all. As such 5th place was pretty remarkable

Being told to ride my own bike I knew I was in Martin's black books, but he gave me all the trick bits. The cut-off flat silencers and the other bits I probably shouldn't say, as it was all down to the interpretation of the rules! And it was just as well it was a 500 as it was a mass start, where you ran across the road to the bike. I don't know if they thought that would split us up or not, but I went down Bray Hill side by side with Hugh Evans actually, and it was pure madness. I frit myself to death. Mick Andrew was meant to be on one of the works Triumphs but fell off in practice and they gave it to Alan Peck so I thought: *"I'll just keep this bloke in sight and make sure he doesn't get away from me, then try to pass him at the line"*. I thought I could slipstream him, but I only beat him as I think he missed a gear, as we were even for speed. He did an article about it afterwards, and was most put out, being beaten by this sidecar racer!

Melvin Rice was a regular aboard an A65. Seen here bringing his very standard model in to a respectable 8th place in the 1967 Production TT

The 190mm Gold Star hub and complicated left-side, rear-brake linkage indicate this is a Lightning Clubman model, fitted with tucked-in, 'Hailwood' pipes. These were de rigueur for anyone racing a BSA twin since the ACU allowed such alterations to 'production' machines on safety grounds. The same was true of raised/rear-set footrests

Back on the mainland July was significant for the appearance of BSA draughtsman Les Mason on his home-brewed Norfire - a Spitfire engine in a Norton Featherbed frame - as well as for wins by Heath at Llandow and Smith at Snetterton. They might not have been so easily won had on-form Chris Hopes been in action, since he was a top Triumph runner at the time, but he was otherwise engaged riding with Dick Rainbow's Chris Lodge to a 5th place on an A65, in Spain.

The Les Mason *Norfire* at its first meeting at Lincolnshire's Cadwell Park

Dave Mason: Looking at the photo now it's quite embarrassing actually, as that frame went through the chrome-plating shop at BSA. A Norton Featherbed frame, hanging up, going across the shop, with all the bosses walking below! And that BSA brake, it used to be single sided. They actually did some handed brake plates at BSA, so we got old Fred in the wheel building shop to press two hubs together, rotated, so the spoke angles were right, then laced those rims on and ended up with a double-sided brake

Hopes (right) in search of glory, out on track at Barcelona, and (left) with fellow British racers. **Chris Hopes:** *That's Dave Nixon stood up, Hugh Evans, John Burgess in glasses, Richard Rainbow looking like a Buddha, Chris Lodge to the right and then me looking across at Dave Nixon*

Chris Hopes: It was a monumental journey, pioneering! And I'd never ridden a Beeza 'till I got to Barcelona, where I had a run in with Dave Degens and Rex Butcher in practice. I was still getting used to the bike and there was this left-hand corner where I overtook Rex. I lost control a bit but didn't fall off, so got 'round and cleared off. But after practice Dave Degens and Rex Butcher came marching over going: *"We've come here to win this race!"* Really bollocking me, but I just laughed it off and said: *"Rex, you shouldn't have been going so slow then"* and I got on really well with him after. Though the race itself was quite peculiar. I was talking to Gary Green as it started, so was a bit slow running across and getting going. But that ended up being a good thing in the end as Pirelli had given tyres to everyone and no one had scrubbed them in. As no one knew about that sort of thing back then and they were falling off left right and centre. Armageddon it was. But as I didn't get such a good start I survived it and don't remember really any problems with the bike at all. And it must have handled, as we finished well up against all those two strokes, which were full race bikes really. Perhaps as I really liked the circuit, which was like Cadwell, just twice as big. I particularly remember coming up the top of the hill, after the start finish line, as where you came into a left-hander everyone was just sitting there at a café, drinking. So, you sort of peeled off just before you hit 'em. It was surreal, but I've never ever heard anyone even mention that before. Having people sat drinking on the racing line, so to speak? It was bizarre. Like after the race when we all went to the Town Hall to get the prizes and there were these guys all in flashy old military helmets and what have you. All pomp and ceremony.

There was probably less pomp and ceremony when Bob Heath took the win at Oulton Park on 29th, the same day as new boy Dave Vickers also won at Cadwell Park. The Cadwell meeting was notable also for Barcelona returnee Chris Hopes taking the win over another new name on an A65, Londoner Clive Wall.

Looking for sparks. Sponsor, owner and one man race team Dick Rainbow looks for life, while rider Chris Lodge does the necessary with a torch. It was a far cry from what endurance racing would become in the 1970s but a form of the sport more in line with what the TT had originally been set up to promote. Testing of the breed

Clive Wall: It took me ages to get anywhere at Cadwell. Chris Hopes came down to Brands a lot and I could beat him easy, so he said: *"Ah you wanna come up to Cadwell Park. That's a real riders circuit."* So, I went up there and I'd been racing a few years by then, and I got lapped. I wasn't happy. I hadn't been lapped for years and years, so he said: *"I'll show you the way round"* but I couldn't keep up with him, as he was very good up there. I reckon I did a season of races before I found out what to do and then I did quite well. '64 was actually my first race but I did the whole of '63, going down to Brands, doing practice days as often as I could. I probably did at least one or two a month at 17s 6d for a half day or 27s 6d for a full day and they were proper race practices, not like track days today, and you'd run into Derek Minter and who ever, getting in their way.

Wall (left) and Hopes (right). Like most of the Production Racing fraternity they were friends off the track but fierce rivals on

I was racing a Gold Star and while there used to be very few meetings at Silverstone in the mid-60s the MCC used to race a thing called the *Speed Trial*. It was actually just a race meeting, under an auspicious name, to keep the old timers happy I think and I went there, as I'd never been. I came up against this guy called Kevin Moyes, he raced this A65, a stock Spitfire MkII, for R H Smith Motorcycles and I had a look at it after 'cos it was so quick down the straights compared with this Gold Star of mine. I thought: *"I gotta get out of this Gold Star, it's just too slow"*. And as I started chatting to him he said: *"Actually I can't justify the money. I'm going to pack up. If you want to come and meet Dick Smith with me, he might help you out"* and I ended up buying half the bike. Off R H Smith, who used to sell me all the parts for it at trade price and used to pay all my entry fees. And if that doesn't sound a lot now, it certainly was back then. Anyway, after that I got pretty good at Cadwell. I'm pretty sure I never came off and I used to pass people all the time into the hairpin, where they just play follow the leader nowadays. I didn't make any friends mind - as you'd be bouncing into it! – but I got to like it up there.

(Left) Easter 1966, at Snetterton, Clive Wall on his Gold Star. By 2nd July (right) he was out on the R H Smith's Spitfire however and by early 1967 he was already appearing in the results

Factory rider

Contrary to popular belief neither Chris Vincent nor Tony Smith were paid racers. Like counterpart Percy Tait at Triumph they had day jobs at the BSA factory, though having time off to prepare for meetings over weekends. Neither complained. Few had such opportunity.

Tony Smith: Within the factory I was initially a Development Engineer and it was all nice, down to earth, bikers. No pretence. It was a wonderful atmosphere to work in as there was no bullshit and they were all good, solid, guys. There was Mick Boddice, Norman Hanks and Peter Brown who was a wizard. A bloody smart guy who was brilliant with engines. I liked to think I was good, but Brown was clever and I'll be honest I spent most of my time initially learning from older men like Peter. These people had years experience on me so I gathered ground very rapidly as a result. They would do something on an engine, I would work to perfect it, alter it, then perhaps even change it back again. I would go in at 7.30 in the morning and they'd be ringing me at 11.00 saying: *"Why are you still at work. Are you coming home?"* Everyone else would have clocked off but I would lose all track of time.

Tony Smith at the 1967 TT. Bar the *'Hailwood'* pipes and alloy tank there wasn't much on his bike which couldn't be bought over the counter. He was already carrying out extensive porting work however which released considerable performance gains. His engines never exceeded 670cc however, even on his open class racer

Evolution of the species. Standard-type profile 10.5:1 A65 piston (Left). Squish piston from a Graham Sanders prepared competition engine (Centre). Unmachined casting for a prototype slipper piston (Right). The beautiful shape of the combustion chamber on the A65 unit meant BSA never had to resort to the massively domed, gas-flow sapping, piston shapes required in other contemporary engines

And Brian was a great guy. I didn't realise 'till afterwards just how much Brian Martin must have put into me, to keep me going, as it was an uphill struggle for him. He actually took over when I was in the Experimental Department initially, but wanted the road race bikes transferred over into the Competition Department and I never really appreciated just how much poor old Bran Martin did for me. You don't at the time, you're so busy with what you're doing and to be honest the only person I ever clashed with was Jeff Smith. Simply because he resented splitting the resources. Before, 90% of the Comp Shop budget went on motocross. So, I was a real thorn in Jeff Smith's side when I arrived. I was taking more and more of that budget all the time, so there was quite a lot of animosity there. As production racing was all pretty low key when I started, so to have any kind of factory road racing bike being supported at all was quite something.

It was a good set up for me too at BSA, as the deal was that I kept the prize money, start money and appearance money and would you believe, as I elected to use my own van, they even paid me mileage and all my expenses to all the race meetings. Even if they were unofficial, non-factory supported races. So every club race too. But when it came to the bikes you could still only build a bike with what was available on the shelf.

For my race bikes I could go anywhere down the production line and pick off bits at that stage, then finish off the machining as I wanted it myself. It was far better like that and there was no money for special parts anyway. So while they had titanium frames for the motocross-ers we still ran cast iron barrels. We didn't have the budget for alloy which was a real shame, because if we'd had alloy barrels, Nikasiled bores like Jeff Smith's 500 single, we probably could have saved another 4 or 5kgs on weight. And if we'd done 180 degree cranks we could have got rid of 90% of the mass of that central flywheel. As we'd not have needed that big weight to counter-balance. We would have lost another 5kgs of weight instantly like that. So there were things which could have been done, but unfortunately that was never going to happen. We were on a budget and they tried to keep things as standard as possible, so they represented the bikes that they sold.

(Left) The yellow colour made it clear the B40 single at Cadwell was prepared on the off-road side of the Comp Shop, since it was *their* colour. (Right) Spitfires for the *Hutch* lined up during testing at Snetterton. In the event they never really threatened, with 1967 being one of BSA's most subdued Hutchinson 100 performances for many years

It was Cadwell the BSA runners were back at again soon after and while Mason, Heath, Horne and another new name, Ray Hole, were all top three contenders a victory eluded the BSAs when Smith pulled out contesting the lead. It was an interesting day for BSA all-round however as Comp Shop employee Graham Horne was ostensibly there to see Tony Smith out for the first time testing an experimental B40 based single, which was reported at the time as: "*Brian Martin's latest private venture*" and it was, being built by Horne on the Scrambles side of the department rather than the road racing. Next day the Road Racer's handiwork did better at Snetterton however where the *MCN* headline read: "*Smith wins on 'Hutch' Spitfire.*"

> "BSA works development rider Tony Smith scored a convincing win on the Spitfire he will be riding at Saturday's Hutchinson 100 in the first production race at the British Formula Racing Club meeting at Snetterton on Sunday. With the machine running perfectly Tony decided not to use it again and for the all comers event came to the line on the Spitfire that John Cooper is due to ride at the Hutch. This developed bad vibration and Smith had to be content with second place behind the swift 650 Norton of R Connolly. Smith then called it a day and retired from the scene with the fastest lap of the day at 88.53mph to his credit."[18]

It was a nice segue to that Blue Riband event itself but it was not to be three Hutchinson 100 wins on the trot. Bob Heath chose to race at his favored Darley Moor instead, winning both of the production and unlimited races and it looked like a wise choice. For once the BSA twin's speed advantage seemed lacking and in the event Smith's 6th place was the best any of the six A65s entered could manage. The Hutch ended up being dominated by John Hartle's Bonneville, which was just one among twenty-plus similar models.

Bob Heath at Darley. Avoiding the *Hutch* proved a wise move

Dick Mann at Peoria. The National win was long overdue for BSA

The other TT

Since their launch the unit twins had struggled in competition in the States. On the dirt ovals Gold Stars were still preferred to A50s, it being the same in road racing too. In TT racing, where dirt ovals were interspersed with turns and jumps, the 500cc over-head valve/750cc side-valve rule did not apply however, and with the advent of the 650cc Hornet the A65 started to make its mark. Dick Mann in particular started to get results and developed his own oil bearing frame for the unit twins. Which was significant, as the standard chassis was certainly not on a par with others. The hard work paid off on 13th August, at the Peoria TT, where the A65 took its first ever National win. The images were used extensively in BSA publicity material and were important, as while the BSA twins still clearly had some way to go to challenge the dominant Harley-Davidsons, they were getting there. They were getting there in another country too, as while Mac Hobson's sidecar results were regularly reported in the press when he crossed the border, other Scottish events rarely appeared. It didn't mean that A65s weren't winning however, with one racer being fairly typical of the breed.

Ian Thomson: There were several people who raced in my area, Murray Warner and Harry McEwan who did the Manx, Billy Kane and people like that, they encouraged me and said: *"You're a good rider on the road, but on the track, that's a different thing."* I'd bought a brand new Lightning in 1966, it was a great bike for its time, first of the unit construction engines and so easy to work on. So I thought; *"I'm going to race this!"* as I'd decided that production racing was the best way to get into it. In the early '60s PR racing was a bit frowned on by some. Not really seen as proper racing. It was later on, when it started to take off, but back then I remember being on the line at Crimond and the commentator was going through the grid of guys on Manxes and Aermacchis and he was quite disparaging when he came to me, as I was on a PR bike. But I came in third place that day and while separate production races started to come in I used to enter the unlimited races too, against Manxes and G50s and this sort of stuff. As depending on the circuit the A65 was quick, it would come out of the corners well and I had really good results.

At short circuits like Gask and Crimond in particular. I don't know what it was like down south but back then you had to join the club to race at any circuit up here. So the Solway club for Silloth, Kirkcaldy for Beveridge Park and that, though I used to go down south to Croft, did Cadwell once and liked Scarborough and I did quite well. I was lucky to have a garage in Airdrie that paid for my petrol but there wasn't much sponsorship unless you were really well known and after virtually every race I'd have new valves and springs, as I was a bit pedantic over things like that.

Race transport 1967 style for a young Ian Thomson

There was actually quite a few racing Spitfires and Lightnings up here. Ewen Haldane had a shop in Oban and raced a Spitfire and there were a couple of Clubmans models around, the gold ones and though it was a long way to places like Crimond some of the English riders used to come up from further south too. Later on there was George Fogarty and Ken Redfern, people like that. But I very well remember Malcolm Uphill coming up to Crimond on his *Bonnie*. He blew his engine up in practice and we thought: *"Oh that's good, he's out."* Put typical Uphill he had a spare in his car and came in 9th or 10th or something in the heat, when I was third or fourth. So I thought: *"Oh, he's not that good then"* as in the production races I was never out of the top five or six. But, 'cors, in the race we never saw Uphill again. He just cleared off! He was very underrated. But the camaraderie was always great at the meetings. One time I had a flat tyre going out to the start, so I borrowed a whole front wheel off a guy with a Lightning in the car park. I had to apologise about the brakes when I came back in: *"You'll probably have none left!"* But that's how it was back then. Everybody helped one another and the racing was really popular. We used to get big crowds at some of those meetings. Seven or eight thousand.

Thomson at Crimond where he was rarely the sole A65. Bill Mercer's similar machine in the background

The crowds were at least that size at Cadwell in September too, as the season came to a close. With *MCN* commenting:

> *"Tony Smith raced his Daytona BSA at Cadwell Park on Sunday and finished 13th in the main event. It is the prototype for racers which BSA will send to America for Daytona 200 early next year and features an Elektron crankcase, a disc rear brake and a Fontana front brake. The motor is based on the A50 twin engine."*[19]

The ex-Daytona 1967 machine with US preference drum front, disc rear, brake set-up

The bike was actually a repatriated '67 model, not a prototype machine for 1968, and what was more significant was that Smith also entered the 350cc single again, which he'd tested for 7-laps of practice around the Manx GP circuit the same month. This was as a precursor to further competitive rides in 1968, which while interesting demonstrated perhaps a rather shot-gun approach to race development at BSA. Solo results in 1967 had been similar to those in the sidecars and while looking on the cusp of real success the factory had failed to secure any of the Blue Riband mainland production events. They'd won neither the *Hutch* nor 500-miler, though Bob Heath had wrapped up the Darley Moor production championship, and Tony Smith had taken 3rd place at the TT, along with a number of high profile wins, including the BRC Snetterton one-hour Enduro title.

BSA were still committed to the twins though and it was announced that Paul Smart had test ridden a production Spitfire and had been signed for 1968. Smart commenting: *"I was very impressed. It certainly has plenty of power and the handling was not half so bad as some people say"*.[20] The handling was still obviously an issue however, as in December, when Brain Martin announced that a 500 would be made available to Paul Smart too he noted: *"It will be similar to the 500 twin which Tony Smith has ridden at a few meetings, but will have a new frame, as the old one was not satisfactory. There is no hard and fast arrangement about the 500, he can ride it when he wants it."*[21]

In fact, he didn't want it and never rode it. He was also to be a lot less complimentary on the production bike's handling once he rode it in anger. But that was all for '68, when Smith and Smart would be accompanied by Mick Andrew if the press were to be believed. And that would have been it too for 1967 were it not for a chance encounter between a budding sponsor, a mechanic and two expatriate Englishmen gone walkabout in Southern California.

Randy Hall: Howard Bare had been an amateur sports car racer in the 1950's. He missed racing which resulted in him purchasing in 1967 this BSA from Tom Cates, who was the National Service Manager and Racing Team Manager for the BSA-Triumph set-up in Duarte, California. It was first raced by two notable southern Californian racers called Bill Manley and Byron Farnsworth in some local

The Riverside paddock was a far cry from Mallory Park, but Gould adapted admirably, winning easily on the ex-Daytona machine

amateur road races. Howard and Bill decided to fit a disc rear brake using parts more commonly used on go carts. It took a few glowing red brake discs, but they finally got the rear disc brake working as it should and the BSA was very competitive.

In the Fall of 1967 two young men from England, Rod Gould and Bruce Cox, came to southern California. It resulted in Bruce going to work for *Cycle World* magazine and Rod as a mechanic at Norm Reeves. I got to know them very well at the shop and particularly in the evening, with all the guys drinking beer. The bar kept a six pack of beer under the counter because the English drink warm beer! Through my Norm Reeves connections it was arranged for Rod to race Howard's BSA. I don't remember at how many and what races Rod raced the BSA but I do remember Rod winning the race at Riverside International Raceway.

Through journalist Cox the result got coverage on both sides of the Atlantic, with the win having unforeseen consequences for the careers of all of those involved.

Rod Gould: That race was the start of things that changed my racing forever. The bike was an ex-factory Daytona machine entrusted to Randy Hall to prepare and Randy - who worked at the same motorcycle dealer that I did while in California - asked if I would like to ride it at Riverside.

Gould's Daytona machine to the front and a more conventional road-based A65 racer to the rear

I had raced the dealer's Honda 450 at Willow Springs and won so we went to Riverside Raceway, practice was OK, and I felt comfortable with the bike. The local ace was Buddy Parriott who rode a 500 Manx and it was a case of who would be second if he was riding. The event was not an AMA event, but run under the FIM affiliated organisation, so a dead engine start. I got away well and to cut a long story short won without much trouble. Buddy was second. The link from this to my future career was that Randy stayed with me for the next few years, resulting in the World Title in 1970. But without a doubt that would not have happened if I had not ridden that BSA A65 at Riverside in '67.

The Riverside ride would lead to Kawasaki and Yamaha deals and obviously finish any prospects of future A65 rides for Gould, but it did set up BSA nicely in the States for future developments. Gould's win had been in an ACA, FIM sanctioned event, while the AMA ran the majority of meetings. As already noted these restricted overhead valve machines to just 500cc in the majority of events but rumors were already circulating that full 750cc engines would soon be allowed in Flat Track, creating real prospects for the A65s to take on the Harley-Davidsons in the future. 750s would be needed for the UK too, since there were rumours of a 750cc Sidecar TT in the offing. But in the meantime it was back to work on the A50s, as for Daytona it was still only 500cc.

A BSA Grand Prix racer? The hobbyists evidently thought so, but that would require BSA to produce a competitive 500cc racer for 1968, on a par at least with Triumph's T100

Vinicombe vindicated - 1968

Les Mason: I was very good friends with Brian Martin, the Comp Shop Manager and as they were closing down the drawing office at BSA, doing the whole thing down at Umberslade Hall, he realized he was going to have a hell of a job getting anything drawn. He said: *"I've had a bit of a chat with Bert Hopwood, and he's in agreement with me, that you can come and work with me and set up a drawing office in the Comp Shop"*. I said: *"Thank you. Thank you very much Brian. That's right up my alley, that will do me a treat!"* Me and Brian had offices next to each other and I worked with Jeff (Smith) and Tony (Smith) and the boys on both the roadrace and motocross side, so anything they wanted making, they'd just come to me with their sketches and bits and pieces. Then I'd draw it and I'd end up being the procuring man as well, as I'd have to go and get it made and make sure it was all done right.

Anyway Ernie Webster said: *"OK I've got a job for you. I want you to work with Paul Ridout on the A50 Daytona twins."* This was the last time they were raced, which was 1968, and we got cracking as Paul had already sketched out a few improvements he wanted to incorporate. I detailed an awful lot of it and I did most of the drawings for that engine, as I was the only draughtsman working on it. It was true that the Daytona BSAs were disastrous in previous years, but things changed in 1968 when Alan Shepherd really got involved.

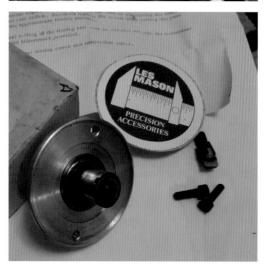

(Top & middle) An innovation for the 1968 Daytona racers was the Lucas remote contact breaker, which drove the points through an Oldham coupling, to eliminate elliptical rotation of the cam. Draughtsman Les Mason was soon marketing his own (bottom), through his Precision Accessories line, as a simpler and less obtrusive alternative

(Top) 1967 cases and (below) three magnesium cases from a 1968 engine, showing respectively the oil pump location area, the special mounting for the remote Lucas contact-breaker assembly and the oil-way for the direct oiling to the end of the crankshaft

Paul and I got into the engines and Alan set up the new frame I had drawn up under his direction. It had a Victor type swinging arm, with a snail cam adjuster and rear axle grabbed by the 4-bolt clamp at the end, and they were superb. Handled a treat. And when Paul designed that last Daytona engine we end-fed the crankshaft, as the boys were already doing that in the Experimental Department under Clive Bennett. But what Paul did was actually design it properly. He was given carte blanche, so it was very good, but it meant that you had to have special crankcases, special covers, special this, that and the other. That engine was virtually a one off, with magnesium crankcases and everything.

There were actually two different frame types developed with the more conventional one selected. The improvement in handling with both types was clear, though testing still presented its own unique set of challenges.

Tony Smith: Daytona is the first week in March of course, so Norman Hanks and I went off to MIRA to do the 200-mile simulation with one other mechanic, I think Ron Smith. We get there and it's freezing, late February and it's Friday. You can't believe how cold it is with the wind blowing across and I have to simulate the 200-mile race. There's no infield, just the oval, we're probably running for four or five laps, something like that and the snow starts to come down. So, in the end I'm just following a little bit of black tarmac in the white and on the banking it goes from a few inches wide to about a foot where the bike's drifting. I came in after the pre-determined half way, 100 miles, and they're asking *"You're not carrying on are you?"* So, I say; *"If we don't finish it now we'll have to come back on Monday."* So, we carried on, refuelled and calculated afterwards that we'd done the 200 miles at an average of 119mph. On an A50. The 500 had a top speed of about 135-137mph and I'd averaged 119mph over 200 miles, in the snow.

The other frame

Norman Hanks: Alan Shepherd had a bum deal really. He was never used to his potential. The last year they did the Daytona bikes '68 he made a frame and went and got Ken Sprayson to put it together. This frame was phenomenal, it was the one we all liked. I can't speak for Tony Smith, but he rode it and I rode it, and I think Michael Boddice may even have rode it and that's the one I would have had. We used to go to Mallory and as BSA used to hire the whole circuit it was only us there. And we used to run this fantastic bike round and round and round. It was the winter and sometimes frosty, so Alan had this car, a brand-new BMW and he'd say: *"Drive this round a bit and make a line"* and Tony, me and Mick we used to do all this mileage on this frame, with him telling us what to do.

Detail showing the oil tank behind the engine on the Alan Shepherd designed chassis

When I was going round Gerards the back-end must have been hanging out as I was actually turning away from the corner. I was doing that naturally and it was only when he said: *"Do you feel it hanging out and feel the revs rising? You need to turn the handle bars away"* that I thought; *"Wow, you're right."* So, by the time we came to the 500-miler I could hang the back end out round South Bank on my own bike, like a speedway rider.

We fell into two camps, Clive Bennett wanted a more standard looking frame which was what we used for Daytona and Alan Shepherd said he wanted this frame, which was stiffer. It was a bit of a fight between the two and I'm not sure what Tony's feelings were, but I always told everybody that Alan's frame was better and so did Michael. At MIRA we'd have people lying down on the edge of the track seeing which came round the corner better.

A paddock photo indicating that Shepherd's alternative Daytona A50 frame was at least practiced at a UK race meeting in late 1967, or early 1968, if not actually raced

Either way this was evidently a very complete machine, since it carried the full USA specification brake set-up as fitted to the final machines sent to America, as well as a bespoke tank and seat unit

It's interesting to conjecture what might have happened had this frame-type been prioritised in 1968 over the more conventional chassis selected for production

Norman Hanks: We tested those last bikes at MIRA and spent hours going round and round and I think at the time the lap record for an hour was held by a Velocette. We were told not to go round faster than 125mph, so we went round at 125mph all the time. In those days the banking was concrete. There was a little stripe between the two strips of concrete, just at the beginning of the banking, so we tried to ride on that to keep it interesting and to keep you sane for the hours you went round and round. Alan Shepherd had made this oil cooler which came down underneath and when we came in this oil cooler was chamfered off completely on one side and we weren't even aware. We were definitely circulating over what the world record was at that time, but you weren't allowed to set world records at MIRA back then.

Dickie Newell on his A50. It failed to go the distance, but Bobby Winters' did and performed very well

Things looked good for the race, but tragically not all testing had gone as well as at MIRA. Around the same time *MCI* announced: *"Alan Shepherd, ex-MZ and Honda works rider has left the BSA factory, where he was employed in their competition shop for the past 18 months."* But it told only part of the story.

Pat Slinn: The building and preparation of those bikes took longer than expected, and a couple of us from the Development Shop had been drafted in to help, as one or two teething problems had shown up during testing at MIRA. The evening before the bikes were to be crated up and dispatched to the US, Alan took the last one to be completed out on the BSA test track, just to check that everything worked. Unfortunately, it was after 5.30 pm and the factory personnel had started to leave, as part of the test track was also the way out of the car park and a barrier was lowered to stop any bikes from using the test track. For some reason Alan had not noticed that the barrier was down and went crashing into it. He was quite badly hurt and the bike was very badly damaged. This resulted in a few of us having to work through the night to repair it.

Ron Smith: He was going around the test track the wrong way. But that was OK as we made sure there were no other testers on the track. We were actually in the Comp Shop looking out the window at him, going round. What happens? The copper comes down, puts the barrier down as all the staff had left and locks it. Course *Shep's* bladdering round the track and at the last minute I think he saw the barrier and got right down on the tank. The alloy tank was squashed in the middle where his chin had like been smashed down under the barrier and threw him off. Unconscious he was. When we got in the ambulance, the three of us, the driver and one of the BSA coppers, he went straight across a red light on the Bristol Road and hit a double-decker bus and wrote the Daimler ambulance off. *Shep* was in the front and his helmet was off. His head was slammed into the front of the ambulance and that was it after that, as he wasn't on the scene again.

It was an inauspicious start and given the A50's previous performances it was surprising that Dick Mann still signed up. But he was BSA to the bone and was backed up by Bobby Winters, Dickie Newell and Don Twigg as the official BSA factory squad. A pre-race accident ultimately sidelined Mann however, meaning Tony Smith got the ride.

> **Tony Smith:** John Hickson was like my champion at BSA. He called me up to his office and said: *"Tony we want you to go to Daytona, to help the team to set the bikes up for the Americans."* He gave me £150 in cash, but within the first week Brian Martin and the guy from Lucas, had spent all theirs as well as mine, as they knew what to do with expenses. I was there to set the bikes up for the American team, I wasn't there as a rider anyway, because Daytona was a specialist circuit, but during testing I lapped quicker than all the factory riders. The trouble was I had a bike that I'd done all the development work on, and it broke a crank the morning of the race, as it had done hundreds and hundreds of miles testing. What BSA should have done is taken one of the other bikes and given it to me, as 4,000-miles is a long trip to end up just a spectator.

Smith was probably right as while Don Twigg and Dick Newell had technical problems Bobby Winters managed a 12th place overall. This was a good 5 laps down on the astoundingly quick Harley-Davidson of Cal Rayborn, but only four genuine 500cc four-stroke machines finished ahead of the A50. The bike's overall performance was far from shabby. Winters was seven places and a full four laps ahead of the Triumph of 1967 winner Gary Nixon, and immediately ahead at the close was double World Champion Phil Read, on a 350 GP Yamaha two-stroke. To further highlight how the A50s had improved, in the 100-mile amateur race which was run two days previously, Ray Hempstead rode into 2nd place on the East Coast backed BSA, which was formerly ridden by Jody Nicholas. This was second place out of 82 runners and it showed what could be achieved in terms of speed and longevity with a little extra development. In the short term however there was a silver lining for Small Heath's sidecar fraternity, in the fate of the less successful Daytona machines.

A Daytona engine with 1968 timing cover converted to 750cc for sidecar racing use. A surprising number of such engines appeared on the British scene

Peter Brown: By 1968 the cases and castings were getting quite tasty. The camshafts and idler gears had needle roller bearings and this stuff kept coming back from America. The good thing about the Americans was that they also made special pieces. Some beautiful con-rods, pistons and valve springs. We used to get this stuff across and the valve springs were supposedly from special steel used on rockets to the moon. Whether that was true or not I don't know, but they were bloody good springs. They were *'rated'*, much shorter than the standard and a smaller diameter as well. What they did was give you a very low poundage on the initial lift but one that then strengthened up as the valves opened further. They were capable of rev-ing higher than the standard spring and there were sufficient of those to go around. They were intended for the Daytona engines but there were a lot of *'spares'*. So, we got our ration!

The problem with the '68 engine was that it had a huge double row roller bearing, self-aligning, on the drive-side. The crankshaft was trapped against that bearing by the alternator so as the engine got hot, and there was more clearance due to expansion, it would allow the crankshaft to resonate. It floated and broke every crank they had. All the engines came back with broken cranks and my eyes lit up as I'd suddenly got a lovely supply of crankcases. They were actually beautiful bearings they used too, but the first thing I did was take them out, throw them away and replace them with just a standard fully floating roller bearing. The engine, built like that, ran perfectly, no trouble, bullet proof. The problem as ever was that they didn't test the sodding things enough.

Mallory Park 5ᵗʰ May 1968 Norman Hanks leads brother Roy. The final result was Chris Vincent from Norman Hanks, Mick Boddice, Roy Hanks and Peter Brown. All on A65s. *MCN* reported it as: *"exhibition stuff"*

Mac Hobson as a blur. He was virtually unbeatable on the northern British and Scottish circuits

Lack of testing was not something which could have been levelled at those using A65s for sidecar racing. Not by 1968 at least. Though there were still alternatives to the BSA twins, particularly for those looking for bigger engines. Before the season had begun Vincent was beaten on December 29th by the new owner of the Greenwood Mini, Andy Chapman. The win didn't mean much - as it was little more than a test day - Vincent reporting at the time: *"I looked round, but there was so much spray I couldn't see any further than my back wheel of the outfit. To be honest I didn't see him coming!"* It showed that the cyclecars would still be a consideration however, as would Norman Hanks' test machine that same day. As he was out on a Hillman Imp car-engined outfit. He would be back on an A65 for a successful season start however, but only in the wake of incredible carnage behind. The 3rd March Mallory Park opener got off to a bad start when Vincent broke his chain and Vinicombe succumbed to electrical problems. Mick Boddice then flipped at the Devil's Elbow leaving Norman Hanks to pick up the win, once Brown had also thrown away the lead.

Peter Brown: The prize money was about £100, but unknown to me a person who will remain nameless was guilty of spreading oil everywhere when we came round the Devil's Elbow in the lead. Back in the bad old days you used to come round the hairpin and knock it in to second gear if you were quick. Dave Bean was a good passenger, he was a big bloke but knew how to let it spin, so I could get into second pretty smoky and if you were really on it you could knock it into third going round the Elbow. But it was all a bit on the edge that day and we hit this sodding oil and spun pretty quickly. I have a suspicion we went round twice and while I can't say we were in control we were still on the ground and I remember quite distinctly - and I know it sounds absurd - but thinking: *"If I give it a fistful just in the right place I might be able to get it straightened up?"* By this time we were at the bottom of the Devil's Elbow though and hit a new bit of tarmac. Dave flew off in a parabola while I decided to abandon ship. I remember sliding down towards the start line, on me arse, looking at my outfit upside down, sliding along, thinking: *"Oh shit we've got to get that ready for Brands Hatch next weekend."*

Incredibly he did, to take the win, with results then being delivered on a regularity reminiscent of the pre-*Mini* era. Vincent won the following week at Snetterton, then did the double over the last weekend of March. Winning first at Oulton, then Lydden, with a 275 mile overnight drive in between. Those wins continued for Vincent up to the TT, though Hobson, Vinicombe and Brown all picked up victories as well, with the other BSA runners never being far behind. These now included Bill Cooper who featured at Castle Combe on 27th April, where one of the few non-A65 outfits at the front experienced the Birmingham Mafia phenomena up close and personal. As while Cooper had come third behind Vincent and Brown in the first race, it was a Triumph outfit in the same position second time around.

Mick Horspole: I remember that one as while I was having a right do with Peter Brown, Vincent was more or less protecting him. I think generally that they stuck together a bit. I went quite well round Castle Combe and while they were a bit faster than me drawing out of the corners I had as good a speed as them by the end of the straight. But it stuck in my mind that day the way they were riding, as while I could pass Browny suddenly Vincent would be in the way, and then the pair would get going again. Vincent was protecting Browny, but then I think they did have a technical advantage too. As they were all working at the factory. Browny, Boddice, Hanksy and that lot, while we never had anything special at all. We never had a full 750 and the first time we had a proper Bonneville engine we had to buy it in spare parts, £105, most of the bits new sort of thing. We had a 500 for the Internationals too, for when the Germans used to come over with their BMWs. But those BSA guys were the ones really to beat. I always reckoned I was the best of the rest though and we used to go down to Brands a time or two and put the cat among the pigeons. But Chris, I think he was a cut above the rest and right good-looking with his little beard too!

Bill Cooper in action. He matched Horspole at Castle Combe with an A65 in one of his own chassis

He was, and was regularly pulled in for publicity purposes by BSA. But for the solos it was a BSA product in a non-standard frame getting all the publicity at the start of the season. With Smith still in Daytona rising star Alan Barnett was in the spotlight, out on Tom Kirby's Rickman Métisse-framed A65 at Brands Hatch, on March 10th.

"Riding Kirby's BSA Spitfire-engined Métisse which was alarmingly fast, he held off Ray Pickrell on Paul Dunstall's 750 Domiracer for four laps. Then as the BSA began to misfire Pickrell forced past and Barnett headed for the paddock."

The machine obviously showed promise and while there were top three places for Heath, Mason and Vickers, it wasn't until Cadwell Park on 7th April that Smith took the first A65 win of the season. Bob Heath then did the double at Darley Moor the following weekend, in an eye-opening performance for another A65 competitor.

Bob Heath lining his Lightning up for Scrutineering. Though updated regularly, underneath it was a '65 Clubman

Mel Cranmer: I would go along to the races as a 16-year-old kid and went one time to Silverstone and saw Tony Smith win the production race on a BSA. There was one for sale locally, brand new, a Spitfire and I bought it. I thought: *"That's the fastest production bike you can get. I'm going to start racing."* But of course, while you might have the fastest bike, you might not be the quickest rider. That first meeting I rode the bike there, Darley Moor this is, sat around in the paddock next to my bike, then did my first race. There were heats for the production race and I think the first twelve went through from each. I think I finished thirteenth, so not good enough to get into the final, however only eleven must have finished in the other heat or something, so I did. And my clearest memory is of coming out of the hairpin, where you've got that long straight after. I'm thinking: *"I'm on the fastest bike you can buy"* but as I came out I got the sensation that I'd got someone behind me. And suddenly Bob Heath's BSA went one side and Pete Davies' Triumph went the other. I couldn't believe how quick they were going. It was fantastic. What real racing was all about, and at the end of the season Bob's bike came up for sale, so I bought it. It was very well put together and it must have been quicker than mine, but it didn't really feel that special. It was just very well set up. It braked well, it handled well, and I remember Bob had a Dunlop triangular rear tyre on the front and an Avon Grand Prix on the back. And while that sounds a strange combination, that's exactly how he rode it back then, so I rode it like that too.

Heath traded his Lightning Clubman in at the end of 1969 as he wanted a Manx Norton and the following Sunday, April 14th, Tony Smith was on a single too. This time a bigger version of the 350 that he had tested in '67. It took 3rd place in the 1,000cc event and it was claimed to have been clocked at 132mph at MIRA. But it showed that BSA had their fingers in other pies and removed the potential for another A65 victory. That was achieved on the last weekend of April however, when Bob Heath was at Aintree, taking the win over Les Mason as a perfect warm up to the 500-miler at Brands on Sunday 12th May. It was the first year that the factories openly entered machines under their own name, but one that Ray Knight dubbed in his regular PR Notes column: *"A fantastic machine-wrecking race."*

For the BSA Group it couldn't have started worse with Tony Smith hitting the deck at Paddock Hill Bend early on, followed soon after by Triumph's Percy Tait. But by lap 31 things were looking up for BSA. 1967's chosen factory riders, Smart and Mahoney, were already up to second place and even though Smart had managed to grind through most of the left-hand silencer, by the 92nd lap they were pressurising the leading Croxford/ Pickrell pair to such an extent that the Norton threw its primary chain in protest and was out. By lap 115 not only was the Smart/ Mahoney Spitfire leading, but Bob Heath, partnered by Alastair Copeland was 2nd, before it all started to unravel. Mick Andrew took his turn dropping the second works Spitfire at Druids, the Boddice/Mason Spitfire was in to the pits having its broken exhaust pipe repaired with Pepsi cans – and sounding like it too! – and then Heath and Copeland started to slip down the order too.

The 500cc version of the BSA single. It would go on to become a formidable weapon by 1970 by which time it was fully on song. It was in truth hopelessly out of date by then however, in comparison to the Japanese opposition it was up against. It still, briefly, led the British 500cc Championship however

Down but not out the Smiths (mechanic Ron and rider Tony) await a scrutineer's adjudication on whether the Smith/Andrew Spitfire is fit to continue, after Tony Smith hit the deck early on

Catastrophically Mahoney was in and out of the pits also, reporting handling problems, before a keen-eyed scrutineer spotted that the swinging-arm was actually completely broken.

Ron Smith: For the Brands Hatch 500-miler we'd had a special swinging arm made. A bit longer or some such, up in the frame shop. Alan Shepherd had arranged it, but the guy who had done the welding had got it all too hot and it broke. They brazed it too hot. That's what the lab said afterwards anyway.

It was a crushing end to what looked like a certain BSA 1-2 finish only a few laps before. Hugh Evans and Paul Coombs took 4th in the 500 class on their A50, while Smith and Mick Andrew clawed their way back up to a similar spot in the 750s. But these were poor recompense given what could have been. The disappointment was reported as etched across the faces of Martin, Smart, Mahoney and sponsor Tom Kirby and there was cruel irony in Chris Vincent screaming across the line to win the 500 class and take 4th overall, paired with Tommy Robb on a Suzuki. Vincent was employed by BSA, but as a tester, not as a racer. Officially he was only racing in his spare time which was the reason he had the prominent 'Vincent BSA' on his sidecar's fairing. Making it clear it was his, not BSA's outfit, he was racing. BSA never asked him to race a solo A65 and he hadn't been impressed with their approach previously, when he was put on an A10 then C15.

The strength of field in the Blue Riband production events amply demonstrated at May's Brands 500-miler. Tommy Robb (Suzuki 500. No.21) who partnered the multi-talented Chris Vincent, makes a move on Derek Minter (Ducati 350. No.22), while three BSA A65 line up astern. 54. Graham Horne; 57. Bob Heath; 56 Les Mason, who shared his machine with sidecar pilot, Mick Boddice; **Mick Boddice:** Every time it rained Les came in. I was riding faster than him anyway but, saying that, I've got a picture somewhere of Les Graham coming 'round the outside of me. And he was on a 250 Suzuki!

Chris Vincent: They weren't interested in getting a second rider in then, like Read or Ivy. If they'd said to me: *"Pick a rider"* we could have done much better, as we provided Alan Kimber at Suzuki with three wins on the trot. Suzuki won the *MCN* Bike of the Year award, and the Super Six really took off in '67. Then they moved me to the 500cc Cobra, with Tommy Robb. It was all so different to BSA as we were equals, we matched each-others times, and BSA never asked me to race an A65 solo anyway. Though oddly, later, they started this 750 racing and were putting up about 500 quid at Mallory. So old Dave Croxford says to me: *"Could you do me one of your engines? Your 750 sidecar engines".* And I thought: *"Actually, I'll have a go myself!"* I'd got left with this really nice frame from when I was racing the REG, don't ask me how, but I had it down in my workshop at BSA actually. So, I set it up on my desk and I was trying to graft an A65 into it. But I worked out I'd got no maintenance prospects, as you couldn't get the rocker box off and that was as far as it got unfortunately. It was a sad story really, as later no one wanted it and I scrapped the bloody thing.

It was certainly an imponderable as to why BSA never asked Vincent to ride an A65 solo, when other manufacturers were queuing up? Perhaps they thought there was sufficient talent out already which was perhaps demonstrated by a Bob Heath taking a double at Darley Moor on 19th May and the Smith/Andrew partnership a second place at Mallory Park the following weekend, in a novel 30-lap production event. This included a Le Mans-type start - with riders running from the outfield to the Paddock building area to collect and start their bikes - along with a rider change. It was the 500-miler Dunstall Norton partnership of Pickrell/Croxford which claimed the winners' prize, but it was still a good ride, as Smith's bike was the one he was taking to the TT and evidently a better example than Smart's.

Paul Smart: In the Production TT I rode a 654cc BSA Spitfire. It was a roadster which the factory said was specially prepared but there was very little special about the thing I could see. I could not believe a works bike could be so bloody bad! I never used top gear and got so bored I wished I had a radio. In the end I couldn't see much point in suffering for nothing and pulled in at Ballacraine. But lovely old Brian Martin, who was managing the team, told me later that I was in fourth place when I retired!

TT 1968: Paul Smart (left) at the bottom of Bray Hill, while Tony Smith (right) pushes Smart's machine through scrutineering earlier on. It was a DNF for Smart and third place again for Smith come race day

To try to match the speed of the Nortons Smith and mechanic Steve Brown (standing right) tried a different fairing on the Spitfire in practice, but reverted to the standard type for the race

Smart was used to thoroughbred Grand Prix machinery and as such the BSA probably felt unsophisticated in comparison and a lot slower than it really was. This was demonstrated by Smith beating all eleven Triumphs entered, including the two most fancied runners, John Hartle and Malcolm Uphill, but as was the case at the Hutch and 500-miler, he could not match the outright speed of the 750 Nortons. The 100cc capacity advantage made all the difference, with race winner Ray Pickrell and second placed man Billy Nelson proving just too fast for Smith, who was pushed back to 3rd place again.

Smith on his standard-faired machine which he rode to another fine 3rd place

The quiet before the storm. The corporate liveried Fred Hanks Equipe undergo scrutineering. It is not recorded whether the baby walker, bottom left, passed muster?

The A65s TT

It was second time round for the production racers at the Island, so the big news for '68 was obviously the inaugural 750cc class for the sidecars. In the UK there was dwindling interest in the BMW-dominated Grand Prix scene and the 750-category reflected better the realities of the day. British sidecar racing was dominated by machines of 750cc and above and the BSA runners were tipped to do well. But it was far better than anyone could ever have foreseen. Realistically unchallenged by any other make of machinery, the race resulted in a unique A65 podium. It was a fine win for the ever popular Terry Vinicombe and John Flaxman and paid sponsor Tom Kirby back for his belief in them and the A65. Of the other fancied A65 runners Hobson got no further than Union Mills, Chris Vincent stopped when leading at Kirkmichael and both Roy and father Fred Hanks were in the pits with problems. The second and third place runners weren't without their difficulties either.

Norman Hanks: I was second and Rose was the first woman to stand on the TT rostrum. But we were lucky, as on the last lap, going up the Mountain, Guthrie's or somewhere like that, it was stuttering on one cylinder. I thought: *"God not now!"* as one of the carbs was hanging off. We'd borrowed some of the fancy Daytona carb-rubbers, but one had split, so every time we went round a left-hander it fell off. But Peter was struggling too, as Dave Bean's leathers had split open.

Peter Brown: In '68 we should have won it actually, but the zip on Dave Bean's leathers broke. He looked like the Michelin Man and it must have knocked about 30 mph off the top speed as a result!

Brown's claim he could have won wasn't an idle boast. Working on A65 engine development at BSA as his day job his motors were acknowledged as the quickest out there, which was demonstrated as the season on the mainland progressed. As while Vincent won at Snetterton the first weekend back after the TT, Brown won at Thruxton, then again at Brands Hatch and subsequently at Castle Combe. Over the same period Hobson won at Gask, Silloth, Croft and Crimond, with the later being noteworthy not so much for Malcolm Uphill winning the headline solo event, as witnessed by Ian Thomson, but for the second placed crew in the sidecars, since they would soon be out on one of the winner's engines.

Pete Krukowski: I changed to A65 engines when a friend appeared with one in 1966 or '67. It was so much faster than my Bonneville and when I asked why, his answer was simple: *"It's all standard parts!"* When I started using A65 engines myself I found it was true. I bought an engine from a crashed Spitfire and it was exactly as the engines I bought from Mac Hobson, except for the inlet ports, which he'd opened out. I have no evidence to support my opinion, but I believe that as BSA had developed scrambles engines for many years it follows that porting and cam design would be influenced by that same experience. Leading to engines such as the A65, which produced a wide spread of power ideal for sidecar use. Norton and Triumph, the A65s closest competitor engines, were developed from solo experience, so may not have had that same sort of power.

750 Sidecar TT podium: 2nd Rose Arnold (soon to become Mrs Roy Hanks) and Norman Hanks. 1st Terry Vinicombe and John Flaxman. 3rd Peter Brown and Dave Bean – with his *'air-brake'* leathers, devoid of zip, in evidence.

Krukowski's was a reasonable assumption about the A65, but probably not so true of the coming breed of engine. Which Chris Vincent experienced on 4th August, when stuck behind the Hillman Imp-powered outfit of Idris Evans at Lydden Hill. He got by, but the commentary had it that the speed of the Imp *"Startled spectators"* and presumably Peter Brown too. Since he was unable or get past at all. It didn't greatly influence the result of the championship though in which there were continued victories for Hobson around the northern circuits, Vinicombe at Thruxton and Hanks at

Pete and Frances Krukowski at Beveridge Park. A65s proved as popular north of the border as south, though not getting as much media coverage

Cadwell Park. Vincent in turn had wins at Brands, Mallory, Croft and Cadwell, but these were not all British Championship rounds. Brown had had a good early season and continued with solid, consistent placings, helped by a win at Brands Hatch on October 6th. He pulled out of the late season National at Mallory Park, when passenger Mick Casey struck his arm on the retaining wall at the Devil's Elbow, but it didn't really matter. He'd already been crowned British Champion, the title back in BSA's hands after the two year, *Mini*, Hiatus.

"What the hell is that?" The late 1960s were a period for testing new ideas and testing the rule book. Roy Hanks does a double take at Cadwell Park, as Jon Worthington's rule bending *Scitsu* gets too close for comfort. Worthington took a win and a 2nd place on May the 19th, while Roy Hanks' best was a 3rd

Last corner, last lap. Mallory Park, October 20th 1968. Norman and Rose Hanks get their A65 up the inside of Gerry Boret and Pete Kennard's Vincent 1000cc as Peter Brown (no.2) can only look on. As was so often the case, Chris Vincent was long gone by this point

The A50's final bow

There was little chance of BSA emulating Brown's National success in America. But perhaps buoyed by the A50's better performance at Daytona, Dick Mann wheeled one out for the second road race of the American championships, at Loudon. Ex-team mate Jody Nicholas was more of an A50 fan than Mann, but as he was no longer in the team he was on a Yamaha and both ended up in the same battle. With the Harley-Davidson of Rayborn and Triumph of Gary Nixon out front they found themselves in a mighty fight with Dick Hammer (Triumph) Ron Grant (Suzuki) and Mert Lawwill (Harley-Davidson). The decision finally went in the favour of Nicholas' fleet Yamaha, but Mann's A50 took fourth with the press commenting that: *"although seriously outpowered, the bike looked and handled beautifully and was well suited to the to the tight Loudon circuit."*

It wouldn't be long before American road racers would conquer the world. They'd do so largely off their flat track experience and those influences still showed through on Mann's A50 road racer, at Loudon, in 1968

If not already known, beautiful handling could no longer be provided by the standard A65 chassis, so while Tony Smith was already toying with an ex-Daytona chassis identical to Mann's, a number of privateers in the UK had already gone down the accepted, default route, of using a Norton Featherbed frame. Les Mason was the most prominent but BSA road tester Malcolm Lucas was soon to follow. The alternative was the Rickman Métisse, with both options showing their potential following the TT. Alan Barnett nipped inside Malcolm Uphill on the last lap, to win on the Kirby Métisse at Thruxton, on June 23rd, while Les Mason beat Bob Heath at Aintree on July 6th. Subsequently there were a succession of top finishes, for the Smith, Wall, Hole, Heath and new name Gerry Millward. With Melvin Rice's 2nd place at Cadwell Park probably his last race on an A65, since he was about to retire. Hugh Evans then took a win on his A50 at Snetterton, on the 4th August, before the Hutchinson 100, which proved a frustrating affair.

With both Paul Smart and Alan Barnett out through injury Tony Smith was virtually alone on an A65 and was forced to accept 4th when oil on his back tyre resulted in some lurid slides and the need to relinquish places. The most interesting feature of the race therefore were the machines behind Smith rather than those in front. As Mick Andrew was on a solitary example of the new Norton Commando and of the nineteen Triumphs, the one on Smith's tail, Percy Tait's, was an equally new and exotic 750cc Trident triple. These bigger 750cc machines were still largely for the future and certainly couldn't spoil BSA's party over the August Bank Holiday weekend, as it marked one of the A65s biggest ever wins. As reported in *MCN: "Tony Smith took the works 650cc BSA twin to its first National race victory ever, when he took the "Cadwell Conqueror" title, at Cadwell Park, on Monday."*

Alan Barnett on the 654cc Kirby Métisse in the specification as used at Thruxton, on June 23rd, to win the Players no. 6 1000cc championship race from Malcolm Uphill on a similarly framed Triumph. Short, parallel pipes, devoid of megaphones, defied tuning wisdom, but obviously seemed to work. An acknowledged stylist of the highest order, Barnett ended up 3rd in the Players Championship by season's end

With a damaged foot Smith needed a pusher from the back row of the grid but then rode through the entire field to beat Billie Nelson's Norton and Steve Jolly's Matchless G50 on the line. It was a hugely significant win since Jolly and Nelson were top line GP regulars and Smith was no longer on a Production racer. His machine was based on one of the returned 1968-spec. Daytona racers, fitted with a 670cc engine, and to further emphasise the A65's credentials as an open class racer, Alan Barnett took the Kirby Métisse

Bill 'Jock' Gow of the BFRC Committee sizing up Melvin Rice's Lightning prepared for Travelling Marshall duties **Derek Jarvis:** I bought that Lightning off Mel which he rode in the 1967 Production TT. HOX 874E. Apparently, Mel bought this machine as *'secondhand'* directly from BSA, using the auspices of Dick Rainbow. I was told not to change anything concerning the cams or timing on it and it went like an absolute rocket

Aussie rules

BSA's performance twins were slow to filter into overseas markets other than the States and the production class was still not yet universally accepted in racing. The English speaking world still constituted BSA's biggest market however and the experience of one Australian racer perhaps epitomised the potential of the Spitfire when the competitive format was right.

Larry Simons at Bathurst 1968. By this point he had a disc brake fitted for the GP category

Larry Simons: In late 1966, the new BSA Spitfire Mk ll Specials arrived in Sydney. I'd been waiting for some time for them to arrive and within two days of them becoming available I'd traded in my 1965 Triumph Trophy on one of three available. My Trophy had been quite fast but the Spitfire was something quite different. Despite some problems with it initially it just got better the more that I rode it and I started by changing the jetting, crept up to 270 main jets, it felt better with that. I then decided to try locking my ignition at fully advanced, because the points cam was a loose fit on the advance unit. This seemed to obtain better performance and from memory I again increased the jetting from 270 to 290, but a slight misfire was there so reduced it back to 280. The engine sounded a little rough like that, especially when idling, so I tried setting the ignition using the timing plug in the alternative A65 upright position. An amazing result, more rattles and clunks but noticeably more performance.

I'd been road racing since June 1965 and decided to enter my Spitfire in the February 1967 meeting at the new Amaroo Park. The Spitfire was still on the *'never, never'* (HP finance) so I only entered one race, the unlimited production race. I started from about the middle of the front row of the grid and from the instant the race started I led, to the finish, the second placed rider about a half lap behind. I got probably about $10 for first place, not much but better than nothing and it was a great result for me. My very first race win and there wasn't a better bike to win it on, a Spitfire, as it was its first appearance in Australian road racing. Although immediately after finishing, a race steward was insisting that I should be disqualified because I had a Honda horn instead of the standard BSA unit that had fallen apart a few months earlier! Commonsense prevailed thank goodness, with a bit of back-up from Paul Giles, father of international racer Shawn.

Following that my next race was our Easter Bathurst meeting on 25th March 1967 and after forgoing the production race, working on my Honda which had cracked a piston in the previous race, my final race was the unlimited. I started from about grid position 40 out of more than 100 starters but battled my way through to 7th place over the 24 miles. The first production bike to finish and the bike still in road trim, mufflers and all. Following that race the *'chief steward'* - our local BSA sales manager - wandered over and gave me a piece of paper with three speed trap figures written on it. 'Not sure of the order now but they were 123, 125 and 128mph. He said very sternly to me: *"Don't show these or discuss them with anyone"* and after told me if anything happened to the bike in a race, they'd cover the cost of repairs etc. Whether or not they would have, I'll never know.

By 21st May 1967 at Amaroo Park, there were lots of rumors circulating that I hadn't taken part in the Bathurst production race because my bike had been modified. In the marshalling area we were given the indication to proceed out to the grid, I pulled the clutch lever in and instantly the lever lost its load as the nipple had pulled off. The wires of the cable had never been twisted over before the cable had the nipple soldered to it. 'Obviously a Monday morning or Friday afternoon production fault, or perhaps after a midday break at the pub? I felt compelled to still take part in the race however, because it just wouldn't have looked good to not start for a second time. But by the time I finally got the bike rolling and into gear, I was probably very close to last away. Doing about only half the normal number of gear changes I clawed my way through the field and almost caught the leader on the last lap, Kevin Fraser, an A grade short circuit and scrambles rider, on a 250 Bultaco Metralla. Despite not having a clutch, I again set a new production lap record and was more than 1.2 seconds faster than any other rider. Unable to find the nipple I asked over the public address system for a cable and eventually got one for my next three races that day. Though I'd virtually destroyed the gearbox. It wouldn't stay in gear after that, the gear dogs were rounded off and it was only when BSA sent me a new C/R gearbox that it was OK again. My final Production race at Oran Park was on 11th June 1967 and was not really a contested race, more of 'a Sunday ride' in semi-wet conditions. I still cut almost a full second off Kel Carruthers lap record, but having then won 'three-out-of-three' production races, I was ineligible to compete in any more.

They were quite strict about the rules and at the time, three production races was all you were theoretically allowed to win. So once I was no longer eligible, from August 1967, I raced the bike in *'Open Class'* races. Which was never any problem, except the Spitfire needed a far better front brake. The original 190mm full width brake, as far as racing went, it just got far too hot and would constantly fade quite badly. My last race on that bike was 5th April 1969. The Australian Unlimited GP. I finished in 4th place, almost without a front brake for the entire race, with a completely standard engine, just running on methanol the same as the other place-getters. The first three places were taken by a 660 Triton ridden by Jack Ahearn, a 1,000 Vincent Manx and a 680 Triton. As such my Spitfire's racing life was just twenty five months but it really was a very good bike as my Mk ll was basically standard. I did virtually nothing to it, so perhaps I was just lucky when I picked it out of the three that arrived in that shop?

Simons' Spitfire with its Honda horn to the top right. Enough to threaten disqualification under the strict Australian production racing rules then in force

Gerry Millward was a new name in 1968 and another rider who came from a background of fast road riding. Seen here at Snetterton in October, he spent five years campaigning A65s

version to Snetterton's prestigious Race of Aces on 1st September. His 5th place in the final might not have looked as impressive as Smith's result, but as he was behind Mike Hailwood, Phil Read, Ray Pickrell and Percy Tait that put it into context. These sorts of results were then replicated by Smith in three season closing performances. On 22nd September Mallory Park saw racing's international royalty arrive for the Race of the Year in which the results read - 1. Hailwood (297 Honda) 2. Agostini (500 MV) 3. Barry Randle (Manx) 4. Barnett (G50 Métisse) 5. Tait (Trident) 6. Croxford (Seeley) 7. Smith (BSA A65). Smith's was the first twin home and he could have done better in the Blue Riband 1000 class event later that day when, having been 2nd to Agostini's MV Agusta in the heats, he came off at the slippery hairpin when holding the same place in the final. It was similar on October 6th where he was 5th at the Race of the South - behind Hailwood (Honda 4), Agostini (500 MV), Read (251 Yamaha) and Pickrell (750 Dunstall Norton) – and at the season ending Squire of Snetterton meeting, where Smith was 5th again. He had been closing rapidly on second placed Percy Tait beforehand however ,when his bike went on to one cylinder with electrical problems. Was he fast enough to have taken the *'Squire'* title? Well he lapped at an astounding 93.81mph, just 2 seconds outside Mike Halwood's outright lap record and showed what a formidable machine the factory tuned 670cc 'Daytona' had very rapidly become.

Tony Smith: That Daytona-framed bike was absolutely wonderful power-wise. The power to weight ratio was great and the handling was pretty well spot on too. I could make it drift all the way round Gerard's and after the bottom straight at Cadwell, you know that left hander up the hill? Well I could have it on opposite lock up there. The engine used a standard Spitfire cam but everything around it, the followers and that, were all drilled out. As before they had the Stellite cap put on the bottoms they were drilled both ways. They were hollow and they weighed nothing, as the vertical tube was all drilled through too and reamed reducing the thickness. They went with some very large diameter hollow pushrod tubes, originally from the States and the other key thing was that I ran Witham springs from America too. Which were very precise on the dimensions. When you think when I first went to BSA the rev limit was 7,200rpm, with these you could go to 9,500rpm, as there were certain things about that engine which were pretty much bullet proof by then and that was one. As I never had one which dropped a valve.

One thing I could have done was run a duplex chain instead of triplex and slimmed down the clutch and run a single plate, but the thing was it was bullet proof as it was. The cranks though were like chrome, polished all over with tiny oil-ways down the centre. I had a big machine from Avery to balance the cranks both ways, cross ways as well, so the thing which was virtually eliminated on that bike was vibration. That just went with the revs, it became like a turbine. I used to run a 54% balance factor and the flywheels were probably half the weight and machined 'D' section. The weighted end had been reduced by about 50% and the width as well, so they really were very light by comparison to standard. With the big ends I didn't worry too much, as while the Daytona racer had an end-fed crank, with the production racer I was quite happy with it on the standard timing-side bush arrangement. I used to monitor the oil pressure on the PR bike and it was always perfect.

22nd September, the Mallory Park International Race of the Year. Smith was 2nd to Agostini on the MV Agusta in the qualifier. The fairing said 500 but the programme said 670cc and even in Daytona specification the A50 was rarely raced. BSA were already experimenting with B40-derived singles (Smith's 350 is in the background) and with the 500 version of the single already being tested the A50 would soon disappear completely

The bush didn't need changing in those days, it wasn't necessary. But I would spend on one cylinder-head, the porting and valves, two weeks work! And on the Open racer I used eccentrics on the rockers, without adjusters. A tiny movement would take off 10-thou' of an inch and they were machined especially. The rockers and the spindles were all separate and you had to have different left and right ones, so you couldn't adjust it from just one side as on the PR bike. By then it was solid, it was sound and the four-speed, close ratio, box was very effective and bullet proof. People said third was too near fourth, but when you're pulling the optimum gearing you don't want a big gap, as the power drops off and you have to wait for it to come back in again. So, as it was, the four-speed, it was actually spot on and I was very happy with the reliability all round. I mean in the early days there were some niggling problems, but that was because no one had used them to the limit. Once you used them hard we got rid of those problems. We had a completely different section of rod for example. The rods got bigger and heavier with additional oil holes put inside for lubrication. They just evolved, as with the piston and the oil pumps. You handed things back to the drawing office and said: *"If you make them like this they'll perform that much better on the road."* So, we did earn our money.

Interestingly a 5-speed gearbox developed by Quaife was rejected by all at the factory who tried it, as being both unreliable and largely unnecessary. Limited numbers would later become available commercially, but weren't necessary for Bob Heath to take routine wins at Darley Moor in August and September. Nor would they have made much difference to Ray Hole, who narrowly missed out on the popular BRC One-Hour Enduro title at Snetterton on 15th September. Instead his machine benefited from the sort of support which could be expected from a normal BSA dealer, for any rider lucky enough to receive it.

Graham Sanders leads Bob Heath, both on BSA A65s. Production racing at Darley Moor was unusual in that it was dominated by A65s, where elsewhere at British circuits Triumph twins were always in the majority

R. Hole (142) D. Draper (72) G. Bailey (68). Ray Hole's Lightning leads at the hairpin, on Cadwell Park's shorter *Club* circuit. Third place Graham Bailey was a regular PR adversary. Seen here on a disc-braked Commando, he was more normally on a Triumph, which was regularly entered as a *'Saint',* in keeping with his day job as policeman

Ray Hole: That race was in absolute torrential rain and although I knew Peter Butler was in front I had no idea how far ahead he was, as you really couldn't see a thing. We all just thrashed round with no idea where we were on the track then, afterwards, someone came up and said; *"You're second!"* And Peter Butler of course was basically on a works bike. A Boyers' bike and there was Dave Nixon out with him as well, and they were both very good. At the time I was working at Vale-Onslow and Peter gave me basically what was a standard A65. A single-carb bike, which over the winter got sorted. Once I'd done it up it had the twin-carb head and high compression pistons and everything else I could get off Lenny (Len Vale-Onlsow) in spares. I built the engine up putting big valves in and everything else that was *normal* if you like, to make a bike go quicker. And it was quite successful. As it was very, very, fast when I'd finished with it. '67 that was. Len Vale-Onslow Senior had this small lathe in the workshop, so I put a reamer on it, pushed the cylinder head on to that and took the inlet ports out that way, right on the limit, as it even started smoking actually, as there was a little hole between the inlet port and where the springs sat. The reaming had actually broken right through. And I had a few different camshafts. I mean I had a camshaft which was meant to be the bees knees from America. But like a lot of these things I found in the end it went slower with it than without it, but it really did fly when it was chiming with the standard cam. When it was at its best you'd be going down the straights passing people like they were going the other way. It really was that quick, as ultimately an A65 was much faster than a Triumph. I won the Midland Production Championship twice and I won the Open Class a couple of times too. I shared it one year - I think with Peter Davies? - and in its prime the Midland Racing Club had about 800 members. The biggest membership of any racing club in the country, which puts it into perspective.

It did and Hole proved his performance claims the following week. By doing the double at Cadwell Park for the last round of the Midland Club's championship, where Les Mason took a 3rd place and fellow BSA employee Graham Sanders a pair of 4ths. Bob Heath then signed off the season with two wins at Darley Moor to secure their production bike championship. The final race, on 13th October, delivered a perfect A65 hat trick, of Heath, Sanders and Mason, but BSA made little of the publicity, nor Brown's National sidecar title, since their priorities seemed to lie solely in promoting the off-road results.

Peter Brown: When I won the British Championship, apart from Brian Martin and Bert Perrigo, as he was still around, I didn't actually get any official works recognition. None of the big wigs came and said: *'Jolly good show'* they'd never even talk to you, as that seemed the accepted norm. The engines were wonderful by then and it always made me wonder why no one from the management came down to ask: *'Why's that then?'* It's that sort of thing I couldn't understand.

South Bank, Brands Hatch. Peter Brown follows Norman Hanks, with third placed Colin Seeley in tow. A perfectly captured image of the art of drift. Each outfit with its back wheel out of line, describing an arc wider than the one the machine would naturally follow if heading in the direction of the front wheel

Solo rider Malcolm Lucas was passenger alongside considerably more experienced Fred Hanks during 1968. Fred Hanks always kept with a *'sitter'*, in contrast to son Norman's *'kneeler'* in the background. But irrespective of the advancing technology and popularity with the fans sidecars were becoming increasingly irrelevant to the export-dominated parent company

Right place wrong time

As Tony Smith's performances on the Daytona A65 would demonstrate at the beginning of 1969 the A65 was ready for the final lift. The production racer was very good and the *'open'* bike he had developed from the Daytona machine was set for the big time. It was never going to happen however, as two corporate decisions conspired against the A65. Firstly, Triumph's Trident/Rocket Three was being pushed forward as the Group's silver bullet and the key to greater success in the American market. Since the triples were seen as opening the way for massively increased sales. From now on triples not twins would be the BSA Group's focus, to the detriment of both the Triumph T120 and BSA A65. The twins were simply old news. Secondly, more and more money would be allocated to recapturing the World motocross championship. Both were decisions poorly made.

The likes of Eddie Varnes were racking up wins, week in week, out on A65s, but in non AMA National events. That would change in 1969

Predicting the sales failure of the three cylinder models in the States might be seen as being wise after the event, but even if the triples had hit their sales targets the profit on each unit sold was too small. The triples were hugely costly to produce, so even with unacceptably high dealer price tags - which put many customers off - they offered too little profit to ever save BSA. Similarly the B25 and B44 singles the motocross programme promoted were small beer for a firm once dubbed the largest motorcycle manufacturer in the world. This was particularly true since American motorcycle sport centred around a different type of machine anyway.

In the US, their version of TT racing and flat track - racing on ½ and 1 mile ovals - was everything and from 1969 rules changed favorably allowing 750cc engines. British twins would suddenly be king. In 1966, '67 and '68 BSA had flogged a dead horse by spending much time and money developing A50 500cc machines, which were never likely to be competitive, but in 1969 it looked like they had it on a plate with the A65.

Swan song for Smith - 1969

Brands Hatch, 2ⁿᵈ March 1969. Smith took 2ⁿᵈ place on his 670cc A65 to Ray Pickrell in the 1000cc race

BSA's lack of interest in what the sidecar racers were doing probably related to their diminishing relevance and lack of connection to the machines being sold on the road. These were by 1968 entirely solos, in which a clearer division also appeared on the track. The development of Tony Smith's Daytona machine brought the realisation that BSA had a contender on their hands, in the growing number of 750/open Nationals, meaning it was left more now to the privateers on the production race circuit. While Smith concentrated more on the new machine.

A freezing 2ⁿᵈ March Brands Hatch saw that put into action where: *"BSA rider Tony Smith almost pulled off the surprise win of the day, when he whittled down Ray Pickrell's apparently unassailable lead to a matter of yards by the end of the 1300 race."*[25] The larger Dunstall Norton got the verdict, but two weeks later at Mallory Park Smith cut that *'matter of yards'* with the *MCN* write-up claiming Smith had won one of the best finals ever seen at the Leicester circuit: *"Which had the crowd gasping."* It was actually Barnett who made the running on Tom Kirby's bike, but Smith pulled his way up through the field, past Ray Pickrell's Dunstall and Percy Tait's Triumph. With Croxford faster between the Esses and the finish and Smith quicker on the Gerard's section these two then pulled ahead, with Smith first under the flag, followed eventually by Tait.

16th March 1969. Fellow factory employees Tony Smith (BSA) leading Percy Tait (Triumph) at Mallory Park on their open class machines. They were regular adversaries and Smith took the laurels at the Leicestershire circuit's season opening event

Frustratingly there were then four *'close but no cigar'* performances for open class A65s. Three of them in a row over the Easter weekend. First Barnett slid off the Kirby Métisse when looking sure for the win at the King of Brands meeting on Good Friday, then Smith did the same at the Master of Mallory meeting on the Sunday. When both he and Dave Croxford, his adversary from the previous meeting at the same circuit a few weeks earlier, went down at the hairpin. Having patched himself up, it was much the same for Smith at Cadwell Park the following day, with *Motor Cycling* noting:

> *"The race could have had a different ending if Tony Smith (BSA 654) had not slid off on an oil slick when third. At the rate he cleaved through the field he looked a likely winner."*[26]

Smith stayed on-board on 4th May however, for the big Cadwell Park *Czecho Trophy* International where:

> *"Cooper, Barnett and Smith were riding like demons to keep Graham out; and the crowd were leaping up and down with excitement. Then, with a lap to go, with Graham notching third place, Cooper over did it at Barn Corner, hit the bank and came dangerously close to joining the ducks in the wildfowl reserve."*[27]

May 4ᵗʰ Cadwell Park. Smith (Daytona-framed 670cc A65) leads Stuart Graham (350cc Padgett's Yamaha) and Alan Barnett (Kirby G50). Graham pipped Smith for the win in the big 1300cc class International event

Unfortunately Graham took the opportunity to get past Smith on his super fast Padgett's Yamaha to take the win. But second place ahead of a gaggle of Grand Prix class machinery showed quite how good Smith's open class 670cc machine was. BSA fans had the right to have great expectations off the back of these performances but due to events unfolding behind the scenes these would never came to pass. In the meantime the production racer's season had got off to a terrific start on 15ᵗʰ March, as even though the weather was foul at Cadwell Park Ray Hole and Hugh Evans performed magnificently. Evans smaller A50 actually leading the race for three laps, the rider having had a bit of an epiphany over the close season.

Hugh Evans: I did a while with the A50 as a proddy bike, doing club races and I was sort of midfield. Then some idiot bought me a book, the whole theme of which was the will to win. I thought: *"It can't be as simple as that?"* but read the book three times over the winter. The first meeting following was at Cadwell. I looked round the paddock and all the usual quick guys were there. But I thought: *"Nah, I can beat this lot."* They were on 650s and 750s, but I thought sod it, the flag went down, I went off like a scalded cat, and finished 2ⁿᵈ. That was when I started racing as opposed to just riding racing bikes.

Evans was a stalwart of the A65/50, though as he raced his machine as a 500 up to 1970 his results got less coverage. The results in the news-papers tending to only cover the larger capacity classes

Where'd they go? Ray Hole showed everyone a clean set of heels at a wet and murky March 15th Cadwell meeting. He took two out of two victories in the production class events with no one else in sight

It was Hole with the best early season form though, as after winning those first two races he had a third at Cadwell on 22nd March and a 2nd at Snetterton the week after. Following which Graham Sanders took a very convincing win at Darley Moor over the Haslam brothers, at the start of what would be a highly eventful next couple of years' for Peter Brown's co-worker in Engine Development. It set things up well for the Thruxton 500-miler, but back on a production bike Tony Smith ran into bad luck once again. Running out of petrol and having to push his 400lb machine well over a mile back to the pits before being carried, exhausted, to the medical room. Undaunted, Smith recovered, got back on the machine he shared with Pat Mahoney and finished a remarkable 4th. It was important since the second, Barnett/ Spencer works-Spitfire was way down, Paul Coombs had dropped Hugh Evans A50 and the only other A65 was 9th and a private entry by Comp Shop employees Hanks and Horne.

Fuelling Steve Spencer's Spitfire, with everyone in corporate livery. The same process on the Smith/Mahoney machine obviously didn't go so well, Smith running out of fuel to lose a possible 2nd place finish

Graham Horne (left), Norman Hanks (right), with Hanks' road bike, Brain Martin's Vauxhall Victor and Bell's corporate livery. Norman Hanks was one of the first to bring Bell full face helmets into the country - after a US foray as race mechanic to motocross World Champion Jeff Smith - and each helmet came with a jacket and bag. It was well flash for 1969

Before the TT there were then minor places at Snetterton for Gerry Millward and at Snetterton and Cadwell for Steve Brown. Steve Brown was yet another BSA employee but his workmates hadn't got off to such a good start in the sidecar racing season. Indeed it proved a bit of a farce, when Vincent, Brown and a number of other top runners missed the first race of the season, as being too late to the assembly area. It left Norman Hanks to chase down eventual winner Andy Chapman in the Greenwood *Mini,* though it was the third placed A65 of new boys Pat Sheridan and Trevor Taylor who got the fans cheering. Re-passing the *Mini* three times around Gerard's in pursuit. Ultimately neither Chapman nor any of the other cyclecars would pose the threat in '69 that Greenwood had in previous years, but the crowd's response set the tone for the rest of the season - the fans and media firmly behind the BSAs – with two new names soon to be associated with the A65 winning at the following weekend's Snetterton event.

> **Stuart Digby:** I remember that meeting as I had an ex-Chris Vincent engine in it for the first time. We learnt as we went along, grenade-ing engines on a reasonably regular basis, until we saw Chris advertising this A10 engine. I went up to see him in Aston and he told me all about it. It was made in the tool room, had this, had that and was a 700cc not a 650. It was a lot of money at the time but had all the dyno and build sheets. So, I said: *"Yeah I'll have it."* On the way back my mate said: *"How you gonna pay for it then. Have you got 75-quid?"* I said: *"I'll ask me dad if he'll loan it. But I'm having it whatever."*

Stuart Digby (left) and Mick Williams (right) at an early Brands meeting on the Chris Vincent A10-powered outfit. It would soon go on to be powered by an A65 and prove highly successful

Anyway, first time out, at Snetterton, George O'Dell parked up next to us with his Mini-van and trailer. I always had a bit of banter with George and he was going: *"I don't know why you waste your time with these BSAs. You want a Triumph."* First race we did everything Chris told us to do. Warmed it up on soft N5 plugs, put in the hard ones for the race then went on to the grid. We were middle to back and when the flag went down the bike wouldn't start. I thought: *"I don't believe it!"* Pushed again and still nothing. So, the marshals came over and said: *"Get on, we'll push"* the bike chimed up and we went around the first two right-handers, round the first left-hander and - I'll never forget it to this day - I can visualise all these bikes across the track, going down the Norwich straight, as by the end of it we were in the lead.

Of course, at the end of the race George was straight round wanting to buy it as George always wanted anything that he thought was better than what he had already. But that one of Chris's was unbelievable. We won a lot of races, no problem, but pretty soon I went on to A65s, as the Boddices, the Hanks, Chris and Peter Brown, they were all on them and everyone thought: *"Oh that's the engine to have."* But those guys were getting them from the factory of course, the current model, and really and truthfully I took a step backwards to begin with. But Peter and Chris always helped me out, with bits and pieces, having bought that original A10 and we got to grips with it in the end.

It was self evident that others had already got to grips, with a bewildering number of victories being delivered pre-TT. Roy Hanks won at the new Staverton circuit, the Irishman Pat Sheridan at Mallory on the first mention of a *Mason BSA*, Hobson at Croft, Krukowski at Crimond and Brown at Castle Combe. Meanwhile, in date order, Vincent took the wins at Oulton, Snetterton, Brands, Mallory, Crystal Place, Thruxton and Cadwell. Then Brands and Mallory again, though these were by no means foregone conclusions. The Master of Mallory race on 6th April included outfits from Sweden, New Zealand and Switzerland with German World Champion Helmut Fath debuting a 750cc version of his four-cylinder URS machine producing reputedly a colossal 101hp. If the announcement was intended to intimidate it failed, since Chris Vincent rode round the outside of him at the Essess, on the second lap, with what seemed like consummate ease. It was normally Vincent's style to start slower and work his way through the field, giving the crowds something to shout about. But at Mallory he made short work of Fath, perhaps as a statement piece, pulling away to win by an incredible 11 seconds. It was definitely a case of *'stick that in your pipe and smoke it'* from Vincent, who was never much impressed by horsepower figures anyway and had by now an ambiguous relationship with his employers, for whom he was gaining publicity and titles with little in return;

Chris Vincent: Silverstone was actually the only place power was important and then the crank webs used to flex and break often anyway, if you pushed the power that bit too high. The engine development bloke at BSA, Johnson, was also brainless. We inherited him from the factory at Redditch and he'd try to lock me out so I couldn't get onto the dyno at all. So I just went out and got a set of keys cut, so that I could go into the test house at night by myself and many times I just worked round the clock. I didn't go in often really though, as I never ever tested them for outright horse power. I knew the figure I wanted, I'd have it in my head, and as long as I was getting that, it was OK. But to do it on your own was easier said than done. I might not have had a gearbox in an engine, as you'd do the final drive for the dyno off the crankshaft, but you know the weight of an A65 lump? To carry that from my workshop, up these steps into Engine Development, on the test bed, weren't easy and at night security would come in, as it'd be so noisy saying:

Thruxton 13th April 1969. Rose Hanks kicking fellow passenger Keith Scott in the backside, while Chris Vincent remains resolutely unperturbed. Vincent was given much respect on the track but evidently a bit less off it

Vincent and Scott at Brands. A formidable partnership, though in truth Vincent had more passengers than hot dinners

"No, no, no you've got to stop." As it was against the Factory Act to be on your own in the test house. I guess in case the engine exploded and what have you? I'd take my bike out too, with no passenger, around the test track. It went left-handed, so I'd feel it round, but I'd test it a little bit harder along the straights and I remember one day I took my TT bike out, which was significant because that one would spin right up. I ripped it up through the revs and I guess they were more than they'd ever heard before. So sometimes after that I'd just go down and test it in the dark, after work, as old Perrigo must have heard it in his office and when I met him on the way back in he says: *"Lovely demonstration Chris, but do you think you could do it out of hours next time, as you brought the factory to a standstill."* But it was a strange thing with Bert, as soon after he said: *"We need to make some cut backs and the axe is over your head. Would it matter if we allowed you to come and go, have everything you want, but us cut you off the wages list?"*

An earlier version of the Vincent A65. There were many incarnations

So, I said: *"Well, not really, no."* As it was a pittance compared to what else I was earning by then. But I came back some time later, after one of my foreign trips, and one of the wages clerks met me in the factory, just by chance, and says: *"Here! Come up and get your wages."* I said: *"I ain't got none?"*, but I went up with this woman and she comes out with a pile of pay packets. Which amounted to good money in those days, and she says: *"Yes you have. I pay the wages round here. Not them"*. And just turned her back and walked off. The thing was I was very popular in the factory. If I'd walk through the sections, people would wave to me and that, so I don't think anyone wanted an argument about it!

TT '69

In the Comp Shop Brian Martin had a more generous approach to his employees, counting staff time at the TT as work rather than leave, even if most of it was on the track. The TT clearly was work for Tony Smith however and with the BSA-Triumph three-cylinder 750cc machines in the wings everyone knew 1969 could be the swan song for the twins as factory supported racers. Unfortunately it was all rather anticlimactic as the works bikes of Tony Smith and Steve Spencer both went out with clutch troubles, Smith when well up the leader board. On the third Works machine Mahoney could only manage 8th while Barnett didn't even start on the Tom Kirby entry due to simply having too many rides. Heath blew his engine when going well and very close to the end, so the highlight was Hugh Evans' 5th in the 500cc race, pipped by just 0.2 of a second for 4th, by Cooper's Suzuki. At a race average of 85.16mph he was tantalisingly close to the 85.90mph of Ron Baylie's 3rd placed Triumph, but 5th was the highest an A50 would ever achieve.

Helen Cooper: When the crane tried to pick the van up, to put it on the ferry, it lifted it off its moorings with them saying; *"What the hell have you got in there?"* It was another WEC outfit, as those were the realities of 1960s international travel. The Bill Cooper A65 equipe in Douglas

Pat Mahoney (top) and Hugh Evans (below) were best A65 and A50 TT performers respectively in 1969. With an 8th and 5th however they were actually the worst results for BSA since the Production TT was inaugurated

As the 'sprog' of the team passenger Malcolm Lucas got to do the honors at the weigh in. He shouldn't have bothered. His rides with Roy Hanks resulted in a pair of DNFs

Champion for a day

The TT was also less fruitful for the sidecars, as while the 750 class had been run concurrently with the 500s in '68, with no shortage of entries, two separate races were run in 1969. It gave the super-fast German machines the chance of a double victory, particularly as some ran bigger engines. Though an A65 came close to a victory again. There was no Vinicombe this time however - he'd tragically died from thrombosis shortly after his '68 win – nor Vincent either, as he went out early after delivering his traditional lap record.

> **Peter Brown:** It was at the end of the second lap that *Siggy* (Siegfried Schauzu) made an unexpected pit stop for fresh googles, his first pair being absolutely smothered in insects. My goggles were smothered but I managed to keep a small area of my right-hand lens clear, which was enough. My dodgy left eye was never much good anyhow and I was used to tunnel vision in the right! Poor Mick Casey was having real problems seeing though and on the last lap he miscounted the right-handers into the Bungalow and was still over the back wheel when we came to the left-hander. My words of encouragement to him, to shift his backside, were so loud that they were heard over the radio commentary being given from the Bungalow. I was later rebuked by my wife Shirley for language that might have shocked old ladies listening in. But when I came into the Parc Fermé someone said: *"We think you've won this one, as Schauzu will be disqualified, for keeping his engine running when he changed goggles."* I don't know the ins and outs, but they had an inquiry on the Sunday and decided he'd won again. As far as I was concerned he had to be two minutes ahead of me, so I sympathised, but *"TT winner for a day"* how's that for a claim to fame?

Brown and Casey round Bradden Bridge on Brown's distinctive *croucher* outfit

It was tough on Brown and on his engine too, as while both he and Vincent forced past Helmut Fath at the Post-TT Mallory international, their hastily rebuilt motors resulted in Vincent's gearbox blowing and Brown slipping back behind Fath and Norman Hanks with a badly smoking, tired engine.

As the season progressed normal service was resumed however. Sheridan and A65 convert Bill Crook had wins at Cadwell, Norman Hanks at Cadwell and Thruxton and Brown Cadwell and Snetterton. Digby won at Thruxton, while Mick Gillett, one of an increasing number of club runners adopting the BSA twins won at Darley Moor. Vincent had wins at Castle Combe, Lydden, Mallory and Brands Hatch by the season's end, but through copious victories pre-TT he'd actually won back the British sidecar title months previously. Hobson also took a prodigious number of victories on the northern circuits, though Pete Krukowski took the Scottish sidecar title this time, through dint of more points north of the border.

For the solos in the run up to the *Hutch* there were good places for several A65 runners, with results at the end of July probably being the high point. Les Mason took a 2nd at Aintree and Graham Sanders two wins at Snetterton over Les Trotter's rapidly developing T500 two-stroke Suzuki. While a good win over Richard Stevens' works Enfield Interceptor was recorded at Cadwell Park. After which *MCN* reported: *"Millward, the day's fastest rider, spoiled the look of his 650 BSA when he dropped it."*[28]

Gerry Millward; I rode an A65 as that's what I'd got, a Lightning Clubman and it was a fair looking piece of kit. I wanted to race, but to begin with it was more like having a few beers and having some fun and when I first got the bike it wasn't right actually, so kept going backwards and forwards to Glanfield Baldet, where Mick Hemmings used to work as a mechanic. It had a habit of braking cranks, well mine did, so I got another from BSA and had to pay a fair amount for it. But after a year that was going too, so I got another free, as it was a recon, though obviously I didn't tell them that by now I was racing it! Then I had a third one go and put an A50 crank in it from Tony Clark Motorcycles in Northampton and it was better with that in it, smoother, it went really well. I put a Spitfire head on it, with the bigger valves and carbs and when I got it I didn't know it was going to have a close ratio gearbox as standard. But it did being a Clubman. So, once I'd sorted it all out it was as fast as a Bonneville, as with the Spitfire head on it was really quite quick. I didn't have a problem with the handling either, though then again, I wasn't quite John Cooper! But that one in '69 was my first race win and I won it quite easily. But the second time out he was up my arse, it was a works bike after all and I fell off at the Gooseneck. I had a few wins after actually. Not many, but a few, at Lydden and Cadwell Park, and one at Mallory Park too, though as that was in a heat not a final, I guess that doesn't count?

Millward slips by on the inside of a Velocette Thruxton at Lydden. There was always a diversity of machines in the production class but the Triumph twins were always in the majority and the chief opposition

As all racers know, they all count, and all BSA eyes were then on the Hutchinson 100 following the bomb shell news in Mick Woollett's Paddock Gossip column under the headline: "*Tony Smith, vanishing BSA works Rider*"

> "Since the TT we haven't heard a word of him. He hasn't competed at a short circuit since May and even plans for him to ride a production BSA in the Barcelona 24-hour race faded into nothingness….when I spoke to Tony who works at BSA he replied: *"I haven't got a bike it's as simple as that."* Being a loyal man he was reluctant to enlarge on this but it seems instead of encouraging his racing activities the factory have been less than luke-warm. However he will be at the Hutchinson 100 on a six-fifty in the Production race. Let's hope after that he'll be a regular on the short circuits once again."[29]

There was certainly no lack of commitment from Smith. 25,000 fans watched him take 5th on his 670 Daytona in the first leg of the Evening News Trophy race behind Gould, Andrew, Smart and Butcher, then subsequently put in one of the rides of his life in the big race, which had been won by the A65s of Hailwood in 1965 and Cooper in 1966.

Smith leads Cooper's Triumph at Thruxton on 11th May. It was much the same on 10th August, though Cooper's Triumph didn't feature on the leader-board this time. Rod Gould managed to get his Bonneville into 3rd place but the Triumphs were never really in the picture. It was otherwise three 750cc Nortons in the top five, with Mick Andrew's Commando pipping Smiths 670cc A65 by inches at the line

Graham Sanders in action on his understated but highly competitive A65. Put together and tuned in his spare time it benefited from the knowledge he gained from working on the machines daily at BSA

Tony Smith: I was sitting behind Mick Andrew on the Kuhn Commando and we were half a lap ahead of everyone else with three laps to go. By chance we were lapping Hugh Evans and Mick went underneath him, touched him, knocked him across the road in to me, and took me off the circuit. I was going down the grass and lost a good 100 yards but only lost it to a photo finish on the line. I broke the lap record trying to do it. Some people thought I'd won it and some thought he had, but it was Mick who got given the result.

Before the season was out Hugh Evans secured the BRC 500cc production championship, signing-off with two wins at Cadwell Park on 23rd August and another pair at Snetterton on 18th October. While Graham Sanders clinched his seventh win on the trot at Darley Moor to win the Darley Moor Production title. Sanders then won again at Cadwell Park on 21st September, with *Motor Cycling* carrying the headline: *"Double and record elude Mason"*. As while Les Mason won the unlimited race over Harvey Porter and broke the lap record, Graham Sanders matched it in the production race, to deprive Mason of the double victory.

Les Mason: Me and Graham had a monstrously good scrap that weekend. Graham had got away well along with someone else – I can't remember whom? Terry Odlin perhaps – but anyway I got ahead and was gradually pulling Graham in. We came round the big long right-hander, after Park, before flipping down through the Gooseneck and I'm right

By 1969 the trophies were racking up for the BSA privateers. Hugh Evan's A50 (above) was invariably the sole 500 BSA on track, but picked up a number of Club championship titles, while Clive Wall's Spitfire (below) also started winning extensively from the same year

up his exhaust pipe. I thought: *"I'm having you here, as once I get under you, I'm in."* As it was the last lap and only a little way to the line. Anyway, 'got him, 'got underneath him, 'flew down the hill towards Mansfield and missed my braking point, as I was going in too quick. So I ran wide and Graham, being the crafty little bugger he was, he just did the duck under I'd just done on him and beat me to the line. My two brothers were there, dancing up and down as they'd seen I'd got him, but it was second place again.

At National level there was one last event at Cadwell that year. Tony Smith was defending his Conqueror of Cadwell crown but dropped a valve in pursuit of Derek Chatterton's swift two-stroke Yamaha. It wasn't the sort of sign-off Smith wanted, as that's what it proved to be. Subsequently he announced he was leaving BSA to *'broaden his experience'*, though in truth Smith had experienced a number of technical issues and accidents not of his own doing, while promises of more competitive machines from BSA had fallen through. He'd not been offered one of the new Rocket Threes which were waiting in the wings and in truth he also had other offers on the table. Though luck was never on his side. He ultimately had a 140mph crash in the USA, spent months in hospital healing and lost his Suzuki ride, recounting: *"They gave it to some kid called Sheene!"* At Small Heath his bikes didn't lie idle long either.

Bob Heath: I was working for Bob Joyner & Son originally and I'd been taking Saturdays off, for racing, when coming to one Saturday Bob came up and he said; *"I want you here because the manager wants it off and you have loads of Saturdays off. So if you don't come in you can have a week off, without pay."* I had a race meeting on so I said to my mates; *"What 'am I going to do?"* They said: *"Look, there's loads of jobs down BSA, you gotta go racing!"* So I went racing and 'cors I didn't go into work on Monday, I went down BSA. 'Got an interview to go on the track, assembly of the Rocket Three, and got the job. It was more money and I was in the factory, and whilst working on the engine line you quite often saw Tony Smith and other Comp Shop staff ride the bikes around the factory. You looked down on them from the second floor assembly line in envy, wishing that were you. But of course the job only lasted six months, as sales of the triples dropped off due to the Honda four coming out, and it was last in first out. I went straight to Lucas and got a job half a mile from where I lived, stripping down starter motors and dynamos for the service exchange programme. I don't know why Tony left BSA but I was in bed about 10 one morning, after working nights, when Steve Brown rides over from the Armoury Road, on an A65 actually, with a message from Brian Martin: *"Was I interested in riding their bikes? If so to come over to the factory and have a talk."* And I thought: *"Oh Yeah!"*

Heath got his first tryout at the final race of the year, the Brands Hatch Evening News International, finishing a good 6th in a race won by Agostini's MV Agusta. However the Rocket Three was the coming thing and that would be Heath's priority for 1970, along with the prototype B50 racer Smith had been working on. From the parent company's perspective the door had shut on the A65 as a factory racer, which was ironic. As on the other side of the Atlantic that same door had just been flung wide open, even if the season's traditional Daytona had been a no-show for BSA. Triumph persevered, but speeds had increased drastically and their T100s made no impact. BSA had made the right call in not racing the A50s, as at long last it was A65 which got the call.

"No substitute for cubes"
- the race for ever bigger engines

1969 saw Jon Biggs 875cc Imp and Fred Barwick's 998cc NSU in the British sidecar results. There would be plenty more big engines like that for the BSA runners to contend with, but it was the BSA factory employees who actually began the capacity arms race, even if starting with standard parts.

Peter Brown: I started off with a standard A65 engine and I don't know what other people did, they probably did the same thing in parallel, but the first modification I did was I thought: *"Why can't this engine have an A10 crank in it?"* I got one from the Service Department and had a bit of a play around, so the first 750 engine I had, seven something cc, was an A10 crank with the standard horrible timing-side bearing, with a sleeve pushed on. It might have been the back end of '67 that. We had it on a test bench then I seem to remember using it for a bit that year too.

Later with this set up people regularly used A70 or Triumph T140 pistons, as a near perfect fit. But prior to this the obvious problem was that the standard pistons protruded above the barrel. One solo privateer found the same solution as used by the factory insiders, with one of the insiders in turn using another clever workaround, with a backward sloping barrel.

Hugh Evans: I had an A50 and when I converted it I didn't bother with a 650 I went straight to a 750. So I got a long-stroke crank, an A10 crank, but then thought: *"Great, now the piston comes out the top of the barrel!"* So what to do? Get another barrel, cut the top fin off that, machine it, joint it, pin it and attach it to the top of the original barrel. Then hone it and you got 750. No liner down it, just honed. It never caused a problem with the rings and no one ever did count the fins on that barrel, to see if it was over-sized, though Ray Knight did come close one day when he said: *"How come your 650's so bloody quick?"*

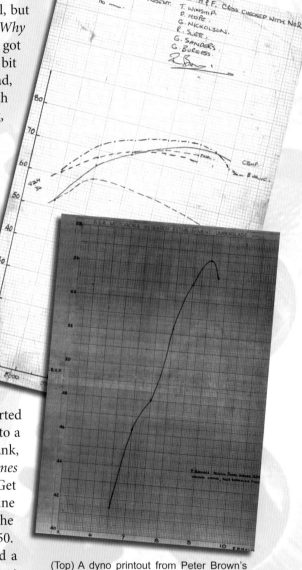

(Top) A dyno printout from Peter Brown's 1970 760cc long-stroke engine, producing 80bhp at 7,000rpm.

(Bottom) It was short strokes too. 56bhp at 9,000rpm for Brown's short-stroke 500cc unit using an A65 top-end on a one-off crank

Roy Hanks: Norman had managed to get a long barrel for his but I had a standard barrel and as they hadn't come out with the A70 piston yet, with the higher gudgeon pin, we cut a fin off a barrel took it down the machine shop and then put it on top, using sealant pegged with counter sunk screws. Then we had it bored to 40" so I had a 770 or thereabouts. Like that the top ring had to be an old one though, because of the lip between the two parts without a liner. So we always carried an abundance of rings about. But then we found if you tilted the barrel backwards you lifted it up high enough to not need that extra fin, even with the standard barrel. You went up about 10mm at the front and 3 mm at the back, but you had to be careful or the cam followers could drop out. They were the bees knees, the right bike to be on like that, though once you went to a bigger barrel as well there was so much torque they used to wear 2nd gear out before you'd left the paddock!

"Skint Racing" was a joke name coined by Reg Hardy but summed up the reality for most racers. While larger BSA engines became routine later in the 1970s they were still a huge investment, beyond the budget and technical ability of most racers, during the 1960s

That next step, as mention by Hanks, to increase the bore, Les Mason achieved with specially cast barrels, later sold under his Devimead brand name. But some special barrels were also cast inside BSA, as 'foreigners'. It could be done another way however, by someone with a good eye for an accurate casting. Again, as explained by a solo privateer - who would shortly appear in the results - when converting a 654 to a short-stroke 750cc.

Reg Hardy: I couldn't afford to buy one of those Devimead barrels, but we used to go to Syd Tapper's scrap yard, in West Bromwich - or Wednesbury was it? - where BSA used to throw all their old scrap castings away. I got a barrel casting which had had the tappets machined but hadn't been machined at all otherwise, as the top fin had sagged on cooling. So, I got it for a song and we bored it carefully, off-line, so we could get as much of the meat as we could round the bore. Then put 79.5mm pistons in. Victor pistons, which were I think .020" over size to make it 736cc. It was about 8mm I had to take off the top of the barrel, as the Victor pistons were shorter. So that meant that damaged fin was gone too and while they used to count the fins at the race meetings, to check if bikes were oversize, of course by then it didn't matter, as they'd homologated the Devimead barrels anyway, so 750 was OK.

Subsequently people have fitted Norton cranks and one-off machined items with both standard and offset big-ends, but the three steps above describe what was pretty much done in the day, to create short or long-stroke 750cc engines, or long-stroke 840cc

Go USA!

Jody Nicholas: '68 I was hanging around Don Vesco's shop and somehow he had wound up with an ex-works bike, that had one of the special frames, made out of Reynolds factory tubing. I didn't actually have a ride at the time so thought it might be a good project to convert the A50 into an A65 and compete when I wasn't busy with the navy and wot not (Nicholas was a Vietnam and NASA related pilot). Don said: *"Sure, do whatever you want"*. I was able to get an A65

Jody Nicholas on an earlier incarnation of the racing A50. His 1969 mount was improved through a larger engine and uprated running gear

cylinder from the BSA Western headquarters and swapped the cylinder-head for one that Dallas Baker had modified. He was an old BSA TT and flat track racer and was working at a BSA dealers at the time. I used the same carburetors as on the 500, which were 1⁵/₃₂", or some odd ball size, and of course that barrel and head fit straight on the A50 bottom end. We didn't change the balance or anything and when we started it, it was smooth. Which for a vertical twin would seem kind of strange, as the pistons were heavier that we put in it, than the A50 ones we took out. But this thing was real quick and had power that was more like a good TT motor. You know, it came in a bit lower down the rev range, but still went right on up to the 8,000rpm that we were running it to. And that was probably the best handling big bike I ever rode. It handled real well and I won every race I was in '69. There weren't too many, as I couldn't get away from the military too much, but I think I rode in half a dozen main events - 'cos remember we had the heat races too - and I won them all. Heats and mains and I was real pleased.

Don Vesco also campaigned the machine with success in non-AMA events, which allowed larger engines in road racing events prior to 1970

The events both Nicholas and Vesco rode in were AFM/ACA sanctioned however, as Rod Gould's had been in 1967. These ran largely to FIM-type rules, permitting larger engines. In the AMA National championships road racer events were still limited to 500cc - while all other disciplines were now allowed 750cc - but changes were afoot there too for 1970.

Jim Rice: I was lucky enough to grow up at a time '66-67 when there were a lot more race tracks in the San Francisco area - Low Dive Friday night, Hayward Saturday night and about once or twice a month Fremont. It was just for trophies but the competition then it was absolutely unbelievable. 400 riders or so would show up for a Sunday race at Fremont and if you won Expert you were riding with a hundred guys to get through elimination for the final race of 12-15 riders, and the calibre was incredible. I went to some of the local scrambles races and thought: *"Man I gotta do that"* so my buddy and I bought a Yamaha YDS2 street bike and to give myself a little bit of credit I eventually got into a main event. At the time I was delivering the San Francisco Examiner. I'd get up at like 2:00am in

Jim Rice at work on a rear tyre. Riders would routinely cut their own tread patterns - and still do - depending on how they liked to ride and the surface of individual tracks

my senior year at high school, it would be nasty in winter, but delivering papers I was progressing to bigger and louder motorcycles and I bought a BSA Spitfire Hornet. It had high pipes with shorty mufflers on it and you could imagine I'd leave it running in Los Altos as it was quicker running around the apartments tossing the papers than getting back on to go to the next apartment. I remember one morning around 2:00am this guy comes out and he wasn't happy. He says: *"If you leave your bike running again I'm gonna kill yeah!"* But I wasn't buying that: *'He's gonna kill me?'* So next time I came back I just left that sucker running as that Spitfire Hornet, I fell in love with it. It was so fast and easy to ride after the Yamaha two stroke I couldn't believe it and as soon as I got that on the race track I was winning regular. I don't want to brag, but really quickly in the sportsman racing I progressed to being the no.1 district 36 area rider in '67. But little did I know how it would open things up for me.

It opened things up as late in 1968 the AMA Competition Congress finally decided that while 500cc machines would continue in road racing until 1970 – thus excluding Jody Nicholas' machine - they would do away with the 500 OHV/750 side-valve rule for flat track events, cutting the A65 loose where the A50 had previously failed. As such for 1969 Jim Rice graduated to the Pros while a new young wild card appeared among the Amateurs, causing quite a stir.

Dave Aldana: In high school here when I was 15 I got what they called work experience. You could do some work in a printing shop, a lawnmower shop, whatever sort of profession you thought you might want to do after school. Well I got a job at a motorcycle shop which sold BSA and BMW. The guy who owned the shop his name was Erv Shivers and his little rule or law was that you could only ride what he sold and I got in on the ground floor as Dallas Baker had a connection with this guy, and tuned a 250 BSA for novices, who were coming up through the ranks. Well I remember going for a test ride at this track, there were three of us on this B25 and Dallas Baker chose me. Even though I'd only ridden a Suzuki 80 up to then. When I got on this BSA while it didn't have as much power as a Bultaco, or Harely Sprint, I excelled in the TT races, though I could not even qualify for the ½-miles. But there was another guy who had a BSA twin, out of a motorcycle shop called LeBard & Underwood, a guy called Lloyd Bowmer. He worked on the bike and had a dyno in his house. One of his rooms it had shag pile carpet hanging from all the walls, to muffle the sound, with an exhaust going out the dry wall, out in to the backyard. It was a real primitive thing. But I rode his bikes on the ½-miles and another guys bike on TT and I won a bunch of races. That's when I got my BSA ride, with Dick Mann and Jim Rice and that. I was still working at the motorcycle shop at the time but I could see that I couldn't have a job and keep on top of the maintenance of my bikes and travel. So I quit college too as I thought: *"I'm gonna ride motorcycles full-time, it's much more fun than school!"*

There were plenty of headlines for Dave Aldana in 1969

A young Dave Aldana (no.38X) the winner of the Santa Fe TT Junior event alongside National winner Eddie Wirth. Both on A65s

Allowing the British 650s in was as big a change in US oval racing as had happened in decades and BSA was quick to benefit. With 3rd places for privateer Dick Mann at both the Cumberland and Terre Haute ½-miles in May, followed by a 2nd at the Louisville ½-mile in early June. At the end of the month, at the Sante Fe TT, Eddie Wirth then led from the start to win on his Harold Seller-tuned A65. Two days after which Mann was 4th at the Columbus ½-mile, which also saw Darrel Dove and Canadian Yvon Duhamel in the final on BSAs too. Rookie Jim Rice then got the big one, at San Jose. The one BSA had been hoping for in America, a first win on a ½-mile oval. Starting on the outside of the front row Rice immediately took control, his A65 stretching out an uncontested lead to the finish, leaving Gary Nixon's Triumph and Mert Lawwill's Harley-Davidson far behind. TT specialist Dick Mann then got 3rd at Castle Rock in the middle of the month, as a precursor to a win at the Peoria TT on August 17th, ahead of the Harleys of Rayborn and Markel. Not to be outdone new boy Rice did it again at Sedalia with another first for BSA. A win on a full mile oval, though this time on a Rocket Three. If that wasn't enough Rice then stamped his mark on the season by placing 3rd at the Sacramento mile, while winning the Oklahoma City ½-mile for good measure. Both times back on his West Coast BSA supported A65. As the icing on the cake youngster Dave Aldana took his A65 to wins in the Amateur class at Cumberland, Terre Haute, Reading, Santa Fe and Ascot, as well as a number of top three placings.

By the end of the season Dick Mann in 6th place was actually BSA's top scorer over the whole, epic, 25 round championship, but it looked good for 1970. The A65s racced in 1969 were less developed than their Triumph and Harley-Davidson adversaries, while Rocket Threes were promised for the less frequent but still highly important road races. Since road races would be opened up to 750 machines in 1970 too.

A65 mounted Billy Eves leads Triumph's Gene Remero

Assisting the privateers

Hugh Evans: Dick Rainbow and I had a reasonable relationship for a long time and through Dick I got to know Tony Smith. So, I then got an *'in'* to the factory from Tony when he went to work there. We had a rapport, and I think the factory liked the fact that I was getting reasonable results on an A50. I was the only one publicising it for them to be honest and I certainly didn't *'ride'* the fact that I was getting support. I think they appreciated that too. I only got on to them when I really needed something and around that time a guy called Paul Coombs did the 500-miler with me. At Thruxton, just before the TT, and threw it up the road. The forks and frame and all sorts of things were bent, so I rang the factory and they said: *"Well, OK, put a list together of what you need. But how are you gonna pick it up?"* At the time I was working at Biggin Hill, the AA had their spotter plane on the airfield and I happened to know the pilot quite well. So I said: *"Are you going anywhere near Birmingham over the next few days?"* And he said: *"Yeah, this afternoon"*. He told me where he was going to be, and at what times he was going to be there, so I rang the factory and spoke to Micky Boddice, to ask if he could get these bits to the airport? *"No problem."* I literally got them the same day. Then later, on the Island, I had an early 5 gallon tank on the bike and it split in practice. I went up to Tony and the BSA guys and they said: *"Well we've got a tank, one of the long slim works alloy ones, with a seat, you can borrow that"*. OK, fine, I thought: *"I'll bring it back to you after the race"*. I happened to finish 5th and afterwards I went back to the guys, with the intention of giving it back. They just laughed and said: *"No that's OK you can keep all that"*. And you know Mike Hailwood rode a Spitfire at the Hutch? Well the factory did some wonderful silencers for him. They were flattened so that they could tuck in under the bike and flattened on the outside, so they tucked under. They ended up on my Cyclone too. A lot of things came down to me like that, so I was always very appreciative of what BSAs did for me at the time. It was great actually, a real friendly association with the factory over the years. So I hope I did some good for them, as I never ever parted with any money.

Clive Wall: I blew up the bike I was racing for RH Smith once. I dropped a valve at Brands, and I couldn't afford a cylinder-head, pistons, cranks and things. So, Dick Smith said to take the engine out, take it apart, go up to BSAs in the van and ask for the race department. I was very young and thought: *"Christ, I don't even know what I'm meant to say"*. But I walked out of there with virtually a new engine! I was on nodding terms with Tony Smith by then, but the guy running it, was Brian Martin and when I went in he was sitting there, reading *Motor Cycle News*. And I thought: *"Wow, he must be important – reading a newspaper at work!"* I always remember that. But he was such a nice bloke. He really was, and I got quite friendly with him subsequently. He said: *"If you ever want anything Clive, just give us a ring. And at the end of the year come up and we'll give you everything you need to rebuild it for the next season"*. It went along the lines of Brian saying: *"What do you need? Tony, give him what he wants"*. A cupboard would open and out would come a load of con-rods and the rest. I never had a complete engine, but I used to go up there and they used to re-bush the cases, line-bore them, new crank, barrels and pistons, con-rods, bolts, new oil pump, etc. To get out the gates they'd say: *"Just throw a blanket over it."*

The Evans and A50, resplendent with its works tank-seat unit

Not all the A65 runners were as fortunate as Wall and Evans. Ted Reading (left) does a paddock plug check, while Len Read (right) lines up for scrutineering at Snetterton. Both supported their racing entirely through their pay packets

It wasn't a fortune to them, but it was a real bonus for me, as they just gave it to us for nothing and obviously it helped massively with the reliability. And with the twin leading shoe brake they showed me what they did with the cams. You just built them up with braze then put them side by side and filed them and finished them by hand, so they were both the same, and that was a real big improvement. I did the same and boy did that make a difference. I had a lot of time for Brian Martin. A nice guy. 'Cos he helped and he didn't have to. I don't know why he did, but I always equated it to the fact that I was one of the few people to really make a BSA work. And Dick Smith had a franchise of course, which has always got to help!

A similarly helping hand was offered to the many sidecar crews now attempting to emulate the results of the *'Birmingham Mafia.'* Vincent, Brown, Hanks and Boddice were not adverse to assisting individually but again the Comp Shop filtered parts out to runners showing promise. With needs be, the assistance running to entire engines.

Ron Smith: One year I had an A65 from the factory, over at the TT, just so I could learn the track, and was in the Douglas Bay Hotel one morning when Brian comes in and says: *"Can you take the engine out of your bike. I'm giving it to a sidecar racer. He's put some rods through on his motor so he'll be taking your engine instead."* So I was stuck with a bike minus the engine! It was in the Comp Shop like that for about six months until I tracked down another engine and actually bought the whole lot myself, for just 50 quid. And it was a good buy actually, as by chance I've still got it!

Titles go begging - 1970

Bob Heath on the Rocket Three production racer. One of the two machines - the other being the B50 500cc single - he was most associated with as a works rider. But he was out on the ex-Tony Smith Daytona twin too

For the 1970 season Brian Steenson was recruited by the BSA factory to race the triples alongside Bob Heath as and when his role at BSA's Umberslade Hall research facility permitted. The twins played no role in the plan and the lack of interest was highlighted when the ACU published the list of approved 'special' parts in April, homologated by factories for production racing purposes. The list for the BSA A65 consisted of just:

> *"Hydraulic steering damper; USA front mudguards & stays; close ratio gears; four-spring clutch; alternative rear wheel sprockets; lightweight alloy petrol tank; BSA Quaife five-speed cluster; remote racing contact breaker."*

The BSA twins were meant to be left to the privateers now, as highlighted on Sunday 1st March when Bob Heath won the 500cc race at Mallory Park on the new factory B50-based solo. This created a lot of speculation, not least as he beat all the established 500 stars and now led the British 500cc championship. But so too did a seeming volte-face by BSA at Cadwell Park at Easter, when:

Dave Mason on the ex-Tony Smith production racer. The sister machine to that used by Steenson

"Andrew slipped up in the Production race. He rode his Commando to a big lead by half distance, but then eased off too much. Before he realised what was happening Brian Steenson and Tony Jefferies, the 21 year-old son of former Triumph all-rounder Alan Jefferies, had pounced. Steenson racing the ex-Tony Smith 650 BSA swept by to win. Jefferies rode his 1969 Bonnevile to a close third. Said Steenson; *"The track was so slippery that I thought I was coming off a dozen times."*[30]

Malcolm Scott: I remember going to Cadwell Park that day and seeing Brian Steenson riding an A65 as he won, but only on the last lap. He was lying third right until the last time round, behind Mick Andrew and Jefferies. I was there as I worked in the same office as Brian as I'd recruited him from Queens University. I went over there to do the preliminary interviews. I was a couple of years ahead of him and they thought it a good idea to send a recent graduate trainee to do the preliminary interviews on the new graduates. So, I went to Queens, and had a chat with Dr Blair on his idea for a rotary valve two stroke actually, and Brian was straight on the shortlist. Anyway afterwards, after he'd won this race, I went up to him in the paddock and I said: *"What got into you?"* And he said, in this broad Irish accent: *"Oh I just lost my temper with it."* As that was how he was. Kind of win or bust unfortunately.

The state of the fairing on Brian Steenson's Rocket Three fairing spoke volumes about his all action riding style. The bulk of the fairing also attested to the sheer size of the three cylinder machine and its lack of ground clearance

The obvious question was why was Steenson on an A65 at all when he already had a Rocket Three at his disposal, prepared for the TT? The fact was one of those involved knew only too well.

> **Steve Brown:** It was a Bank Holiday Monday, at the end of March when he won at Cadwell and Brian would have been a champion had he not been killed later at the Island. You can see from the photos of the three-cylinder bikes there that while Bob Heath was just kissing down the fairing of his Rocket Three production racer, Brian's was completely worn away, he had it so far over. So Brian could have used that Rocket Three at Cadwell, but he preferred to use the twin, as it was a tighter sort of circuit and the A65 was much better there.

It made sense and it also meant a last, final, victory for an officially supported works production A65 at a National meeting. It would all be privateers in the class from then on, who featured early on in the season with wins for Evans and Millward at Cadwell Park and Sanders at Darley Moor. Other A65 racers including Thomas, Prior – better known as a Triumph rider – Brown, Wall and Mason all took good places too, with the Mason in this case being Les' younger brother, BSA production tester Dave.

Dave Mason: I used to play in a band, a rock band. But I wanted to race bikes so took my Rickenbacker guitar to London, sold it and came back and bought the Norfire rolling chassis off my brother Les. I sort of cut my teeth on that, then went on to order a Rickman Métisse chassis through Vale-Onslow in Birmingham. It was blue. American racing blue it was called. The lightest chassis you could get. £350 with disc brakes. I went down to Rickman's to collect it, I couldn't wait it was so bloody trick. Though we moved the engine back, to get the chain run as short as possible and we built the first ever short-stroke 750 into that. I got it into my head that I wanted to build the best bike that I possibly could, having been trounced by Harvey Porter's big Norton the season before every time he got on to a great big long straight. I thought: *"We need something bigger. How are we going to get more oomf?"* At the time I was doing engine inspection work and I was walking up and down one day looking at this shot-peened con-rod on the 'A' Group engine production line. Next to it you had the 'B' Group production line and on it they were building a batch of 441cc Victor Enduros. The semi-motocrossers, with the little yellow and silver tanks on. So I'm looking at this beautiful piston, the slipper one, and thought: *"Why can't I have a couple of those in a twin. I wonder if it'll fit on the con-rod. Is it the same sized pin?"* And it was. It went straight in. I waited until lunch then went up to Les' office. Waving this thing at him his eyes went wide as if to say: *"I know where you're going with this!"* and the next thing the guys are getting the engine drawings out. They're rolling out the tracings and after a few minutes deliberation Les says: *"Leave it with me!"*

Les Mason: When I built that first engine up you could barely tell it wasn't standard. If you got down at the side and had a look, it was short and there was more material around the cylinder bore, but that was it. Anyway, we put that engine together and made some carb jetting mistakes at a test at Mallory initially. But then took it down to Lawford Heath, a little airfield near Rugby and David said: *"You have the honour. You try it."* We'd rev-ed it up beforehand and it sounded good, so I leapt on and disappeared up this runway and it was an absolute adrenaline rush. It took off up this bloody runway like a scalded cat. I'd never been so fast in my life. Turned it round with a grin from ear to ear and rushed back to where Dave was, who said: *"From the sound of that I think you've got it about right!"* I said: *"Well I'm saying nothing. You get on it and tell me how much better it is than the old 650?"* He came back and said: *"If I can't do any good on that I want shooting."*

Dave Mason (left) and Malcolm Lucas (right) at work on Mason's Rickman

Dave Mason rounding the Cadwell hairpin. It was odd that more competitors didn't pick up on the Rickman A65 resulting in only 12 full race versions ever being made

He did do good too, as did Les, as by chance a few days later he took a win on Tony Smith's ex-works racer, out on loan from the factory, at Aintree. Though sadly the purpose for which it was originally lent never came to pass.

Les Mason: The only time I had access to a works bike it was the ex-Tony Smith *proddy* racer, which eventually our David rode, when it went to Joe Rowley at The Motorcycle Shop, Tamworth. What happened was that I always fancied racing at the Barcelona 24hr, at Montjuic Park. So a lad who had come to work for me, John Miller, he and I approached Brian Martin. As I was still working at BSA then. I said: *"John and I would like to do the 24hr so would it be possible to borrow that bike to do it on?"* If he could ever help anyone he would. He was honestly one of the nicest human beings I ever knew, so he said: *"I think we can do that. I can't give you any expenses or that, as I don't have the budget, but there's no reason why the bike can't go missing for a week or two"*. So we arranged to have it the week before. I had it at home for a week, to check it over, then took it to Aintree to shake it down. I had my own bike there too so I said to David Miller: *"OK I'll race my bike in the open class with my meggas and you ride the factory bike in the proddy bike race and in the open class as well if you like"*. Well he fell off. I got a fairly good start and was gone and when I came round after the first lap the bloody ambulance was out on the side of the track. The yellow flags were waving, but they didn't stop us, they just waved us past and I can remember as we came round, the first left-hander after the start, glancing to the left as I could see the Spitfire parked on the side, on the bank, and I thought: *"Bloody hell John's fallen off it. We're meant to be going to Barcelona on that next week!"* That was my first thought. I never thought he might be injured which I should of, of course, as the ambulance was on the track.

Tragically in dropping the works machine Miller broke his back, demonstrating that the attrition rate on the UK's short circuits was just as high as anywhere else. It didn't stop Mason going to Barcelona however, as a result of what transpired almost immediately after.

Les Mason in action on his own production racer at Aintree. The megaphone exhausts indicate that this was probably in an open rather then production event

Going the distance

In that years' 500-miler there were two CB750 Honda fours, six of the new Norton Commandos, the sole works Rocket Three - ridden by Brian Steenson and Pat Mahoney - and a number of Triumph Tridents. In fact, there were 23 Triumphs of all types in the combined field of 61. There were just 3 A65s so it was worse odds than usual and worse still for the sole A50 of Hugh Evans and Paul Coombs. They were up against riders of the calibre of Barry Sheene and Dave Croxford on a Kawasaki Mach III and the Eddie Crooks entered Suzuki T500, ridden by Stan Woods and Frank Whiteway. Bary Ditchburn was in the mix too and they were all aboard machines which exemplified the changing face of British short circuit racing. Nevertheless at the 2½ hour mark, the Evans BSA had seen most of these off, was up to 2nd place and gaining on the leader. It was not to be. The engine cried *'enough'* on lap 71 and that was game over in the 500s. It was similarly tough in the 750 class where privateers battled it out against full factory machinery, ridden by the cream of British racing. But while massively outgunned and outnumbered the A65 pairing of Graham Sanders and Don Jones climbed steadily up the field to claim second in the 750-class by the end. Though the results in the weekly papers failed to tell the full story.

Mel Cranmer: The BSAs were all lined up as the first bikes in the line if you like, all together, and there was myself and Tony Carlton, I think Hugh Evans, and Graham and Don. I'd had an accident prior to the race so Tony set off first and I'd said to Graham and Don that there wasn't much point us getting in each others way so I said: *"You pit, then we'll pit the lap after. You come in and get away, then we'll bring Tony Carlton in."*

Cranmer on the ex-Bob Heath Lightning

Don Jones in the saddle as Graham Sanders and assistant check the rear chain. By 1970 the BSA A65 looked like an unlikely endurance racer, but even with the advent of the Honda 750 four and Laverda and Moto Guzzi twins, it gave a good account of itself in 1970

> So, Graham and Don - I can't remember which way round they were riding - they pitted, they changed rider, and we then stuck out the board for Tony to come in. As he went past he looked at the sign and promptly crashed at the very next corner and retired. As he'd have to have pushed round for a whole lap and I had a bit of an injury anyway. Graham and Don were doing well though, then Don crashed too, *on the last lap!* It was on one of those very fast bends as well, just before you got to the chicane, and it's all slightly up hill. So, he had a reasonably long push, but pushed the bike in and just got over the line in time, getting a massive round of applause from everyone as he finished.

It was a staggering result and totally out of the blue, but in comparison top three places, indeed wins, went without comment among the sidecar racers. Who, on cue, delivered victories thick and fast again, as soon as the season began. The only real question here was who would come runner up in the championship to Chris Vincent? A couple of new patterns did emerge however. Firstly, the number of competitors switching over to BSA power was growing exponentially while, secondly, a top three made up of A65s in '69 was increasingly becoming a top six in '70.

The first of those patterns was clearly on show at the opening meeting of the season at Cadwell, on Saturday 21st. With wins for Peter Williams and Ken Vogl and top three places for Bill Crook and Mike Gillett. A text book example of the latter was delivered on Easter

Sunday at the Mallory Park Carreras National. Where the final result read 1st Vincent (BSA A65) 2nd N Hanks (BSA A65) 3rd Brown (BSA A65) 4th R Hanks (BSA A65) 5th Sheridan (BSA A65) 6th Rust (BSA A65). The most obvious point of interest here being two times British Grass Track champion Bryan Rust's first appearance on an A65. Subsequently there were victories the following Monday for Boddice at Crystal Place, Vincent at Oulton and Norman Hanks at Cadwell. They didn't win everything however as the extra capacity of Chapman's *Mini* denied Hobson and Roy Hanks another win at Cadwell and another big engine put the cat among the pigeons at Thruxton on 12th April too.

Martin Davenport: The Hanks, they were all right, and Peter Brown's bikes had good power. But I don't think they were a patch on Vincent. Vincent was a God back then. I might be wrong, but Vincent was a step up on everyone else and what used to happen a lot was that Brown used to tag on to the back of Vincent. So, the results were often Vincent and Brown, Vincent and Brown, but all those BSA boys were quick. They knew those BSAs backward, though I was never really interested in one myself. I'd got what I'd got and persevered with it. I was doing it for the fun of it and green as grass really, so their brakes and chassis were better than mine, but the rain was a bit of a leveller at Thruxton. That day Chris Vincent won, but I didn't mind the wet and I think the conditions perhaps suited the power characteristic of my bike more, as my Vincent pulled from nothing. I was in second place, ahead of Boddice and remember going onto the grass coming out of Church, on the last lap and Church is the fastest corner of the lot.

Rust leads Sheridan round Mallory Park's Devil's Elbow, though Sheridan got the nod at the line

My passenger apologised after-wards, as he thought we were already through the corner, so had got off the back wheel and we lost traction. I couldn't see anything for mud and stuff being thrown up all over but, somehow, we got back on the track, more through luck than judgement and Mick Boddice was just in front. Which is where that picture would have been taken, going into that last chicane. I thought: *"Well, "I've gotta beat you no matter. It's do or die."* My passenger, Bernie Booth, ended up shoulder-barging a few straw bales,

Boddice leads Davenport at a horrible, murky, waterlogged Thruxton. The BSAs didn't always win

but we got past and in the pits Mick Boddice came up after and said: *"I couldn't see anything going into that last chicane."* So, I showed him my goggles, as they were covered in mud, and I said: *"Mick, I couldn't see anything either!"*

Martin Davenport this time with David Morrall, at a Snetterton Bemsee (British Motor Cycle Racing Club) meeting. Noise restrictions? Just look at those pipes!

100% concentration from Bill Cooper. A top competitor and top chassis designer/constructor who learnt his skills through a Derby Rolls-Royce apprenticeship

The following weekend was a mix of old names and new, with Hobson winning at Silloth, Bill Crook at Cadwell and Bill Cooper at Darley Moor. With the third place finisher behind Cooper being another recent A65 convert:

> *"Bill Cooper, Derby's International sidecar star, rode at his local track Darley Moor, near Ashbourne, on Sunday and in winning the 'A' final set up a new 8-lap record speed of 65.43. Bill also saw his WEC frames fill second and third places, piloted by Mick Gillett and Brian Mee, all three using 654 BSA motors."*[31]

Brian Mee: I started out marshalling, Mallory, Snetterton and that, but I always had the urge to race. My first ever outfit we built ourselves, but it wasn't very good, so we got Owen Greenwood to do a frame and then, when we got the Beezer, I got Bill Cooper to build me one. As at the time an A65 was definitely the best, the way to go. It was obvious going from the Triumph, there was no comparison. Really for a sidecar the Beezer was the bees knees as it had more grunt. You didn't need a heavy reving engine like for the solos, but grunt at the bottom end, and that's what the BSA had in spades. Though of course, Chris and the factory boys, they were using 750s when we were on 650s, then they were on 850s when we went on to 750 and we'd never find out, as there was definitely a

Brian Mee seen with an unfamiliar passenger at an early season practice session at Lincolnshire's Cadwell Park.

Brian Mee: John Ripon was the editor of one of the local news-papers, the Loughborough Echo and he wanted to have a go round as a passenger on a sidecar outfit, to see what it was like, for an article on local racers for the paper.

That photo was taken going into Mansfield and we were really wrapped up. It was so cold there was ice round the carbs and to be honest I think he found the experience a bit challenging

Birmingham mafia. They were the ones you wanted to beat. There was Chris, Brownie and Micky Boddice. And Norman and Roy were great too. They really raced, they were the tops. Max Deubel, Schauzu, Scheidegger, Camathias and that, they were a different story again as while they all had factory Rennsport BMWs when you consider what Vincent had got in terms of machinery against them, he was incredible. That guy was a hero, a lovely man too, and of course just a brilliant racer.

Vincent demonstrated that in the run up to the TT with wins at Castle Combe, Cadwell, Brands, Mallory and Oulton. Over the same period new names Mick Whitton and Ray Bell appeared in the minor places along with all the usual suspects. With wins among these also for Crook (Oulton Park and Darley Moor), Sheridan (Castle Combe), Hobson (Croft), Krukowski (Crimond) and Rust (Cadwell). Rust's being probably the most impressive as over Hobson.

Bryan Rust: I had some good scraps with Mac. He was a bit of a hard lad, but when Ben Pocklington was doing the tuning, the first and second year we had the BSA, it was going really well. The riders take all the credit but it's the mechanic that gets you there and if it hadn't been for Ben I wouldn't have been in those places to take those wins. He'd spend anything up to two hours making sure the timing was absolutely right and on the A65 he tapered the flywheels, shimmed the crankshaft and used a 66% balance factor I think, and it didn't vibrate at all. That altered BSA, I tell you what, it would do 9,500 revs and we were having to roll it off, though it was using all standard BSA stuff inside. We always kept the standard bushes like on the A10 because as long as they were put together right you never had any problems with those engines. It was like Alf Hagon always used to say on the grass: *"There's nothing special about it, it's just well put together."* But what was surprising was that they started as a 500 and 650, then 750, 850 and that, yet there were still never any problems. Most engines couldn't take that. A Triumph certainly couldn't.

Mac Hobson at Cadwell Park. At any circuit north of there he was virtually unbeatable

At the TT Peter Brown *was* the mechanic and came home 2nd again though he was never able to threaten Schauzu, finishing three minutes down. The ever improving Cooper was next A65 across the line, followed by Hobson and Krukowski which showed that you no longer had to come from Birmingham to make an A65 both fast and strong and capable of challenging for a win. Which was amply demonstrated back on the mainland on 18th July.

Bill Cooper on the Isle of Man. A top racer, he was also one of the go-to men for an off the shelf sidecar chassis, a great many of which went on to house an A65

No.2 Peter Brown (Rocket 3) No.49 Idris Evans (Imp) No.25. Stuart Digby (A65) and No.1. Chris Vincent (A65). Peter Brown's troublesome, fairing-free A75 revealing the large oil cooler necessary as well as the large forward mounted oil tank. **Stuart Digby:** Brownie always had his oil tank there, to keep his tea warm between races

Stuart Digby: The first time I realised that they were all beatable was at Castle Combe. We were on the front row of the grid and I thought: *"They're going to come past us like the wind."* But I was still in the lead going into the first hairpin, the right-hander, then Chris came past, then Norman I think. But Browny crashed into us going around the right hander, so we went from one side of the circuit to the other and onto the grass. But we chased after him and behind was Idris Evans. One of the first with an Imp. An Imp which ran backwards actually, but that was the first time I realised, though we were outside our comfort zone really, that we could do it. I'm not saying that we were as quick as any of them really. Vincent, Browny, Hanks, they were all 7-8 years older than me. I was just trying to pick stuff up off them, and they always seemed to drive away from you, but once you'd got close you knew you could do it again. Though Chris was definitely the best rider in the period. I don't think he had anything better than anyone else – Browny's motors all had Daytona bottom ends, while Chris' were standard - he was just a better rider.

Brown's engine wasn't all it could be that day however, as he was using a motor he wasn't familiar with and one which ultimately never really suited a sidecar, though many tried.

Peter Brown: At Umberslade Hall they imported a lot of boffiny-type people from the aircraft industry. They were clever people, but they didn't know anything about motorcycles. One day I had a telephone call from on high, from one of these people:

144

"Would I please stop racing the twin cylinder engine, it was not considered a good advertisement". So I got a brand new triple engine with the instruction that I must stop using these nasty old twin cylinder engines, and in due course and with much hard work we managed to get about 70-something horse power. With the A65 I ended up with about 85hp and the torque on them was

An overheated Peter Brown enjoys an ice cream more than his Rocket Three. It was returned to *'the management'* in pieces

colossal. But anyway, the proof is in the eating, so I went to Mallory for the first meeting and this triple got so hot it was untrue. And slower and slower and I finished 9th. And I have *never* finished 9th. We then went to Castle Combe and again it was getting hotter and hotter until, fortunately, it blew itself to pieces. I came back to Umberslade and said - I was probably quite succinct – *"you'll find all the bits in the box"* and they never asked me again.

The combination of pudding-basins and full-face helmets indicate changing times for Norman and Rose Hanks, at the 'Brands Hatch backwards' Hutchinson 100 in 1970. Norman Hanks was one of the first to import the new Bell helmets after a trip in support of the works BSA motocross team. But his bike reflects other American influences too. The remote points drive and pressure release valve, immediately below it, visible in this photo, indicate Daytona A50 crankcases. These incorporated the first 'official' end-fed crankshaft oil system ever used by BSA. Unfortunately, like many other good ideas developed in racing on the unit twins, it never made it into mass production. The Mini rear wheel would soon appear across the board in sidecar racing however

Success wasn't just about engines of course. Chassis design was evolving, wheel sizes were getting smaller and wider and both affected the riding style. This was nowhere better demonstrated than at the Hutch as while one pairing didn't win they had all the style, with *MCNs* front page headline: *"Mrs Hanks is hero of the Hutch"* matched by a huge Norman/ Rose Hanks photo, their outfit's sidecar wheel hovering over the infield grass:

> *"Phil Read collected the money and the glory at Sunday's Hutchinson 100 but it was a house-wife called Rose Hanks and her brother in law Norman who had the crowds cheering for them at Brands Hatch. They put up the best British sidecar performance to finish third behind world champion Klaus Enders and fellow German Georg Auerbacher on their BMWs, beating Siegfried Schauzu and Chris Vincent"*[32]

Norman Hanks: Chris used to say a trained monkey could do the job. But that was just Chris and I don't think even he believed it. With the passenger, you mustn't think about what the passenger is doing. You've just got to concentrate on what you're doing, as if you're concentrating on what they're doing, then you're not doing your job. Roy's later passenger Dave Wells was the best example of a good passenger. Roy would just go barreling into any corner you like and if Dave thought Roy hadn't got it quite right he'd alter it. He'd just move his weight forward, backwards, whatever, then the back would start to turn like a broadside sort of thing until it was pointing where he wanted it to go. Roy would just be holding on to the handle bars, as a passenger steers the bike nearly as much as the driver. And there were different eras. In the period of 4" tyres, if the back wheel was gripping the 4" inch tyre at the front wouldn't steer. It would just push on. As the tyres got bigger the passenger had to come further to the back. But basically, if the front stuck to the ground you could make the back do anything you wanted. You could steer with the throttle, by spinning it up, but if you haven't got the front stuck you're going nowhere. They were 16" wheels when I started with Manx Norton brakes and the like, then we had discs. Mick Fiddaman made a *'build it yourself'* frame kit. I had a swinging arm off him with all the components to make new wheels as what he cleverly used was all Mini parts. He had a cast iron Mini hub and disc then you put a Cosmic wheel on and suddenly you had a 5" times 10" wheel with almost twice as much rubber on the road. As soon as we all started fitting wider tyres we were doing exactly the same as we were with 4" tyres, but quicker.

Changing design as demonstrated on Ken Vogl's machine. Lower and with smaller, wider wheels. The rear made possible by off-setting the engine to the centre of the machine

Rust and Carter at Snetterton the day they beat Vincent. It might seem odd that other top racers should have such clear memories of beating Britain's No1. sidecar racer, but it happened so seldom for any of them it was always a stand out event

Those wheels were only just coming in so it was a much more conventional 16" wheeled outfit which put in a memorable performance only a couple of weeks after the *Hutch*. At the Snetterton Race of Aces Sheene, Read and Carruthers won the big solo races but a relative new boy took the big sidecar prize.

> *"Tall and bespectacled Rust and passenger Keith Carver (sic) bombed their 670 BSA outfit round the 2.71 mile circuit to blitz Chris Vincent's old lap record by 1.4s"*[33]

Bryan Rust: Snetterton was always the fastest circuit and we got about 7,500 revs on the clock in practice halfway down the old Norwich straight. I said to our lad: *"I'm halfway down the straight Ben and I'm on 7,500. On Maximum, and I don't want to give it anymore."* We needed another gear on it - it was under-geared – but we didn't have the sprockets so, I just thought we'll go out for the ride and see how we got on. And I broke the lap record. Then Chris broke it back, then I broke it again and broke the race record too and it was the easiest ride I'd ever had. I just went out with a relaxed attitude and was expecting for them to come by, down the old Norwich straight, but my passenger was saying; *"Slow down, slow down"*, as I had such a lead. But I thought: *"Bugger that."* I just kept riding as I had been, as I thought: *"I've practiced harder than this!"* and that was the only time I ever beat Chris as I rightly remember.

It was and to cap a poor weekend for *The King of Drift* his gear linkage came apart in the 500cc race, won by Pip Harris. Prompting the British Champion, currently engaged in building a new garage, to comment: *"I think I'll give it up and concentrate on my cement mixer"*.[34] He didn't of course, with the 20th September Mallory Park Race of the Year being one of his finest performances. Early in the race his machine spluttered to a halt as it left the Esses and stopped. Checking both the petrol feed and ignition he and his passenger Peter Williams – a sidecar driver himself -

Chris Vincent at Cadwell Park in September 1970, by which time the British championship was all but in the bag. He always rode with the prominent *"The Vincent BSA"* on his outfit as he was effectively a totally independent runner by 1970, with no formal factory connections

eventually got the outfit going again and then, suitably fired up for the challenge from stone-dead last, started to tear through the field in pursuit. He broke his own lap record and with two laps to go he caught and passed Norman Hanks and Brian Rust, who were then battling for the lead. This, over the course of just 10-laps, each of which took less than a minute to complete. It left Chris Vincent leading the British Championship - the points being Vincent 75, Norman Hanks 40, Sheridan 36, Brown 33, Hobson 32, Boddice 22 - with the obvious talking point being that the race result mirrored exactly that of the season opening Mallory result, the top six again made up entirely of A65s.

The other talking point at Mallory Park was probably Pat Sheridan in 3rd place in the championship. He quickly appeared out of the club racing scene but was immediately into his stride at National level

On October 4th Vincent won from Brown and Hanks at the Brands Hatch Evening News Race of the South, where the Hanks in question this time was Roy. Demonstrating some hard riding in front of the Grand Prix triumvirate of Auerbacher, Schauzu and Wakefield, he was reported as having his front wheel virtually on Peter Brown's sidecar platform he was racing so hard, trying everything bar low flying to get past! The final race of the Championships at Snetterton finished Vincent, Brown, Harris (BMW) Roy Hanks, Wakefield (BMW), Rust and Sheridan and perhaps encapsulated the character of the whole season. Massed ranks of A65s crowding out the thoroughbred BMWs and anyone else who dared try interfere. As a result, *Motor Cycle News* tipped Vincent as the man to topple the solo runners in their prestigious *"Man of the Year"* competition, noting that even after a decade at the top of his profession he had taken 18 top level National wins and had only failed to top the results at that level at the TT, Hutchinson 100, Scarborough International and Dutch TT. It was a pretty astounding set of results which couldn't possibly be matched in the solos. Though, as would soon be shown, two overseas results came close.

Solos galore

In the UK Post-TT there were multiple wins for Hugh Evans, Dave Mason, Clive Wall and Gerry Millward. There were also good performances by new boys Derek Whalley, John Hands, Steve and Lester Harris and BSA road tester Malcolm Lucas, who was now out of a sidecar passenger's seat and onto a solo. In this case a Featherbed A65. In a sign of the times Tony Smith's Snetterton lap record dating back to 1966 was broken by Dave Nixon's Trident, in winning the Shell Production championship race, though Japanese machines were still yet to make their mark in the bigger capacity classes. At the annual BRC One Hour Enduro, at Snetterton - in which Clive Wall's Spitfire finished 2nd - the speed trap on the long Norwich

The remarkable John Hands exemplified the sort of racer who campaigned their road machines on the track in the early 1970s. The ex-paratrooper worked on the A65s and A50s of the Royal Artillery Display Teams during working hours. What made him unique can be seen on the left-hand handle bar of his machine. Having lost his left hand in an accident he raced with great success with just one, putting both clutch and brake levers on the right-hand bar

Ted Reading was another out on a BSA in 1970. He'd soon be on an ex-Clive Wall machine, once Wall traded on

straight recorded Hugh Evans' A50 at 108mph, a good 10mph quicker than the fastest 500 Suzuki. It indicated that while on paper the twins were looking technologically out classed by the new machinery appearing, there was plenty of mileage in the BSA A-range yet.

This was perfectly demonstrated at Cadwell Park on August 22nd where the results read 1st Clive Wall (654 BSA) 2nd Gerry Millward (654 BSA) 3rd Mick James (650 Triumph) 4th Phil Haslam (650 Triumph) 5th Hugh Evans (500 BSA). Wall and Millward were also involved in one of the most dramatic encounters towards the end of the season, at Lydden, on 20th September. Wall slipped past Clive Smithers' very fast Commando on the last corner, to win by a wheel and recorded the fastest lap in any class that day. He also wrapped up the BFRC championship. But Millward had also briefly led that day.

Clive Wall: There weren't many of Dick smiling. I think that must have been the day I bought half the bike off him?

The image may not be crystal clear but the intention is. Gerry Millward deep into Lydden's Devil's Elbow, riding at ten tenths and up the rumble strip in 1968. A similar move at the same corner in 1970 nearly put one over on Wall and Smithers. By chance No.37 in this photo is Hugh Evans, on his trusty, and almost totally unique, racing A50

Gerry Millward: I remember that one quite well actually as going into the Devil's Elbow, before you run up to the hairpin, I went around the pair of them. I thought I was going to drop it but got past them only for my twist grip to come off. So, I slipped down to third again. Clive won the Championship that year and I got 2nd and we all went up to the do at the Café Royal. That was early 1971, January or February I guess. It was quite posh with Paul Smart giving out all the trophies and in fact, I've still got mine in the loft somewhere. Two A65s, 1st and 2nd was unusual, as A65s were few and far between. Most grids were full of Triumphs back then, so that's why I met Steve Brown and Dave Mason from the factory and how I got to know Steve Harris too. As like with the others we got chatting as it was a bit unusual having two A65s at a meeting among all the Triumphs and that. We met at Cadwell, the BFRC, British Formula Club I think it was?

Lester Harris at Snetterton. The tucked-under A65 exhausts were the first product Harris brothers ever made

Steve Harris: At the time we started racing, in 1970, if you were going to go racing anywhere else but Hertfordshire you would have bought a Triumph Bonneville. But Dick Rainbow had this shop in Ware, and when he was at his peak, BSA used to come down and just give him heaps of A65 cylinder heads. He'd modify this one this way and that one another. It was all a little bit of trial and error, but parts obviously weren't a problem.

Lester Harris: Tony Smith, the local hot shot, had come through him so when Steve decided to go racing, Dick says: *"Why don't you use a BSA and we'll build it here?"* And that's what happened, as production racing was popular. Really popular. And on the face of it, the production racers, they looked like a standard motorcycle. But the really competitive bikes, the factory bikes, I mean everything was different. Absolutely everything. There was a lot of prestige involved and they did whatever was necessary. Because the factories, they really wanted to win.

Steve Harris: Yeah, the factory bikes were quite different. To give you an example, I went to work for another local motorcycle dealer, Les Rugg, who had Longstaff's. He said one day, out of the blue: *"There's a bike here for sale in MCN. Buy it"*. It was Malcolm Uphill's Bonneville. You know the Isle of Man one, from the TT100 tyres adverts. But over time it got modified back to standard, as gradually we couldn't find the bits. Everything was different on it. Every damn bit of it. It was a genuine one-off. Well, maybe not a one off, but one of a handful, while the A65s were always pretty standard. That timing-side main-bearing for example, that phosphor bronze bush, we punched a rod through the front and welded it up four times I think. But Dick was obviously a talented bloke when it came to putting engines together and he built an A65 which I raced for a year and then I sold it to Lester.

Lester Harris: We had this idea that we'd start making things, like exhaust pipes, frames, whatever, that would allow us, if we weren't good enough to earn a living out of racing, to at least pay for our racing. But of-course it actually finished it. All the experienced chassis people and tuners said the current bikes coming out were too big. We erred towards the bigger bikes, and we were young enough and foolish enough to think that we might know better, and over a time we obviously did, as that's how we've arrived with our chassis business

as it is today. But those pipes on the A65 pictured - which came out and are tucked right under the bike, then came back out again - we made two or three sets of those and they were actually the first thing we ever sold.

Steve Harris, Brands Hatch, 15th August 1970. Self-made pipes and 190mm Lightning Clubman brake in evidence. Steve and Lester Harris would go on to found a leading chassis company and later manage their own Grand Prix team

Clive Wall picking up the 1970 BRC Production Championship award from Paul Smart in early 1971, at London's Café Royal, in Mayfair. The venue indicated the status of the Championship at a time, when a number of the clubs running Production Championships outside of National meetings had memberships nearer four figures than three

Production racing - small numbers, long odds

```
EVENT 3 - Production 175-1000 c.c.          - 2 -          TIME    SPEED   Pts.

 1    1    D.J. Nixon        741 Triumph T150      12.44.4   89.34   10 + 3
 2    2    P. Butler         750 Triumph T150      12.51.2   88.55   9
 3   10    J. Vincent        649 Triumph 6T        13.06.0   86.89   8
 4   33    J. Kanka          750 Triumph T150      13.14.0   86.01   7
 5   32    P. Darvill        750 Honda C.B.750     13.20.6   85.30   6
 6   30    F. Hodgson        654 B.S.A. Spitfire   13.20.8   85.28   5
 7   27    P.J. McKinley     668 Triumph T120      13.23.8   84.97   4
 8   36    D. Cash           750 Norton Commando   13.26.2   84.71   3
 9   24    H. Robertson      650 Triumph T120      13.33.4   83.96   2
10   18    P. Wyncoll        745 Dunstall Atlas    13.36.2   83.67   1
11   15    T. Smith          745 Norton Commando   13.37.6   83.53
12   12    C.R. Smithers     750 Norton Commando   13.45.4   82.74
13   38    L. Phelps         650 Triumph T120      13.45.6   82.72
14   39    D. Chambers       650 Triumph T120      13.45.8   82.70
15    3    K.G. Buckmaster   649 Triumph T120      13.47.4   82.54
16    5    R. Prior          668 Triumph T120      13.48.0   82.48
17   17    R.J. Harrington   490 Triumph T100      13.54.2   81.87
18   29    J. Witt-Mann      490 Triumph T100T     13.55.0   81.79
19   28    D. Simpson        609 Norton 99 SS      14.10.8   80.26
20   23    W. Thomas         490 Triumph T100T     14.11.4   80.21
21   31    P. Huzzey         500 Triumph T100T     12.53.2   6 Laps
22   14    D. Forrester      250 Ducati Mk 3D      13.18.4
23    4    R.L. Stonely      250 Ducati Mk 3D      13.36.2
24   66    R.P. Sinclair     650 Triumph T120      13.37.6
25   26    S. Jackson        650 Triumph T120R     13.47.8
26    6    M.J. Hemmings     750 Norton Commando   13.52.2
     Fastest lap: D.J. Nixon 1 (741 Triumph T150) 1 mn. 46.4 secs. at 91.69 m.p.h. CLUB RECORD
```

A set of pretty normal production racing results, from the Bemsee run event at Snetterton on 25th October 1970. Among the twenty six finishers a sole A65 was pretty much par for the course. A ratio of ten Triumphs for every BSA was the best any A65 racer could hope for, making their results all the more remarkable

There were never many solo racing A65s. At the same meetings in which the likes of Smith and Hodgson, Heath and Wall took victories, they were often the sole A65 on track. Hugh Evans was *always* alone on an A50. These machines would be regularly pitted against twenty or more Triumphs, along with the disc braked, 750cc Nortons which were able to compete through Paul Dunstall having registered himself as a manufacturer. Legitimising non-Norton parts. So why so few A65s?

Triumphs were hugely successful as pre-unit machines and when they went over to unit construction the knowledge and most of the parts could be swapped over too. It was an almost seamless transition for anyone moving from a T110 to a T120. The A65/50 motor had no carryovers from the A10 however, so when moving on the likes of Pete *PK* Davies - one of the most successful pre-unit BSA twin runners - went to a unit Triumph rather than unit BSA. Similarly, for those riding Gold Stars there was no continuity in transition to an A65/50. It was a whole new thing.

Another factor was that BSA never supported the A65/50 with racing parts. For the engine there were no special parts lists, no factory options and no tuning guides from the Competition Department. Who to begin with didn't even prepare the factory's own competition engines. Triumph in comparison supported privateers to a far greater extent. The 'Thruxton Bonneville T120 High Performance Specification' parts list of 1965 ran to over 100 parts, unique to the Thruxton model. A revised list appeared in 1967, as did one which was 'works only'. This contained a selection of non-standard parts fitted to bikes directly overseen by Doug Hele and which stayed within the Triumph factory. These modifications didn't meet the ACU Production rules, but they were used all the same. Additionally many tuning firms existed which built on the Triumph twins' popularity and longevity, while only Eddie Dow marketed parts for the BSA twins, with these being largely cosmetic.

The final factor working against the A65 was that while BSA scrupulously followed the ACU guidelines in producing 200 Lightning Clubman, they never produced another dedicated production racer again. BSA's policy, from 1966 onward, was that any privateer wishing to enter an A65 in a production event had to buy a Spitfire from a dealer's showroom and carry out any tuning work themselves. Triumph in comparison never bothered with the ACU requirements. After an initial batch of 52 Thruxton Bonnevilles – well under the stipulated number - Triumph built a small number of new Thruxtons every year to 1969, with factory produced racers existing before the official Thruxton designation was created too. Many of these were updated to the latest specification annually with MAC233E, which won the 1969 Thruxton 500-miler and Malcolm Uphill's famous *"99.99mph"* 1969 TT winning Bonneville, being good examples, as actually '66 bikes updated. This was possible since Triumph had a race shop dedicated to maintaining the T120 twins, which also supported dealer entrants.

In comparison BSA had two, or a maximum of three bikes updated annually and these solely for the higher profile production races. Dick Rainbow and Tom Kirby were the only dealers to seriously campaign the unit twin independently and only one factory supported bike, Tony Smith's, was campaigned on a regular basis around British short circuits. The adage that *'to finish first, first you must finish'* never held so true and with more Triumphs entered than any other make – regularly more than half the field – they were always more likely to achieve greater success. It was a virtuous circle for Triumph and one BSA never seriously countered. Which was a shame, given that on a bike for bike basis the BSA A65 actually had a higher victory rate than the Triumph Bonneville in production racing and continued taking championships after the Triumph twin was supplanted by the triple.

Snetterton 19th March 1967 was a rare case of multiple A65s on the grid - No.3 C Wall, No. 78 I Hesketh No. 146 M Burgess and top right, with number obscured, the omnipresent Tony Smith

Manx Norton mounted Bob Heath (left) lines up alongside Graham Sanders' A65 in the Darley Moor paddock. Les Mason would rue joining them at the September meeting

The racing career of another man making parts for the A65 also finished around the same time as the Harris brothers' but for far less fortunate reasons. On a day by chance which saw another A65 new boy, Reg Hardy appear in the results too.

Les Mason: The reason I avoided Darley Moor was I'd gone up there one time and didn't like the look of the place. It was inherently dangerous. Like a canal with earth banks all around the track. Anyway, there was some reason Bob Heath, Graham Sanders and me were all vying with each other at the time so I thought: *"I'll go!"* and of course that was when I had my big one, which virtually finished me off. Some kid got off from the starting line, going like a bat out of hell, a Triumph twin I remember, but he arrived at the Esses just before the top hairpin faster then he'd ever been in his life and the next thing you know he's going down the road with the bike bouncing back off the bank. So, there's this rider and bits and pieces of bike blocking the road right as we're going into the Esses. Bob Heath's right with me, we're wheel to wheel, so I straightened the bike up, hit the earth bank and it flew up in the air. My brother Dave was on the other side of the circuit, at the pits and saw the bike in the air, in bits and pieces it went up so high. I opened my eyes thinking it had gone very quiet, saw the tank flying over my head and then all hell let loose. I was off work for four or five weeks, all plastered up, and while I started racing again it was with indifferent results. I realised I wasn't willing to push it to the limits again. The bravery, the adrenaline, whatever it was, had gone out of the window by then.

It was to the benefit of A65 racers everywhere, as it meant Mason could set aside more time for his nascent tuning business - Precision Accessories which would go on to become Devimead – but in the short term it also meant that the Darley Moor title went out of A65 hands for the first time since 1966. It went to Phil Haslam who would not only have a fierce struggle with Les' brother Dave the following season, but also a rider who took a lukewarm 6th as the lone A65 at Snetterton on 28th October. There were extenuating circumstances behind the poor showing however.

Frank Hodgson: I'd been on a Yamaha at the time and I'd won one or two club championships. Northern based ones around Cadwell, Croft, Carnaby and the like. A friend of my father's, a freelance journalist, said would it be OK if he put the word around about me and eventually he got me on York Sport Television. On a programme on up and coming riders and stuff. It was Fred Dinenage who came to see me, we went to Cadwell Park with the camera crew and luckily I won. '69 it would have been. People ignored me before - I thought it was because I was a northerner - but when I got on TV people were like: *"Oh Frank Hodgson off Yorkshire Television"* and were writing to me asking if I'd like to ride their bikes and that. Actually, Mal Carter had offered me an A65 before, which he was racing himself. He was doing alright actually but gave it to someone else who came about 10th and of course Malcolm was effing and blinding about this so said to me, as he knew me: *"You take it out and show him how to do it."* Well it was terrible this bike and I came about 6th and he was: *"What are you doing. I've spent all this money on it and I was gonna offer you me Yamahas I'm just buying."* So, he offered them to Phil Haslam instead, who obviously went on to be really successful. But it was probably for the best, as eventually I got this call from BSA and that's how it all started. They said: *"Come down, have some talks with Brian* (Martin) *and see what he thinks. As fingers crossed he'll let you have a bike."* Which I found out was Brian Steenson's. The thing was at the time BSA were building his new 350 overhead cam and they wanted someone to thrash it, but I had to prove I could ride a four-stroke bike first and this is how it all came about.

Early days at the Croft chicane. After the machine came back from its first visit back to the factory the Spitfire only ever had the top half fairing fitted.

The ex-works A65 as most adversaries faced it. Half fairing and to standard production racing specification, including all mudguards, stays, rear light and bracketry

So, they let me have the bike on loan, to take wherever I liked, to see how I got along. Hopefully to come back to get this other bike for testing. That part never materialised of course, as the project never went that far. But I got the A65 and I was just so grateful at the time as I was a just a nobody picking up a factory bike and I'm sure some of my competitors didn't believe it when I told them where it had come from.

Steve Brown was the first BSA guy I got to know as this fella came up at lunchtime, after practice, and he just started tinkering around with the bike. So, I says: *"Er, can I help you?"* 'cos I didn't know who he was. He says: *"How's it going?"* So, not knowing who he was I said: *"Well, to be perfectly honest, it's terrible. It doesn't handle right, it's got a bit of a misfire and I can't start the damn thing."* As in them days the races were nearly all push-starts. I remember bumping it and it locking-up and was nearly last off the grid really, like that poor result at Snetterton. The trouble was that early on, like Tony Smith, I couldn't get it off the line with a dead engine. Well anyway he said: *"Actually I work in the Competition Department at BSA"*. So I said: *"Oh don't say owt!"* As I thought they might have the bike back off me. Well he went on to say: *"The bike you are actually racing is an old bike, that's been in a corner and no one's touched it since Brian Steenson had it."* And what must have happened were Steve told Brian Martin when he went back, as I got a phone call from BSA saying: *"Please would I return the bike"*. I thought: *"Oh no, I've blown it."* Because all it were, was a loan of the bike. I wasn't a works rider. It was just an ex-works, factory bike on loan. But anyway three or four weeks later I get a phone call saying: *"Can you come back to the factory? Your bike's ready."* I was gobsmacked. I couldn't get down there quick enough. Well first meeting I had after that it was at Aintree and the bike was fantastic. And it had these new TT-100 tyres on it too, as the ones Brian Steenson had were these more triangular ones, and it didn't seem to handle right. They put these new tyres on and I remember Steve said: *"You won't be able to out ride those!"* But I gave it a good try and I won the race, first time out, and I was thinking: *"this is fantastic"* as it was fabulous after that. It was a lot sweeter, and the rest of it was history as they say.

It was, but that would be for 1971 and in 1970 there were two big *'what if'* stories still to run.

Tested to endurance

Though Graham Sanders and Don Jones had never raced overseas before, following their good result at the 500-miler they thought they'd make the trip to Montjuic Park in July, for the annual Barcelona 24-hr marathon. It constituted the second round of the FIM European Coupe d'Endurance Championship - forerunner of the World Endurance Championship - and they were duly rewarded. Against experienced continental opposition they hammered their A65 round the twisty street circuit, for 24 punishing hours, but apart from a broken head steady and regular chain adjustment their private A65 ran like clockwork. As at Thruxton they rose slowly but inexorably through the ranks and while it wasn't exactly hare and tortoise stuff a carefully paced race paid dividends:

> *"With only half an hour to go Don Jones on the BSA which he shared with Graham Sanders, had worked his way into fourth place and was only 30 seconds behind the Honda. His pit displayed encouraging signals but Norman Price was fully aware of the situation and held off the challenge, keeping the BSA team in fourth place. It was nevertheless a brilliant effort for their first year in international endurance races and sufficient to take them to the top of the endurance championship table with a five marks margin."*[35]

They finished third in the critical 750 class, five laps clear of the next Honda Four of Urdich and Pogolotti, indicating as at Thruxton, that an extra 100cc, more gears, better brakes and twice as many cylinders counted for little in the gruelling discipline of endurance racing. In what looked like corporate opportunism Sanders and Jones then suddenly became the 'Works' team for the final round in France but there was a little more to it than that.

Don Jones (21) a blur of speed in pursuit of the A65s nemesis. Peter Darvill (5) on the Honda 750/4

Steve Brown: Graham worked in Engine Development at BSA, so he was privy to everything that was going on and a good mechanic too. He used to build his own twins and they were super reliable. But Graham didn't have an entry for the Bol d'Or 24-hour race. They got turned down. But Bob Heath did and he had a clash of dates. The same weekend he had a race at Mallory Park in the British 500cc Championship, in which he was doing really well, on his B50 500 single. So I said to Brian Martin: *"Why don't we swap the entry, for Graham and Don to do the 24hr race?"* As you couldn't change the bike, but you could change the riders. As such we went to the Bol d'Or, with the works Rocket Three, instead of Graham's own A65. Les Mason was sort of managing, with me and Ron Smith along. They needed to finish in the first six to guarantee the win, and after a few hours they were, but then they crashed, then ran out of petrol, and eventually finished well down. It was just all so unfortunate really.

Ron Smith: I don't think Graham Sanders ever really got any official help off the factory before that, though I guess he got odd bits and pieces. But I went to the Bol d'Or with them for that one and one of them, Don I think it was, got thrown off in the night and came back with no lights. We'd got a spare fairing, but someone had fibre-glassed the headlamp in wrong, and it was like riding round with a search light on after that!

As a result they finished well down but the points they'd already scored were sufficient for them to claim an impressive second place in the championship, against better supported and funded opposition. Factory 750cc Laverda and Guzzi twins made their first appearance in 1970, alongside the Honda Fours, but BSA made nothing of the publicity since all the points were scored on the twin and interest was only in the Rocket Three. It was a sad end and begs the question of how things could have ended if Sanders had been able to ride his A65 at the *Bol*?

Mel Cranmer: I know that Graham reckoned if he's taken the twin, they'd have won the championship. I actually used to send Ray Knight snippets on production racing for his column, from Aintree, Darley and the like, as up here we weren't really covered. And I know in one of his *Motorcyclist Illustrated* articles he quoted Graham Sanders bike being timed at 134mph at Snetterton and said: *"It went by me like a train"*. That bike was bored out to the maximum that you could get, which was 670cc with +40 pistons, but apart from that it was just the work that Graham did on it which made it so fast. Playing around with exhaust pipes and such. There was no big motor or anything like that, but Graham said he had 74hp out of it, so when he decided to pack it all in, I bought the whole lot.

Sanders at speed on more familiar turf, before the machine was taken over by Mel Cranmer

Flat out.....turn left

A huge European title had been lost betting on a fickle BSA triple and incredibly, a few months later, it was a case of déjà vu USA. Jim Rice had put together a stellar season in the American Grand National Championship in 1969, as had Dave Aldana as an Amateur. They were seen as the coming force and with changes in the rules for 1970 BSA provided them with works Rocket Threes for road racing. Both they, stalwart Dick Mann and new boy Ken Pressgrove, had been developing their own A65s for the TT and Flat Track events which made up the majority of the season's programme, and while the veteran Mann had been using a frame manufactured by himself for a while the others had also found their own preferred chassis combinations by 1970.

Jim Rice was to excel on the A65 in 1970, ending up with 2nd in the National AMA championship. If he'd kept on the twin instead of the Rocket Three at the Sacramento mile, it could have been No.1 he was wearing

Dave Aldana: I started racing my A65 as an amateur with a standard frame which was, to be honest, a load of shit. But I made it work better. By pulling the steering-head back, changing the head angle and putting different wheels on it. But it was still a piece of shit. It was awfully heavy and kept throwing me over the side all the time. But with the Trackmaster frame it was one of the best handling bikes I ever rode and I was very successful with it.

Rice in his 1970, #24, livery. Over the jumps at Ascot

Generally the Trackmaster/A65 looked like a winning combination and early season results only confirmed it. The BSAs seemed to outclass the aging Harley-Davidsons and for once had the edge over Triumph too. Rice won the first race of the season at the Houston TT on February 6th and BSA kept things rolling when Rice won again, from Mann, at the Atlanta ½-mile in April, with Aldana taking 2nd at the Cumberland ½-mile in early May. on 31st Rice then won the Reading National on the ½-mile oval by over half a lap, being followed home by Larry Palmgren (Tri) and Dick Mann (A65). It was generally a good day for the A65s with Ken Pressgrove in 4th, and privateers Billy Eves and Royal Sherbet in 7th and 8th respectively.

At the end of June Charity Newsies National, Ohio favorite Ronnie Rall came 2nd on his BSA and while Rice could only place 6th it put him head of the standings with a 3-point lead over the unlucky Mann, whose transmission had locked up even before he'd gone out in the heats. That gap widened on July 5th when Rice won at the San Jose ½-mile, from Jimmy Odom's Triumph and Chuck Palmgren's Yamaha, as Mann trailed in last and Dave Aldana took 5th having taken out the hay bales and fence on turn one in practice. Mann then pulled it back again the following Saturday evening at the Castle Rock TT. He won, ahead of Don Castro's Triumph and Mark Brelsford's Harley and suddenly Rice was 25-points behind Mann, while Romero had bumped Aldana on the third BSA back to fourth overall. On July 18th TT racing continued at Ascot Park, Gardena, where Mert Lawwill's Harley took the win from Gene Romero's Triumph with Dallas Baker bringing his A65 in third.

The first championship race on a full mile track was at Santa Rosa, California, on July 26th where 1969 winner Rice did it again, with Jimmy Odom in 2nd on his Triumph and Larry Palmgren's Yamaha 3rd. Next up it was the 20 lap ½-mile at Cumberland, where Mert Lawwill took the victory from Dave Aldana and the consistent Larry Palmgren. Ken Pressgrove was the next best A65 in 7th and Jim Rice 12th. It was much better for the A65 racers on August 16th however, at Terre Haute, Indiana, where around the ½-mile circuit rookie Aldana took the win, from Rice in second place. On August 21st veteran champion Bart Markel won his only National on the year at Santa Fe, on his Harley, but Rice was 2nd again which moved him back into the points lead. This stood at Rice 397, Mann 389, Romero 332 and Aldana 295 and with the points so tight as it wasn't all about winning. Consistency paid and while the three main A65 runners had all been picking up points when not in the top six so had Triumph's Gene Romero. He had so far failed to figure at the front but was always there or thereabouts and running a full 750 engine against the BSAs 650cc since, as ever, Triumph were ahead of BSA in playing the rules. The Triumphs had 750cc Sonny Routt Barrels fitted, with Tricor's Service Manager Rod Coates having 200 engine numbers stamped with an additional T, to make a class C rules compliant engine. The T120RT.

The famous Peoria TT was next, the following Sunday and Rice took his 6th race win of the season. He was followed home by team mate Aldana in a reverse of the Terre Haute result, and while Romero brought his Triumph home in 3rd, the win now gave Rice a whopping 60-point lead over the ever consistent Dick Mann. Romero struck back with a first win on the Mile track at Sedalia Missouri on August 30th however, leading Triumph team mate Castro and Rice over the line. This result jumped Romero past Mann in the standings, but it didn't really matter for Mann too much. He broke his leg in a tangle with Chuck Palmgren's Harley-Davidson and as far as BSA was concerned he wasn't a full works rider anyway. Rice was and he still held a good championship lead. September 6th was perhaps a landmark date in AMA racing as Larry Palmgren took his only win of the year at the huge 1⅛th mile Nazareth Oval. The 50-laps proved a real machine wrecker and it was a landmark as Palmgren took the win on a Yamaha twin, while battling with Rice on the Cates Rocket Three. The triple let Rice down however, by breaking its primary chain on the 13th lap, leaving it to the Triumphs of Nixon and Castro to pick up the 2nd and 3rd places. It was such a race or attrition that Rice was still credited with 12th place - since only 8 of the 20 finalists actually finished - but the lost points drew Romero closer in the title hunt. Next evening the championship reconvened at Indianapolis, where the state fair closed with the AMA professional mile race. Dave Aldana took the win to consolidate his 4th place in the championship standings but as the season drew to a close all eyes were then on the big-purse, Sacramento mile, with events famously covered in the film *'On Any Sunday.'*

Dick Mann at the Sacramento mile. He fought through the pain of his broken leg to win his heat but flagged in the final

Blowing the title care of the BSA Rocket Three

By this point BSA's decision to bet on rookies Rice and Aldana was looking good. Both were doing well on their A65s and Rice had actually won a third of all the races so far that season. He looked confident on his home tuned twin from the very first race of the season but the factory prepared Rocket Threes, on which the riders were never allowed to work, were a different kettle of fish. They were a bit of an unknown quantity, but had the extra 100cc which Triumph were running on their twins. That and factory pressure tempted Rice, with unfortunate and disastrous consequences.

Jim Rice: I was pretty confident going into my second Expert season, after winning three Nationals on my home built 650cc and there was much more competition back then. I remember at the San Jose mile there would be riders show up, may be 140 for 40 qualifying spots but the Trackmaster frame with the BSA 650 twin engine in it made for some great racing. I was my own mechanic, 'still am and I always got as much pleasure out of working on the bikes, preparing them and that, as racing them. Dick Mann and guys like that prepared their own stuff too, worked on their own equipment and it was a very special time. But while I did my own preparation and development on the twins, with the triple it was a case of: *"Here it is, check it out."* And after I'd won at Sedalia in '69, BSA were keen to push the three. The BSA/Triumph organization focused on promoting its three-cylinder street bikes to consumers. Winning results sell motorcycles and my mile win on the Tom Cates Trackmaster triple stood alone.

Even though my twin was a very reliable bike, I also liked the three-cylinder on the mile, because it was fast and had a straightaway advantage. Dick Mann and Aldana had stuck with the twins and my three-cylinder and twin practice times were similar. Within a small interval of each other. I reluctantly chose to ride the three-cylinder and later paid the price. The motor width was the problem. As what would happen on a mile, on a turn, you'd go in at 130-135 mph with a good groove and you were constantly fighting with the primary case touching down and unloading the back wheel. At the same time as you were trying to finesse the throttle. Trying to get the power on while fighting out of the turn. So, you'd get to stand it up a bit out of the turn which took a toll on your cornering. But the pay-off was on the straightaway, especially if you could get behind another rider, as you'd go flying past them.

Jim Rice in happier time at San Jose in 1970

A blurry ending to Jim Rice's season. The Rocket Three goes over the barriers while Rice hits them, to the middle of the frame, upside down. Like Sanders at the Bol d'Or the obvious question was: *"What if he'd kept to the A65?"*

After winning two TTs, three half-milers and the San Jose mile on his A65 the switch to the triple was ultimately ill-judged. Struggling for the last qualification place Rice crashed into Chuck Palmgren at the finish, which was captured in perpetuity on film. Rice's season was effectively over and BSA's chances of the title were gone.

> **Jim Rice:** Well it was a tough one for me as my goal was always to be No.1 and Gene Romero and me had had this battle going on for several races leading up to the Sacramento Mile. With just a few races after that the writing was on the wall. That really messed me up as Gene won the Sacramento race and the Ascot ½-mile and I ended up second overall. How am I with Gene? Well I always put it this way. We never really hung out or did chit chat. We had more what I'd call mutual respect, by giving the other person space!

In those last two races Aldana was 4th and Jody Nicholas 12th at Ascot where, as Rice said Romero won. While Rice was 4th and Aldana 6th at the Oklahoma City ½-mile. Romero came 2nd however, behind Brelsford's Harley, and as such it was all over for the injured Rice and team BSA. After leading the championship for nearly the whole season the title went to Romero and Triumph. Interestingly for BSA's prospects in 1971 however the final amateur race at Oklahoma was won by another BSA runner moving up through the ranks.

> **Don Emde:** One sad thing that happened in 1970 was the other member of the BSA factory team that year, Ken Pressgrove, was killed at a race at Louisville, Kentucky. Ken only raced flat track races, so it's hard to say if BSA would have kept him on the full team in 1971, when they added the Rocket Three for road racing. He was a nice guy and a fast flat track rider and I felt a bit that his loss kind of opened the door for me.

The unlucky Ken Pressgrove. BSA's nearly man

I got started in 1970 at Ascot Park in Gardena, where all of the top west coast riders raced. As there was a weekly schedule of ½-mile dirt track races every Friday night from April to October, plus once a month on a Saturday night or sometimes Sundays during the day there was also an American-style TT race at the same track. They had an alternate ¼-mile oval section of track inside the ½-mile oval and a course joined the two, with a jump and left and right-hand turns. It was a fun track and once a year there was also the points-paying TT National race. I won about 5-6 Amateur main events at Ascot that year and late in the season at the National, my Amateur time was the 2nd fastest time overall, behind only Gene Romero.

Emde following his 1970 Oklahoma win

At season's end I won the Amateur final at the last AMA National of the year at Oklahoma City. Triumph rider John Hateley and I were the top Amateurs at Ascot with, end-of-the season, John beating me out for the flat track Amateur title and I beat him out for the TT Amateur title. Though one thing worth noting about the BSA and Triumphs in AMA racing was that until late in 1970, both brands were limited to 650cc's because that's what the street bikes were. But there was a provision in the rules that if 200 kits were made and available to the public, then a 750cc kit could be installed and used in racing. For Triumph, that was an easy thing to do, in fact I think some accessory manufacturer was already making them. So the Triumphs got a little faster late in 1970 since the BSAs were still 650s.

Everyone could see the A65's prowess on the ovals and the deficiencies of the Rocket Three. BSA had been chastened not just because of their mistake with Rice's triple, but in not matching Triumph's increase to 750cc. There was also one large elephant in the room. Dick Mann had won at Daytona, but it wasn't on a BSA at all. No longer an official rider - he was riding the A65 on the dirt purely out of choice - the only spare Rob North Triple available was given to Mike Hailwood, contracted especially for that race. As such Mann had been forced to look elsewhere for a ride and ended up winning on a Honda 750 Four. Honda was over the moon, but BSA had learnt their lesson. For 1971 in would be solely A65s on the dirt, for Flat Track and TT events, with the Rocket Three confined to tarmac. Critically, veteran Dick Mann would also be back on the pay roll. There was promise of a 750 twin too, to make up for that 100cc deficit.

The coveted #1 plate - 1971

Brands Hatch 3rd July 1971. Motorcycle racing had never been so popular, with meetings at upward of a dozen circuits every weekend. Derek Whalley's unconventional Montesa-framed A65 (No.53) was ineligible for production racing but good enough to take two 3rd places in the 1,000cc events

Everything looked rosy State-side but by 1971, though it was not widely known, the BSA ship was in choppy waters. As such whilst support for racing in America continued with all guns blazing - as that's where most BSAs were sold - Bob Heath pretty much campaigned the factory triples alone in the UK, with the racing efforts increasingly directed from Triumph's Meriden Headquarters. Privately entered triples, both Triumph and BSA, were appearing on British race tracks in greater numbers, but by and large big twins still ruled in the burgeoning production racing scene. There was still no ACU sanctioned National title but Shell Oils started to sponsor the Bemsee championship as one of the first companies to pick-up on the category's increasing popularity. There was also now a British 750cc championship.

For the BSA privateers racing started at a chilly Cadwell Park on 7th March where Frank Hodgson failed to read the BSA script, by beating Mick Burns Jervis sponsored Rocket Three, resplendent with its exotic four leading shoe front brake. Hodgson clearly had the ex-works A65 sorted and took other wins in March, April and May, at both Cadwell and Croft each month. Those good results continued for others in April too, with Hugh Evans taking 3rd at Snetterton on 4th April, on a machine now entered as an A65. Since he'd converted it to 750cc over the winter and this was its maiden outing. Sunday 25th was perhaps the best day's racing that month however with Clive Wall second at Lydden, a machine's length behind Brian Edward's Triumph. While at the Snetterton MCRC event Dave Mason's 2nd and 3rd on

Frank Hodgson's style was unmistakable and unusual for a production racer at the time. As he was as much off the bike as on, in a style which would become more common in the 1970s

his Rickman A65 got him off to a good start in the hunt for the 1000cc championship. Other good non-production bike results were the fourth places of Malcolm Lucas on his Featherbed A65 and Martin Russell on his unique Bandit. An A65 engine in the frame of one of BSA-Triumphs abortive 350cc Bandit/Fury twins.

In the production class there were wins the same day for both Frank Hodgson and Dave Mason, Hodgson on the ex-Cooper/Steenson bike and Mason on the Tamworth Motorcycles ex-Tony Smith machine. It meant two *'works'* Spitfire victories the same day, albeit a year after they were officially retired. Hodgson was then at it again on 22nd May at Cadwell Park, where he won twice and Steve Brown followed up with a 2nd place and a win of his own.

Lucas with his Norton-framed A65. His was one of just a handful campaigned

Dave Mason on the ex-Tony Smith PR racer taking the inside line round the Cadwell Park Club hairpin. He used the same bike to take a 1st and 4th on 25th April, to go with his 2nd and 3rd places on his Rickman version at Snetterton

Steve Brown: I used to be in three or four clubs back then. The Bantam, British Formula, Midland, etc. so we used to be at the same sort of meetings as Frank. I used to tell Brian Martin back at the factory the results and they were very good at helping people out. They put it all down to *'advertising'* and when I was working there it was easy to buy things as you used to get a receipt with a stamp on it, signed over to you and bikes were always available too. What Brian used to do was stamp parts up that he sold, so frames were CDF, Competition Department Frame, and engines CDE, each followed by whatever number was next on his list. Another good thing with being at BSA was that the chroming and plating shop, it was just free to walk through, anyone who wanted to. So, if you wanted anything chromed you just saw the charge hand and for a packet of fags or whatever he'd say: *"Yeah OK then. I can do that."* But getting back, Brian was always very helpful and one time Frank had trouble with his engine and I rebuilt it for him in the Comp Shop. He was racing the following week and I was as well, so I took my bike in my brother's van, put Frank's engine in as well and if I remember rightly he put it into the bike in the paddock and then went out and won both races. So it could have been that day. As I remember I got a good start in my first race and there were three or four of us, four I think, circulating together, getting in each others way, as we were all about the same sort of speed, and on the run down to the flag, I got second. In the second race I got a good start again and later, halfway down the straight, I looked around and I couldn't see anybody so thought: *"They must have stopped the race?"* But there was no one waving any flags, and it seems everyone else had either just had a bad start or got crossed up with each other. So I just cruised round to win. Though my first win was reported in 1967, at Snetterton. I'd rode my bike up to the track, like lots of people did back then and was under strict instructions to just learn the circuit and take it easy. So, was having a steady old ride. I came up to the end of the race, to the chap with the chequered flag, and just as I crossed the line Bob Heath was about to lap me. But the chap who was doing the reporting, he was in the bar, so all he saw was the chequered flag dropping and these two bikes crossing the line almost together. I was about three feet ahead of Bob so in the results, in *Motor Cycle News*, it was: *"First place Steve Brown. Second place Bob Heath"* though it obviously wasn't!

Heath was quick in '67 but faster still by 1971, when against expectations he wheeled an A65 out again for three Nationals in a row around Easter. Perhaps as all the works triples were in action in the first round of the first ever Anglo-American Match Race series? On Good Friday he took the 670 Daytona to 5th in the British 750 Championship event. He then went one better at the Mallory Park Rothmans National, on 30th May, as while the works Tridents of Percy Tait and Tony Jefferies led the field home Heath only lost third place to Charlie Sanby on the last lap. The following day Heath used the Daytona machine once more at the late May Bank Holiday Monday, Brands Hatch International, to take 5th in the Superbike race and 8th in Evening News International, where Cooper won from Read and Sheene. All of

Best known for his work on the BSA and Triumph racing triples, Steve Brown seen here on his own 1970 registered production racer. He was a regular PR competitor when time off from 'official' race support allowed. It was similar for many of the BSA employed privateers from Hanks to Boddice, having to fit their racing around other duties

Bob Heath sweeps around Mallory Park's Devil's Elbow in trademark-style, leading Dave Croxford, John Cooper and Barry Sheene. Opposition didn't come any tougher than that

them were on two-strokes and the strength of the field can be gauged by the fact that Heath finished on the tail of World Champion Kent Andersson's Yamaha 350. It also demonstrated that while BSA might formally have favoured the triples the 'staff' didn't always agree.

Those staff still included the usual suspects in the sidecars, which saw wins come regularly early in the season. March saw Vincent win at Oulton and Thruxton, with Norman Hanks victorious at Mallory and Cadwell. At the latter Pat Sheridan won the handicap race, and as a result of some very heavy time advantages a few new names were also able to shine. Including Blake and Rudd in the minor places, with Rudd's result being virtually his first outing on a brand-new machine.

Sheridan leads Vincent through Hall Bends at Cadwell Park, where more often than not the programme now depicted Bryan Rust after he'd defeated the Germans there previously

Terry Rudd and Henry West on the 654cc BSA. While they soon moved on to bigger, more powerful engines, as with so many others they found it didn't necessarily deliver better results

Terry Rudd: I did two years as a passenger and eight years as the driver, initially on a Triumph, as everyone and his dog was on a Triumph back then. Pre-unit Bonneville engine, Norton gearbox, AMC clutch, the same as nearly everybody else. But it was then that the BSAs came in and that's the way I thought I'd go too. There was an element of following what the Birmingham boys were doing, a little bit of that, but with me I just thought the A65 was a beautiful looking engine. The look of the rocker box cover, the head and the unit construction. So Bill Cooper from Derby did one for me, put a roller bearing in, because you had to get rid of that right-hand shell bearing, as we were always told: *"If you don't, you'll have trouble".* But the engine had a lot of pluses and just looking in my results book, for 14th March 1971, I remember now that we only ended up in that handicap race as the oil tank burst on us in the race before. So, we got a good handicap and won the grand sum of £5!

The factory boys were probably after a bit more than that and collected it over Easter. Norman Hanks winning at the Good Friday round of the Anglo-American series then at Cadwell, with Vincent taking the second Anglo-American round on the Sunday when Brown won at Crystal Palace. Subsequently at Castle Combe it was Vincent again, picking up after a run of 'mechanicals', while Mick Boddice took the win at the new Gaydon circuit from Bryan Rust. Who perhaps had a less hard nosed approach to his racing.

Bryan Rust: At Gaydon I said: *"Give my prize money to the best clubman."* I had an International license and that, so I thought: *"This is a bit unfair."* As you'd get a bit of prize money, even for the heats, at club races back then, when of course nowadays they get nothing even for a National. The sidecars *could* make money but there again you could go all the way down to Brands for just two races, 200 miles each way and get

Gaydon was typical of the circuits opening up. In the early 1970s new venues appeared regularly due to the huge popularity of motorcycle sport and the demand for racing venues

Roy Shipley, Peter Rust (sponsor), Ben Pocklington (tuner), Bryan Rust and passenger Keith Carter

nothing. As the only start money I ever got was from Charlie Wilkinson at Cadwell. Even after that one I won at Snetterton over Chris Vincent I didn't get any start money. I didn't even get a free entry! But back in the old days there'd be at least 5,000 at Cadwell and old Charlie would take a dust bin bag full of cash to the bank in Louth afterwards. I guess I wasn't forceful enough to ask for more?

But we had the best days to a certain extent and it was no good going for the easy money. If you wanted to get better you had to go where the competition was and I went all over as that period it was always good racing. You only had to leave a gap and someone was taking your place, so you used as much of the corner as you needed. If you were sideways they daren't come past, as you had the narrow wheels then and you could drift it. That was the fun time, the late '60s onward, as the racing and circuits were bloody good and soon after that you needed money to get involved.

In May 25,000 came for just that sort of racing, to the Cadwell International. Agostini was the big draw but the crowd were treated to a fine display of Birmingham formation flying, even if Vincent lost his clutch late on and slipped back, to leave the final results 1. N. Hanks 2. P. Sheridan 3. M. Horspole (Triumph) 4. C. Vincent 5. R. Hanks. 6. S. Digby. Next day Norman Hanks won at Croft too, in the absence of circuit specialist Mac Hobson, to pick up valuable points for his title challenge. John Biggs second place on his 875cc Hillman Imp was a sign of the times however, as budgets increased in the search for BSA beaters.

It was Peter Brown picking up the tinware and cash at Mallory Park on 30th May, at the Rothman's sponsored National

It was then Peter Brown's turn to bounce back from some indifferent results for his first National victory of the year at Mallory Park. Mick Boddice was second and Bill Cooper third with passenger Frank Dean in the chair. Cooper's machine was interesting for its smaller wheels than was normal at the time and as a result his chassis were soon in demand. After the Mallory results it left the early season Championship standings as: Norman Hanks 48, Peter Brown 45, Chris Vincent 35 and Roy Hanks 25. Though Sheridan added more to his tally on Monday 31st May, at Brands Hatch, clearing off for an easy win. It was not to be sniffed at either, as Auerbacher could only manage 4th on his Rennsport BMW and *MCN* noted the fast Birmingham twin: *"Gave Pat Sheridan and passenger Phil Smith, on Les Mason's 750 BSA, their first International win – and they haven't yet won a National!"*[36] There was a new kid on the block and it was a nice sign-off

Bill Currie's 8-valve Weslake disappears out of shot, leading Sheridan (12) Boddice (3) and Williams (15). It was Sheridan taking the win in front of the packed crowd however, the first for a *'Mason BSA'*

Frank Dean: Early 1971, Mallory, was the bike's first race. Hence the unpainted fairing. It was the first race we did with small wheels and we carried two outfits, one on top of another, in a Commer J2 van. It was a bit of a tight fit!

for the ever improving Irishman before the TT. But that proved as disappointing for him as for the notoriously mechanically unsympathetic Chris Vincent. Vincent was only interested in winning and nine years on from his last Isle of Man victory he got pretty close again.

"The sweet roar of the BSA star's engine as he started his final lap sounded good.

Auerbacher's clutch would be severely punished by the tight corners at Ramsey Hairpin and the Gooseneck and it seemed unlikely to survive the mountain climb. All Vincent had to do was keep going. But it was not to be. The BSA seized just a few miles in to the last lap at Glen Vine."[37]

In 1971 Peter Brown (14) with 2nd fastest top speed must have had high hopes, as would Mac Hobson (39) behind. In a race of massive attrition however none of the riders pictured – including Ronnie Coxon and Pete Hardcastle – finished

Peter Brown: He used to go to the Isle of Man with the intention of beating those bloody BMWs. But he couldn't get out of his short circuit mind-set. Now on a short circuit both he and I could beat them, but you couldn't beat the bastards on the Isle of Man. Being a more practical person maybe I knew a BSA twin engine was going to be lucky if it saw the end of three laps. Consequently I didn't used to gear for a top speed of more than at about 6,000rpm. It went into overdrive then and gave it a rest. I went to the Isle of Man to finish rather than put in whatever a lap speed and break down. I knew it was next to damn impossible to beat the BMWs, so I over-geared it and it plodded around. I just went as fast as I could and if that happened to be enough to win the race so be it and if not, tough. So I didn't understand this attitude that it was so important to win, especially at the Isle of Man.

Mick Potter (left) and an *'exploded'* view of Roy Hanks' 1971 A65 engine. It shows that much was standard, down to the alternator and flywheel, though an end-feed, oil supply to the crankshaft is visible

That win or bust mentality unfortunately seemed to permeate the BSA runners in '71 with Roy Hanks' performance probably being the standout. He fought hard with the BMWs of Luthringshauser and Butscher to be third on the first lap and looked good for a podium place before his engine *'let go'* spectacularly, meaning the first BSA home was actually Mick Potter's in 8th. As some consolation Vincent took 6th in the 500s, but it was really a TT to forget. Sheridan obviously wasn't too put out, as he picked up where he had left off when back on the mainland, and in some style, at the 13th June Mallory Park MCN Superbike meeting.

There were seven A65s in the top eight that day and while Norman Hanks outdid Chris Vincent before the line for second spot, no one was able to match Sheridan. Who was hiding a secret weapon, in the form of a crankshaft and barrel that everyone outside of the factory would soon be fighting to get hold of.

Les Mason: Over time I think we had a dozen or so A70 cranks. We got one for Brian Rust but the first one that we put in an engine was for Pat Sheridan. As after Pat won the International at Brands Hatch he was leading the second race when the A10 crank he was using then broke. Which we expected, as it wasn't strong enough really.

Pat Sheridan examining the rear of his machine following a DNF. Transmission problems rather than engine failures were the bugbear of the BSA twins once engine sizes grew

But he was so good, mechanically sympathetic, that he stopped the engine so quick it hardly scraped the big-end shells. The crank had broken straight through the big-ends, but hardly touched the shells. At the time I'd got this one A70 crank and thought; *"That's the one I want to use, to go in for him."* So, we did, and put it together for the post-TT. As he had the smaller 750 engine in for the TT itself. So, when he got back to the mainland we had this one ready for him and I remember him coming out of the Elbow. Vincent talked it all down afterwards saying: *"I must have missed a gear or something"* but Pat went past him, front wheel pawing the air, smoke coming off the back wheel it was so quick, as that was the first *really* big one we did.

Sheridan at rest and at speed, exposed sidecar wheel and *'jet'* helmets on the later outfit

Chris Vincent at Castle Combe on 17th July. By this time Vincent was already getting itchy feet and was looking at options to get back on to the Grand Prix trail again

Vincent was clearly not cowed however and perhaps inspired by his performance on a 500 at the TT he ventured over the channel to take an even better 5th at the Dutch TT, having held 3rd early on, on a standard A50. He'd experienced blown head gaskets in practice on the experimental Keith Blaney's 8-valve DOHC A50 he was meant to be racing and the combination of results was probably enough to convince him to go back on the GP trail in 1972. For 1971 however the A65 results continued, with wins for Krukowski at Beveridge Park, Brown at Castle Combe and Boddice at Wroughton. The latter meeting being most notable for the appearance of Jones and Bailey's aerofoiled A65. It was then on to the Hutchinson 100 for a pair of standout rides from the Hanks brothers. Each ending up with a win apiece.

The Jones/Bailey A65 complete with front aerofoil. Various attempts were made with aerofoil but they were banned before their benefit could really be tested

Opposition took many shapes and forms. Bill Cooper's A65 in a *Mogvin-Mini* sandwich, at Cadwell's Gooseneck

Hanks: I'd tried to engineer a draw first time out. We'd trained for that meeting as we thought we were pretty good. We had a technique of drift, which was like a Vincent drift, but taken to the extreme. We could drift anytime once we'd set it going. It was round the long circuit and people got tired, but I couldn't shake Roy off, so I thought: *"I'm not going to try now"*. I suppose he was waiting for a mistake or something, but as we came out of the last corner I thought: *"This would be good for a dead heat?"* I led it the whole way and engineered a dead heat and then they gave it to Roy!

So, in the handicap race, there he was behind me again, but I thought: *"No chance, there'll be no dead heat this time"* and got there first. But blimey if they didn't give us both a ride round in the car after. It being such a good performance, that they thought he deserved a ride round again. That was bloody typical that!

Norman and Rose Hanks in a posed photo for a non-motorcycling publication. There was still titillation in women being involved in the sport

Joining the Mafia

Roy Hanks: One year at the TT we had Dad's, Norman's, mine, Chris Vincent's and Peter Brown's bikes, all in this coach garage. It was an honour just to be in the same place as them and then I managed to put the outfit on its roof round Keppel Gate of course. I came back and Chris Vincent is in front of all of them, with his arms folded, and just shakes his head and *"tut, tut, tuts"*. They were just winning everything and when I started racing they all used to lap me. All the *'names'*. The first time I wasn't lapped in a final was at Brands Hatch. As I was coming to the line I could see the marshal ready with the chequered flag, so knew the leader was there behind me. It was probably 1966 on the full circuit and as far as I was concerned this was the day I'd made it. Back in the paddock I was chuffed to bits, then the dreaded Chris Vincent comes around and says; *"I had to slow down for you there, to let you get your last lap in!"* But later Norman went as mechanic to the BSA motocross team and while he was away I went with his bike as well – as we were still into pulling heads and barrels off between races, making a 500 then a 650. I used Norman's bike for the first time and it was like

Roy tows Norman or Norman pushes Roy? There was always sibling rivalry in the Hanks clan though they more often than not worked with each other than against

Norman Hanks leads Vincent, leads Brown. The archetypal 1960s front three

an E-type Jag compared to mine. First time out I think I finished 2nd. I managed to beat Pip Harris to the line and thought *"I'm The Man!"* And then we went to Thruxton and for some reason Thruxton and me just clicked. I really loved this long back straight, hanging it all out. There was Norman, Peter Brown, Pat Sheridan and Chris Vincent and it was like a freight train. I only finished third but I broke the lap record. Of course, Chris Vincent came along afterwards and said: *"You won't hold on to that for long son!"* but then I won one and it was like: *"Wow"*, as up until 1970-odd I hadn't won a race really. I hadn't a trophy to my name, as I was up against these top guys. But the bikes got better and better and I'd got an engine comparable to the others and ended up winning a good one. The Hutchinson 100 at Brands, on the full circuit, backwards. The continentals were all there, but Norman led from almost the beginning and I kept just close enough that he kept looking behind. And on the last lap - I think it was 12 laps or something mad on the long circuit – he went into what was Clearways and looked behind, and waited, so we came along the bottom straight side by side. We tried to cross the line together, but they gave me the win. 'Got me laurels, did the lap of honour. It was great. But it was in the handicap race when I realised quite how competitive Norman was. As I came to peel in to Bottom (now Graham Hill) Bend he banged into me and sent me off on to the grass. How I didn't go into the bank I don't know but as we came up to the hairpin I came up behind him again and tried to get inside. Thinking: *"Does he think I'm a German or something?"*

Into Paddock and there was no messing this time, the gloves were off and when he got back into the paddock he said: *"Don't you ever try to beat me again!"*

Roy Hanks demonstrates the art of lofting the sidecar wheel on a left-hander.

Though unfortunately in this case he's just about to flip it at Brands Hatch to the detriment of passenger Gerald Daniel

Peter Brown, Norman Hanks and Mick Boddice. Castle Combe, 17th July, 1971. The taller profile of Brown's, more traditional, *'croucher'*, outfit is clear, but it never hampered his progress. Less aggressive than some on track, he was tactically good and benefited from his own superbly constructed engines. No one ever questioned that Brown's were the pick of the bunch. Hanks was one of the known hard men of the track winning the British title the following year, while Boddice's skills were demonstrated through no less than 9 TT victories, among 20 top three placings on the Island

Passenger Neil Shilton underneath while Ken Vogl in leathers works on his machine behind. Every penny (right) had to be accounted for

Following the Hutch there were two wins for relative newcomer Ken Vogl at Cadwell on 14th August and a second for Sheridan behind the four cylinder URS of newly crowned World Champion Horst Owesle, at an exciting Silverstone meeting on the 22nd. 27,000 fans saw Chris Vincent ride round the outside of Owesle on the grass, on the first lap around Woodcote, but then lose out when he had to pit for fuel after developing a leak. There was actually as much excitement off the track that day as on, as a flurry of protests were then put in concerning engines being variously below or above the 500-750cc capacity stipulations. Owesle's URS presumably being under and Sheridan's perhaps over? None of them were upheld however, even if it was known there were plenty of 'big' A65s around by late 1971. This was all overshadowed by proceedings the following weekend however, as while Vincent won ahead of Peter Brown at the Snetterton Race of Aces International, the next day, Bank Holiday Monday, August 30th, went down as one of the blackest in British motorsport history.

Bill Crook and later partner Kenny Arthur on their A65 at Oulton Park on a subsequent visit

Interestingly Kenny Arthur would go on to ride with two more ex-A65 sidecar pilots. With Jock Taylor to take the overall sidecar TT victory in 1978 and with O'Dell to win the TT and 1977 World Championship

In 1971 Crook was involved in far less joyful proceedings following the Oulton meeting

Bill Crook: The bikes were going about 90mph along the straight approaching the bend. At the 100yards marker I braked for it, but Sheridan didn't appear to do so, as the gap between us widened. As he entered the bend the back of his combination turned right round and it ran backwards off the track and then bounced back on to it. I took the inside line and ran up a bank to get out of the way. It was the only course open to me.

That was Crook's report at the inquest following a five machine accident at Oulton Park. It resulted in Sheridan, his passenger Phil Smith and Gary Bryan's passenger, Peter Pritchard being killed. Bryan himself received life changing injuries, while those of Derek Booth, Bill Crook's passenger, were also serious. Incredibly the race was re-run, with Vincent setting a new lap record in the process of winning by over 17 seconds.

Chris Vincent: Being a racer I should have been up the front somewhere really, when it happened, but I wasn't. I'd been reinstalling the fibreglass fairing before the race and I'd got the actuating arm on the clutch in the wrong position as a result, so the clutch was slipping. I was actually ready to pull out when they crashed so I was able to go out and won the re-run. So my bad luck, was my good luck that day.

Vincent was hard but practical and there was little room for sentimentality among other riders too. Sheridan's outfit had been a good one and the engine very fast.

Pat Sheridan as the paddock remembered him. A talent which shone brightly if briefly at the highest level

Les Mason: George O'Dell bought the complete lot I gathered, though as I was in a bit of shock afterwards I lost track. But from what I know now George O'Dell bought it all off Pat's wife and sold the engine which was in that original outfit and I think it might have been Ken Vogl might have had it. As the engine O'Dell then raced was one he got off somebody which had a magneto conversion on, which we never used, as we used Lumenition ignition. It wasn't actually a big engine Pat had in when he was killed either. The International at Oulton Park was a 750 limit. So he had a 734, as he couldn't use the big engine, though I'm sure there were a few who were!

Ken Vogl: When we tried it, could we get this damned thing started? It just kept locking up. But eventually we got it going and wow it was the fastest thing. Before I blew it up! We go out for the first practice on the Club circuit, did a steady lap round to see what it was like then, next lap, I started going. Park, I used to go down the gearbox a lot there and would then be waiting for the bike to build power to get 'round Chris Curve. Well, with this engine I accelerated out of Park and I suddenly had to brake! What a beauty. Oh, it accelerated. Quick round the Gooseneck down the hill like a rocket and I was still only on half revs. But turned right to come back, round Charlies there, and it just went *Whoof!* Well, the barrel had sheared off. It was still bolted down, but the sheared part had come up and the two exhausts pipes, which were under my frame, it bent them flat. But afterwards someone said: *"Didn't you know that was cracked? It was when George O'Dell had it."* So that's how that engine finished. A shame as I was never able to build another one like that and it really was fabulous. The quickest thing I'd ever been on.

Vogl and Shilton heading out onto the circuit at Mallory Park. Although on a tight budget Vogl's was always one of the better turned out machines and regularly up at the front by 1971

Chris Vincent was happy to talk to the press but was an enigma in many ways

That was of course later, and in the meantime, and in ignorance of the events on the other side of the Pennines, Norman Hanks took the sidecar victory at Cadwell, while new boy Nev Riley was first at Croft. With the pall of that dark Oulton weekend still in the air Sunday 4th September then saw the main protagonists turning up for the penultimate round of the British Sidecar Championships at Castle Combe. Vincent pulled away to take the victory – Castle Combe was a favored circuit - but the all-important battle for points was actually going on behind.

Norman Hanks: That year, Michael Boddice knows, if there was a moment I lost the championship that was it. It was Castle Combe. Vincent was in front of us, not far ahead but there was no way I could beat Vincent round Castle Combe, but I could beat Brown. He had a fast 650 so I just followed him, followed him, followed him. Those photos are the last corner on the last lap, and as I came down, as I was just turning to go inside of him, Michael came straight up the inside of me, because he'd obviously been doing the same thing, thinking: *"I'll have him on the last lap."* He stopped me going up the inside of Browny and I ended up fourth, instead of what I think I should have been, which is second. It was racing. I was trying to do the same to Browny, as Michael did to me. So, I got a right huff on at that meeting and I wouldn't speak to any of them and it was some time before I'd even speak to Michael. I said: *"You knew I had to beat him?"* But it's racing, I shouldn't have left the gap. When we found that picture I put it on my iPad. 'cos we go away on holiday with Michael now and I'm always at it with *"You cost me the championship!"*

Mick Boddice: Yea I beat him that day at Castle Combe. A fast circuit. We used to work together, and were brought up together, and afterward he never spoke to me for a month. But we were working in the same place with motocrosser Jeff Smith and Jeff says; *"What's wrong with you Norman? You race to win races, not championships. Man-up."* He was on full lock and there was no air pressure, with no fairing on. So, he never went to Snetterton, Castle Combe, or Thruxton again without his fairing on after that!

Vincent won again at Mallory Park on 19th September, after a big crash at Scarborough, and the following weekend it was Vincent again at Cadwell, while Mac Hobson won at Croft . The Cadwell meeting was actually interesting for the result in the handicap race, since Dick Hawes got his Hillman Imp powered outfit into 3rd and Rudi Kurth his 3-cylinder two-stroke Crescent into 6th. Machines like this were yet another sign, if one was needed, of the changing times, but it was still three A65s in the thick of it. With Terry Rudd 1st ahead of Brian Mee, for whom consigning Roy Hanks to 5th was an even greater achievement.

A season in three photos. Sunday 4th September 1971, last corner, last lap, Castle Combe. Norman Hanks (45) tries to go up the inside of a wide drifting Peter Brown (57) but Mick Boddice (3) slides inside them both

(Top) Mee at speed with Colin Newbold in Brian Mee's helmet and Brian Mee in what looks like Ken Vogl's? There was plenty of sharing and mend and make do in the early 70s paddock. (Bottom) Brian Mee with assorted tinware

Brian Mee: I remember that race as we'd changed the front wheel and going around in practice it had rubbed through my front brake pipe. As it was all hydraulics by then. So, going into the last corner before the start-finish, Barn, we went shooting by Roy Hanks, much to his surprise. Afterwards he said; *"Bloody hell, you're going fast today aren't you?"* So I had to tell him I'd actually got no brakes! But I had Devimead do me an engine by then, a 750, a Les Mason special, and it was good. Rusty borrowed that bike at Cadwell one time for the handicap race and at Silverstone someone else borrowed my Beezer too. We did those sorts of things as we were all mates and the sidecar blokes all stuck together in those day, they really did, the camaraderie was great. But you still wanted to beat everyone, and Roy Hanks was one of my heroes. Never said a lot, a bit like Chris. 'ust got on with his racing, but I really wanted to beat those guys and that day, Roy, I did.

The shape of thing to come. Jim Todd's Saab-engined machine ridden by Terry Rudd in subsequent seasons. Cadwell (left) and Snetterton (right). New engines were appearing at the same time as chassis development was moving on, threatening the A65 stranglehold on the British sidecar racing scene

Terry Rudd: Oddly, though I won it, I don't really remember that one too well, but I did the meeting prior. The Snetterton Bank Holiday International. We pulled up late for the practice proper, so we went out virtually on our own. And then the rev-counter broke. So, I just had to ride it as best I could. But when we came in we were shown *"P1"* and I couldn't believe it. And in the race - I have it written here in my notes – it says: *"Leading the race on the first lap, passed by Chris Vincent then Pete Brown. Should have finished third or fourth, but due to having a carburetor fall off, didn't."* The thing was really flying that day, and the Birmingham boys were all on full 750s of course, so we were soon on to Jim Todd's 841cc Saab ourselves. With mixed results really. Dale Ward had that gleaming aluminum looking Saab by then, which was the bee's knees, but ours was never perfected to its potential. We had problem after problem, but those sorts of machine were the way things were going. I think Mac Hobson was one of the first to get rid of his BSA and put the four-cylinder Yam in and the difference in speed was just chalk and cheese. It was phenomenal really. I remember at Cadwell seeing that Yamaha going down the straight and thinking: *"We're going to do nothing against that."* By then I guess you could still have a go with a BSA if a Yam was spinning up like, in the wet. But me and my passenger, who funded it between us, we just decided that if this was the way things were going to go we just wouldn't have the funds to do it.

Rudd did actually persevere until 1975 and while the A65 was sorely tested by then, in 1971 it still had its nose ahead. As demonstrated by two A65 wins over the first weekend in October. Vincent won initially at Brands Hatch, from Roy and Norman Hanks, but was beaten in turn at Lydden the next day. On a very fast outfit Norman Hanks was able to get inside him at the Devil's Elbow, on the last lap, using an engine he hoped would bring him the British title the following weekend at Snetterton.

It was a three-way fight between Norman Hanks, Peter Brown and Chris Vincent and you couldn't put a fag paper between them. The championship hadn't been this close for years and *Motor Cycling* announced with historical inaccuracy that with things so close Vincent *"cannot afford a tactical race."* It couldn't have been more tactical if he tried!

Norman Hanks: In '71 they taught me a lesson. My dad had a big-bore 750. I had a long-stroke 750. So, I had my dad's top half on my bottom half at the Lydden meeting previously. And I beat Vincent and Brown. But it showed them what I'd got, so I think they devised a plan for the last meeting at Snetterton. I had a bad start and got mixed up with loads of people, including Bryan Rust, but thought: *"Calm down now. Don't panic. You've got this big 840 thing under you."* As I knew that I'd got the legs on them. But I think Vincent deliberately let Brown lead? So, Vincent was in front of me going: *"Have a look at that gap there. Oh no. Too late. Bad luck."* Blocking me. So, it got to the chicane on the last lap. It's not like it is now, but a proper chicane. With built up banks and Vincent held it in tight all the way round Coram's. So, I had to come around the outside. He suckered me into that. Knowing that he could then just drift across the road and leave me looking at a grass bank. It meant me losing enough momentum to end up third. Brown, Vincent, then me. And what that did was make me third in the championship too. Which is why Vincent let Brown win, as Vincent was still first and Brown was then second in the championship. They'd worked out exactly what they needed to do. But it was bad racing by me, as I should have known better.

Perhaps it was bad racing, but it was also tactically brilliant by Vincent. Since even had Hanks got by Vincent with his big engine - which was a distinct possibility, given his Lydden performance a week previously - with Brown too far out in front for Hanks to catch, it wouldn't have been enough to have affected the overall results. As Bryan Rust pointed out, having been barged off track by Hanks earlier *"Vincent was a wily bugger!"*

When men were men and chicanes were made of railway sleepers. For those unfamiliar with 1960s chicanes John Crick's A65 leads the similar machines of the Hanks brothers through at Croft. There was zero margin for error

Vincent was National Champion again, but there was change in the air. And nowhere better exemplified than in the results of the two final meetings of the season. Ken Vogl was second to the rapid KGB Imp of Peter Williams at Cadwell on Sunday 10th October, while Brian Mee was second too, at Darley Moor this time, behind the Imp of the Hardy Brothers. It wouldn't be so easy in 1972.

Roy Hanks battles with the Hardy Imp (above) at Cadwell Park and the John Biggs version at Croft (below)

Clive Wall at Lydden. He was a bit of a circuit specialist at the tight Kent circuit. He racked up wins up and down the country in 1971 however, with Brands Hatch, Snetterton and Cadwell Park featuring heavily

The more it changes...............

New machinery had been appearing among the production racers also, Tridents and Commandos specifically, but Japanese machinery too. The top PR A65s kept scoring however with Clive Wall and Frank Hodgson in particular trading victories over the summer. In June Wall won at Lydden and Cadwell, while for Hodgson it was Cadwell and

Darley Moor. In July wins at Snetteton and Cadwell for Wall were matched by victories at Snetterton and Aintree by Hodgson. Then 24th July threw up a couple of new winners, even if one of them was only temporary.

The all-action style of Frank Hodgson at his home from home, Cadwell Park. He was good elsewhere but almost unbeatable at the Lincolnshire circuit

Hugh Evans at Brands Hatch 1971. By now with TLS brake, Firebird pipes, and a few more CCs

Among the solo runners Hugh Evans had been overshadowed by Wall and Hodgson in recent meetings but he won at Brands Hatch that day. Evans had been on a 750 since the beginning of the season and his machine was borderline production eligible. Since while his engine conformed, loosely, to A70 specification, his chassis was older, so probably did not. The same day however Reg Hardy fell foul of the same rule book at Darley Moor, as having won a tight-fought Production race against larger capacity machines he was then stripped of the award due to *"the fitment of non-standard parts."*

Reg Hardy: Mine was a short career unfortunately as I was an apprentice tool maker and I'd got no money. No money and no van initially, so I used to borrow a painter and decorator's, to take me about. We called ourselves Skint Racing and talk about shoe- string. I bought an old Morris Van, split screen, and the old front seat used to fold down. So we took the front wheel out of the bike, dropped the back wheel into the foot well and as the petrol tank was gone - it was rusted through and we couldn't afford to buy a new one – we put a five gallon drum in the back with a tube running down from it to the engine. When we arrived at tracks we would smell the cooking bacon and think: '*you bastards*' as we couldn't afford anything. We were struggling to afford a sandwich. But that's how it was back then.

My original bike I bought for 200 guineas, an A65 Lightning Clubman. There were only 200 made allegedly, but you got the close-ratio box with them and in the club I used to go to, The Kavern Club in Walsall, well there were three of them. But when I said I was going to go production racing everyone said: *"You'll do no good with that, you've got to have a Triumph Bonneville"* but I thought well, Vincent's won seven British championships on one, pulling two people around, so if it'll pull two people around, it'll certainly pull me. And that race at Darley Moor was my very first win, until I was disqualified! What happened there was that in the qualifying my exhaust broke, the silencer, so I put the meggas on instead. There was a bloke there who was on a Rocket Three, Bill Lloyd, and I rode my pants off to beat him.

But it was racing for money, not trophies or plaques that day and a chap who was fourth, on a Norton Commando, it was him who put an objection in. So, they pushed my bike up to be checked, put a stick up the exhaust pipe to see if it had any baffles and said; *"Sorry lad!"* But the only reason the guy objected was that as he was on a Norton Commando and a Commando was such a bloody expensive thing!

Early days for Reg Hardy at Darley Morr

Racing an A65 to win

Clive Wall: The first A65 I had was half mine and half RH Smith's. Then I saw advertised what was reputedly Ron Chandler's Hutchinson 100 Spitfire, from when John Cooper won the race. It seems he said: *"I will never ride that bike again, it handled so bad, it was evil."* Well I didn't know any different, as I'd never raced anything else; *"Hey, it's got to be OK, as John Cooper won on one in the Hutch?"* So I bought it off an ex-BSA employee, though it wasn't actually anything special for a factory prepared bike. It had a bog-standard head and rockers on it, but it had all the right bits and a brazed frame, when the normal ones were welded. It wasn't lightweight like Tony's, but it had the under-sump pipes, the right seat and the big long aluminum tank, though I never knew how they got away with using those in Production Races, as there were only ever about five of them ever made? But the reason my bikes were quick is as I came from an engineering background and had done an engineering apprenticeship. My dad was an engineer and had me adjusting tappets on his car and that when I was eight years old. So, it sort of gets into you a bit. When I first got the A65 I had it for two years - this is the original one - and we did the motor, properly, in the middle close season. I knew Allen Dudley-Ward quite well so gave him the head, and the tappet adjuster, where it goes through the rocker arm, you can drill a third of the middle out down to the hardening and you can halve the size of the locking nut. Well if you put that on four rockers that saves quite a bit. Simple stuff like that. Polish the cranks polish the rods get a proper bloke to set up the balance for the whole thing - which Dudley-Ward was very good at - and as a result mine didn't vibrate much. And we used to shim the gearbox then they never dropped out of gear and we looked at other ways to lose weight too.

I didn't get any trick cams or anything out of BSA though, so after that it was just riding hard. Lydden I was ever so lucky. It's a weird place, but I learnt a lot there, as you could ride in the Open races really close to very, very, quick people. It was such a short circuit there was nowhere they could get away from you. There were no 120mph corners, where good people would be 5mph faster, so if you could get away with them, even at the Lord of Lydden meeting say, you could still finish 7th or 8th on a production bike and it was a real eye-opener to see the differences in what people did. I remember following Steve Jolly there and when you went into the hairpin at the top, he would get half way round, pick the bike up, squirt it at the bank, then drop it down again and pull four-foot away. I started doing the same and all of a sudden, you'd find another ¼ of a second a lap, though Crystal Palace was actually the first place I ever won any money. I just turned my eyes off to how dangerous it was there you know, as while it was a beautiful circuit, lovely circuit, it had a three-foot run-off, then six-foot railways sleepers. I saw people fall off there, two or three times, who didn't get up. I tell you that sure focuses the mind!

The Wall Spitfires. The original 190mm braked MkII to the front, subsequent ex-Ron Chandler MkIII to the rear

Like Millward and Reg Hardy, Mick Fletcher's A65 also fell foul of the Production rules in 1971. Fletcher's by dint of him altering the frame tubes under the seat to allow for unobstructed air flow to the carbs. The 4LS front brake might also have condemned his machine to the unlimited class, which a later disc certainly did.

Fletcher's bike was representative of the machines being raced by 1971 however, since the production classes were becoming increasingly competitive so ironically the Open ones could provide richer pickings

That 25th July Darley meeting was also notable for Mick Fletcher's A65 appearing in the results, though Derek Whalley's performance a couple of weeks after, at Snetterton, was probably the standout performance of the up and coming racers. On Saturday 7th August, riders were greeted by torrential rain at the Norfolk circuit, but undeterred Hodgson took two easy production wins over Norton hot shot Mick Hemmings and fast man Mac McMillan. It was Derek Whalley who caught the attention however by taking his unconventional A65 to a similarly decisive victory over more fancied runners in the 1000 cc event.

Derek Whalley: I bought an A65 in 1966, brand new, from Claude Rye and used it as my go to work and for down the Busy Bee, the Cellar and that. But later it was stolen on Northumberland Avenue just off Trafalgar Square, taken away, crikey! Two months later the police recovered it from a front garden in Kent. The engine was lying there but the rolling chassis had gone, so a mate from the Bee, Paul Castle, who was racing a Tricati at the time, said; *"Why not come racing? Have a word with Bob Innes."* He worked in the mews up Harlesden and helped a lot of lads out with work on their bikes and persuaded me to put the engine in this Montesa Impala frame. He grafted it in and created a tank for it as the original wouldn't sit on with the A65 engine. Anyway, it looked atrocious but

that's how I started racing seriously and I perfected what I called a three step start. As it was one, two, three and bump and *'whoof'* it would go. It was great for a quick start. We refined it in to a good short circuit racer in the end and that one at Snetterton I remember I got a good start, got away well. The only problem was we had these meggas on it and crikey it was real stop and go on the power. It went very well, pulled really well with straight-through pipes, but with those meggas I

Derek Whalley at the 1971 Lord of Lydden meeting where he pitted his Montesa A65 in the same open races as Clive Wall tried his production bike

had on that day, I don't know why, but it was really hairy. No low down grunt on it at all. But I'd treated myself to my first set of triangular tyres, so they were fresh and stuck like glue and to be honest the only thing that really let the bike down by then was the front brake. At Snetterton that day, as it was wet, it was OK, but I put an entry into the Manx Grand Prix around then and got refused, which was probably just as well. As God alone knows what it would have been like with that brake going down Bray Hill.

26th June at the Brands Hatch BMCRC event. A pensive Derek Whalley awaits the start. 2nd place in the 1,000cc event was his reward this time

Derek Whalley, no.53, second from the right, Brands Hatch, 3rd July 1971. He got two third places for his efforts

Ironically for the officials who refused Whalley he'd later go on to win on the Isle of Man, but in the meantime the ding-dong trading of wins between Hodgson and Wall continued, though largely at different circuits. Wall had victories at Snetterton and Cadwell, the latter a triple win, while Hodgson won at Snetterton, Croft and Cadwell, before Dave Mason popped up with a win at Cadwell of his own. The August Bank Holiday weekend then saw a win for Evans at Cadwell, two for Wall at the same circuit and one for Hodgson at Croft. Hodgson then won at Cadwell, Aintree and Cadwell again, before a big showdown for Dave Mason on October 10th to decide the Midland 1000cc Championship.

On 10th October Malcolm Lucas (left) took a pair of 4th places at Cadwell Park on his Featherbed A65. But with his two victories Dave Mason (right) took the MCRC 1000 championship over Phil Haslam. It has to be said both knew the A65 backwards, being employed by BSA as production testers at the time

Dave Mason: I had to beat Phil and Terry Haslam to win that championship and Phil was a legend at the time. It was the final round of the championship and it all rested on that one day. It was all on that one race at Cadwell. I remember going after them and caught Phil up and went by him, but made a mistake at the hairpin and he came by me again. There were still a few laps left to go and I thought: *"bloody hell I've got to get past him. I need these points"* you know, and I caught him up into Park, followed him down towards the Gooseneck and he braked just a little bit too early for Mansfield. And I just went by, going: *"don't let it run wide, don't let it run wide"* and got out and I had another lap to go. I thought: *"keep it neat. Keep it tidy"* and can always remember 'cos I could hear all the lads shouting at me, at the hairpin, from when I cocked it up a couple of laps earlier. I'd sort of come into the hairpin too hot, I had the back-end scampering around and snaking, so I couldn't get in as tight as I wanted to and Phil got in underneath. As he saw me in trouble on the brakes, as I'd over run the left-hander, the kink. Oh, it was good fun that one and I'll always remember Mal Carter, who sponsored the Haslams, a rough diamond car dealer from Halifax, coming round after, wanting to buy my BSA Metisse off me. He said: *"What the hell have you got in that?"* But I just said: *"No mate, it ain't for sale!"*

Dave Mason at speed on the first ever short-stroke 750 A65 engine, in the second only Rickman A65 race frame built. Graduate apprentice Dave Pillborough made the barrel casting patterns, with the first barrels going to Les Mason and the second to Norman Hanks. It wasn't long before Les Mason had his own versions in production

Clive Wall, trophies and the big no.1 plate. Winning multiple championships was no mean feat given the quality of the opposition by 1971, both in terms of riders and machines on circuit

In all the excitement it could almost be forgotten that a Mal Carter associate, Frank Hodgson, won the production race ahead of the 750 Nortons of Pete Lovell and Mick Hemmings that day too. Though that was it for the domestic Production racing programme since Clive Wall didn't bother attending the final BRC championship race at all. Even with stern opposition he'd won their Championship already.

Clive Wall: Peter Butler, Ray Knight and a bloke called John Hedger, a mate of mine, they were the men to beat. And while Tony Smith and Dave Potter had moved on by then, Phil Haslam was still racing, so I got involved with him a few times too. I particularly remember he had a massive crash in front of me as he came out of the Gooseneck, at Cadwell, down the left-hander, at the bottom of the hill. But he was quick, definitely. Just a very quick rider and when I won the championships, '70-71, Mick Hemmings was in there too, as well as Ron Wittich. He was another quick one, but then he did bin it a lot. I mean all the regular guys were there when I took the titles, but once you'd been racing a few years you just sort of shuffled your way up to the front. You just ended up winning and I took the BRC Production Championship, '70 and '71, along with the British Formula Production class. That was in 1971, when I won their 1,000cc championship as well. So, three in one year in 1971. I honestly can't remember who I beat to first place in each case, but I knew it was bloody hard work, as of course with the amount of Triumphs which were out there they had so much feed-back. Good old Len

Read used to ride an A65 - he wasn't particularly quick but he was a real A65 man – so he used to rock up everywhere, but otherwise it was still 80-90% Bonnevilles which were racing. I think the BSA might have had a little bit of extra grunt coming out of the corners but the Bonneville was easier to ride and the 750 Norvil Commando, when it came out, it was even better than the Bonneville. As by then true 650s had gone in the UK for production racing. You had to have a full-blown 750, as there were Laverdas and Hondas as well as other

Len Read loading a recalcitrant A65 into his van at Snetterton. Close inspection reveals a lack of cylinder-head and barrel alluding to a catastrophic end to proceedings. Note also, the number-plate and rear light as required on production machines

Japanese stuff coming through by then as well and my A65 was still a dead standard 654cc. That 15% less capacity or whatever it was, was a lot, so I felt I had to move on. I raced against Clive Smithers a lot in 1971 and it was his bike, a Commando, which made me say to Dick Smith, my sponsor: *"Dick, we gotta have a Norton. It's like 10 mph quicker and it handles!"*

But those A65s must have handled too, as they won numerous production and open/1000c races over 1971, resulting in no less than eight championships. There were admittedly a lot of clubs running championships by 1971, but eight was more than half of those for which A65s were eligible. Clive Wall took the BRC Production class and both Production and 1,000cc classes in the BFC. Frank Hodgson took the MMCR Production title while Dave Mason took their 1,000cc class. Hodgson also took the Racing 50, Waterloo & District and Nottingham & District Production titles. With the passage of time and closure of some clubs, the details are now sketchy, but Hodgson more than likely won the Pegasus and Skegness championships too, meaning a grand total of ten club championships. The only major titles A65s hadn't taken were the Racing 67 and Bemsee crowns. And that was just the solos of course. Chris Vincent won the British sidecar title - with five A65 in the top six. Vincent; Brown; Norman Hanks; Roy Hanks; Mick Boddice – Pete Krukowski had won the Scottish version, and there were club sidecar championship wins too numerous to mention. But in truth and with all due respect to the riders concerned, these were all small beer in comparison to what was being delivered on the other side of the Atlantic.

The BSA works team line up at the Houston Astrodome, 29th January 1971. About as far from a wet Mallory Park mid-week practice day as was possible to imagine

1971 and the Grand National Championship

In 1971 the BSA Group made a huge investment in the American race programme, which consisted of seven road races and fifteen off-road events. But what remained surprising about their approach was reflected in Jim Rice's comments on 1970 – *while I did my own preparation and development on the twins, with the triple it was a case of: "Here it is, check it out."* As while the money BSA were spending was huge, bar the development of the A70 - which was too little and too late to affect results - absolutely nothing went directly into A65 development by BSA themselves.

Dave Aldana: It really wasn't a works team in the sense that we got works engines or whatever. When I think of works teams and factory sponsorship, if it was Honda or Kawasaki, you'd get specially built engines from the company, that had been dyno-tuned and modified for the best results. But that wasn't the case with BSA. We were works riders in the sense that we got money from the company. A salary. But with that salary we were supposed to develop our own motorcycles, well I think we were. That's why Jim Rice did his own thing and Dick

Aldana in full works livery for 1971. Seen by some as a bit of a loose cannon, his reputation belied a wealth of raw natural talent

Rice, Aldana and Mann at Ascot 1971. With their numbers indicating where they finished in the 1970 title hunt

Mann had a connection with Megacycle cams, Jim Dour, who helped him develop his. At my end I did what I guess any other BSA guy did, which is what I did previously. I had a guy called Dallas Baker who helped me with suspension and exhaust systems, as he'd done some development of his own, but just through a motorcycle shop, as there really wasn't a factory engine that I got which came in a box or anything, with special parts and special things done to it.

They gave me $25,000 in 1970, which was a lot of money, but I didn't spend it on my motorcycle, I spent it on real estate, some property and got involved in that, which I'm glad I did. So my bikes were pretty much stock. I mean they had high compression pistons, but just whatever BSA sold at the time. I think they were like 10:1 pistons you could buy through any parts catalogue and I ended up with just a stock cam and a flowed cylinder-head, by a guy by the name of Ted Hubbard who did a lot of BSA development work. I did have a couple of cranks with Carrillo rods on them, but I bent and broke them too, like the normal ones, so they were not bullet proof. And at the very, very end, because I had trouble with the primary chains breaking, I finally had a better chain, as Jim Rice had developed what they call a Hy-Vo chain, like a Toyota cam chain. But that was it. In comparison the Triumphs had special cams and valves, and ran with big GP carburetors, while on the A65s we just used Amal Concentrics. 32mm, which we bored out to 33mm after we found out they were doing that with the triples. When we got to Daytona we saw the carbs on the factory triples and we thought: *'Hey we can do that, take it out a millimetre.'*

Aldana chases Terry Dorsch over the big jump at Ascot

Preparing an A65 for Flat Track and TT

Don Emde: Over the winter of 1969-70 my dad was building two A65s for my upcoming Amateur year in dirt track racing. Keep in mind that at this point I was not a factory rider, just a privateer riding a BSA. By then a stock A65 frame was out of date so my dad, Floyd, ordered two Trackmaster frames and got the popular running gear for it, including Ceriani front forks and the wheels made by Howard Barnes. They were the adaptable type with the same quick change knock-off nut that would hold either a rear sprocket, or for TT, a disc brake rotor, so the same wheel could be used front or back, and at a flat track race, you could run the wheels on one side for practice and heat races, then turn them around for a fresh side for the Main event.

Floyd and Don Emde. The only father and son to have won the Daytona 200. Here with Don's 1970 flat tracker

The engines we started with were both salvaged from wrecked bikes that came into our shop and they were totaled out by the insurance companies due to the excessive damage. But the engines were fine, so in addition to some assistance we got from BSA, my dad knew Tom Sifton from way back in the 1940s and early 1950s from when Tom was tuning Harleys. By 1970, Tom's performance business was more about BSA and Triumphs than Harleys and he had a line of cams and all the cylinder head parts such as valves and springs for the A65. So Floyd talked to Tom on the phone at length a few times and not only did Tom give Floyd his setup, they worked out an arrangement where Floyd would have fresh cylinder heads at our shop, but also he sent Tom some extras and Tom would get them ready to ship down when needed.

While Dave Aldana's bikes tended to have primary covers by Carl's Speed Centre Jim Rice and Dick Mann favoured the version made by ACK in San Jose. Floyd Emde made one out of his wife's frying pan for son Don, which was the approach taken by many adopting the A65 for flat track, as initially there were few off the shelf parts available.

They had the inlet and exhaust ports all smoothed out and had his Sifton valves, springs and keepers all installed. Tom also sent a sketch for the exhaust pipe dimensions. Jim Rice and his race tuner Mike Akatiff by the way, had worked at Sifton's shop for a time, 'not sure when they left, but I think that's where those two got working on Jim's fast A65 that he won Nationals on in 1969. Jim's A65s were like no other. They were high revving and had straight exhaust pipes. I remember one of the cams that Sifton offered was for that high-rev combination, but the other way to go with the A65 was the torquey style motor, that was strong through and coming off the turns. Those used megaphone exhaust.

There were two related problems with the stock A65 for dirt track racing. One was that the clutch case of the left side was so wide it would catch in the dirt. This was known before I was an Amateur, so someone - maybe Sifton or maybe Cates or Tryon at BSA? - told Floyd that a narrower cover needed to be made to avoid that problem. We were about a year ahead of some nice cast covers that came out, so to get going for 1970, Floyd made a cover from a flat aluminum plate, and to fit over the clutch itself he robbed a frying pan from my mom's kitchen cupboard and welded the base of the pan to the plate. I recall my mother being not too happy with my dad about that, but I think he bought her a new one and maybe took her out to dinner, to smooth things over.

The other problem, before we ever fired up our A65s, was that we were told that the three-row A65 primary chain was no good for racing, and that not only would it break when revved fast, but that it would take the main engine cases with it when it did. The solution was to convert to the twin row chain used by the Triumph Bonneville. So Floyd machined off the third row of teeth on the clutch and engine sprockets and also I recall he drilled some holes in the main crankcase that allowed some lubrication to flow back and forth. Being also Suzuki dealers Floyd had obtained some of the high tech Mikuni magnesium body carburetors and we ran those, as most BSAs were still with Amal carbs then.

Emde ran a Triumph duplex primary chain but many like Rice and Aldana went to the Hy-Vo inverted tooth type

One big decision was whether to power the ignition from a magneto or battery. We had no access to a dyno, but were told a magneto would drag some horsepower from the engines, so the battery would help produce more horsepower, but the batteries was a continual problem, even leaving me with a dead engine on the line at one big race at Sacramento in 1970. Plus we had to keep recharging batteries from a portable battery charger. Looking back I'd probably had gone with the magneto if I knew how much trouble the batteries would be.

But Gene Romero I know what he did when he got the money from Triumph, he spent his money at a place called CR Axtells. He did development, dyno work, he spent his money making his bikes the best that money could buy and he was rewarded with the championship in 1970. 'Cos when he got to those long miles he did well, when he couldn't normally hit his arse with both hands you know, because now he had a full 750 and *horse power*. And when I got on the Norton later, Ron Wood built that Norton just like a Triumph. As by then CR Axtell had fully developed the Triumphs and knew what combinations of which bits worked. So even though my bike said Norton on the side of the gas tank, inside it was all Triumph. So to get back to our BSAs, the bottom line is we didn't do much. It was like a lot of things, leave it alone if it works and those BSA A65s were probably unique in that regard. 'Cos Gene Romero's Triumphs were very, very, modified, like my Norton that I rode after, all *very* special.

Don Emde: When I joined the BSA factory for 1971, my rookie season in AMA National racing, my deal was like Jim, David and Dick's, where we were told that for road races all we needed to do was show up. They would bring the bikes and the mechanics. But for the TT and Flat Track races, we would be using our own machines and mechanics. So for 1971 the only thing different than what me and my dad were already doing was I would get any parts free that were in the BSA parts or accessory catalogues and I got a pay check on a per race basis. Which I kicked in for dad, to help pay for our gas and other travel costs. The day I signed my contract at some swanky hotel in Beverly Hills, they were up front with me that I was getting what Aldana and Triumph rider Don Castro had gotten last year, but that my salary would go up next year if I did well enough to stay on the team.

But as we got going in 1971, I soon found out that my BSA A65, a bike that was pretty competitive in the Amateur class in 1970 was a little short on power against a full field of Expert riders. This was a really competitive time in American racing where 50-60 Expert riders might show up at a flat track National or even 80-100 at a TT, like the Houston Astrodome. Only 48 even made it out of qualifying and it was all cut down to 18 for the Main event. The riders made most of the difference in the results, I never felt that any brand was superior to the other, though some machines stood out a little. As David

Emde at Houston. Always seen as a better road racer than dirt rider he appeared on the scene at the right time, since Americans were picking up more on European-type racing

pointed out Gene Romero's Triumphs were always fast, as was Jim Rice's BSA, but they were both smart guys and great riders and worked to come up with some great overall packages. The Harleys weren't necessarily any faster than us, there was just a lot more of them and Harley's race manager Dick O'Brien did a better job than his counterparts at Triumph or BSA to share the knowledge and learning with any or all Harley riders.

Jim Rice at San Jose. It was generally accepted that his A65s were the class of the field in 1971

One thing that BSA *had* learnt in '69 and '70 was that they needed a bigger twin. It was promised but it would be slow in coming and perhaps only available in '72. You would think BSA weren't trying with the twins, particularly given how close they were to taking the big prize in 1970, with that certainly being Mann's take on things. Perhaps as he knew more than the others as to what was going on behind the scenes?

Dick Mann: In those days, they did not want me to win. The rest of the world didn't know it yet but BSA was belly-up. They knew it and did everything they could to make sure that Romero finished ahead of me for 1971. They wanted a Triumph to win. The BSAs were only 650cc, the Harleys and Nortons were 750s. We didn't get the 750 until late in the year but it was a little disadvantage. Those BSAs ran really well. When we got the 750 twin? It was like cheating.

To prove it Mann kicked off in style taking his A65 to a win at the Houston Astrodome TT, followed by a victory at Daytona on the Rocket Three. It was a fantastic start and Mann continued to pick up points in all of the disciplines. 2nd at Road Atlanta, 3rd at Loudon, 8th at Terre Haute, 12th at San Jose, 1st at Kent and 5th at Castle Rock. He then went through a bad patch breaking a crank at Ascot, being left on the line along with other riders after a confused semi-final at the Corona ½-mile. There was more mechanical trouble at the Livonia mile and he was then unable to qualify for the Sante Fe short track final. Those bad results dropped Mann from number one spot at the end of July, to third by mid-August, with both Romero and Rice leap-frogging him. At Pocono and Talladega Mann hit back, with back to back road race wins which promoted him to the head of the points table again, with a good 5th at the Ascot ½ mile for good measure.

Mann at Houston

Theroux, Mann, Gillespie and Nicholas at Corona. A messed up start meant none qualified for the main event, but it was a rare hiccough for Mann

Triumph's Romero came back with his own back to back wins at the Oklahoma ½-mile and Nazareth mile, but Mann took good places to limit the damage to his lead. Then what should have been a big final shoot out at Ontario turned into a bit of a shambles. John Cooper took the highly lucrative win but Mann finished 9th overall after a multi-rider, oil-induced fall, clinching the Championship when Romero was unable to remount.

Rice and Aldana finished 3rd and 4th respectively in the final standings as while they'd not won a race between them they had scored consistently. Meaning as in 1970 it was just one Triumph but three BSAs in the top four. Mann's victory was bitter sweet however. The series was televised on ABC's Wide World of Sports, so it gave huge publicity for BSAs big twins which Mann had ridden in the majority of his points scoring rides. The machines in the showrooms now mimicked American flat track styling, right down to their oil bearing frames but unfortunately, due to a litany of design and production line foul-ups, there were few in the shops when they were needed. BSA won the title but they had already lost the sales war. Worse still the huge joint BSA-Triumph US racing programme had inadvertently contributed to the demise. The tragedy was neatly summarized in a letter from Pete Colman to *Cycle World* magazine in 1976.

Pete Colman: *"In 1969, our US President, Peter Thornton, asked me to develop a racing program(sic) which would win all the Grand National Championship events. He asked me how much it would cost, and I presented him with a budget of $240,000, to sponsor two four-man teams…After corporate headquarters had added certain promotional and public relations expenses the cost of the season increased to a staggering $400,000.*

In 1971 I was directed to reduce the budget which forced me to cut the two teams to two riders each. Our efforts did not go unrewarded as Dick Mann captured the No.1 plate for BSA and our three other riders came second, third and fourth. Not bad for a non-racing company.

208

To win races is great from a public relations point of view but it's a waste of money if you can't back your wins with the right product, at the right price, at the right time. Our factories in England were promising some 50,000 motorcycles annually, plus good supplies of parts. Unfortunately, we received only small quantities of both. Unfortunately, again, our advertising campaign, racing and other expenses were geared on 40,000 sales and huge losses resulted."[38]

The situation was hard to believe. 1971 was the most successful year ever for the A65 in racing, yet with the parent company in turmoil no attempt was made to build on the success in the UK. While advertising in the States - bar one advert following Mann's Houston TT win - was built almost exclusively around the triples. 1972 would be a case of defeat from the jaws of victory.

Faded and tattered? Aldana and the rest of the BSA crew had just had a fantastic year in 1971. But unbeknown to the majority the story behind the scenes was one of collapse and decay. BSA was about to become history

Chapter 10

The last title - 1972

Bob Heath on the ex-Tony Smith 670cc Daytona A65. Though in this case fitted with a bigger Peter Brown built motor. He used it to good effect at the very early British 750cc Championship opener, at Oulton Park on Saturday 26th February, finishing ahead of both Dave Potter and Tony Jefferies

In 1971 BSA had new road models and a huge racing budget. They'd come away with the US Grand National title but little else than debt. BSA wasn't quite gone, but it made no odds. No twins would be made after Christmas 1971, so A65 racers suddenly found themselves campaigning obsolete stock. For some it wasn't all bad news however.

Frank Hodgson: I was contacted late 1971 saying that they were in a bit of bother and were going to have to recall the bikes. I also had to send all my achievements for Brian Martin to have a look at, press cuttings and that. I thought: *"Oh I've lost it!"* then he was: *"Oh you ain't been going too bad then"* and came up with a price I couldn't refuse. I got the chance to buy the bike back, end of 1971, and when I got the invoice it was for £25! Brian was a right gentleman. If I paid £25 they'd send the log book and I could keep it. And when they did I looked at the name in the log book, and thought: *"Was that possible? Would he really have had his name on the bike?"* as the registered name on the log book was John Cooper. Of course, once we got the bike we could do what we wanted, as before that we weren't allowed to touch it. We'd put petrol and oil in and that was about it. But it was all such a shame it came to such a quick end, as they were getting very successful with the threes and I wonder what might have happened for me if they hadn't gone bust? It was sad, but I was just so grateful that they gave me a chance.

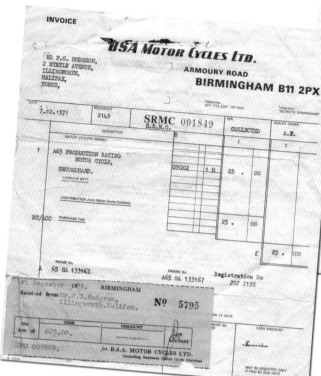

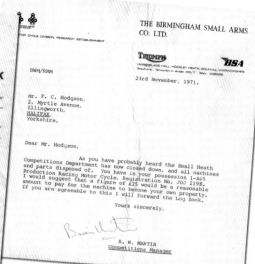

Even at the time £25 was a ridiculously small amount of money, when new machines were ten times that price

Hodgson used the investment to advantage carrying on 1972 where 1971 had left off

Hodgson used that opportunity to best advantage, as while the opposition was becoming stronger the virtues of the A65 still shone through. That was demonstrated at the first National meeting of the season, where Bob Heath took the now ex-factory Daytona racer to second behind Percy Tait's (still) works Rob North Triumph Trident, in the British 750 Championship round.

Bob Heath at Oulton Park in early 1972. On leaving BSA it was the Daytona twin Heath chose to buy

Bob Heath: Tony was pretty clever really and got that bike well sorted. It had got 19" inch wheels in it when Tony had it, as it came back from Daytona and Tony made it a 654. I rode it a few times in 1971 and then the triples came along, but it was converted to A70 750cc spec, with direct oil pressure fed big-ends so I could use it in British unlimited. But I put 18" wheels in, so the next problem I had was the frame. The frame if you look at the front the

Heath and the Daytona 670 at Oliver's Mount, 2nd July 1972. One of his final 1972 rides. The compact dimensions of the machine are easy to see

down tubes they're narrow, but at the back they're really wide and the tube used to hit the deck. So, I said to Ken Sprayson: *"I've got this problem is it OK to cut the tube?"* It was and it wasn't an issue after I put flats on it, but the reason I asked Ken Sprayson was that he'd made the original frame in 531 tube when it was first done for Daytona. It had a fibreglass oil tank with a battery tray off the front of it, done by Screen and Plastics - as they used to make all the fairings for BSA, in Leopold Street in Birmingham - as well as a big Fontana out of the Rocket Three racer on the front. Triumph bought a load of brakes from Italy, then sent two over for our bikes, as the first lot of F750 triples had drum brakes. But then they came out with discs, so one of those big drums made in onto that A65, as before it only had a smaller Fontana when Tony had it. But I tell you what, that was a bloody good bike. It really was. It could see a triple off on the right kind of circuit, as it was so much more nimble.

Nimble enough to defeat Dave Potter's all conquering Kuhn Norton in the process and while Heath's machine subsequently saw little action, later in the season another Daytona framed machine would. In the meantime the country where those machines had been designed to race was seeing a lot of change in '72, even as BSA continued the hard sell on the road bikes.

Even in victory BSA found it hard to acknowledge the part played by the A65 in taking the US 1971 AMA title.

It was all BSA Rocket Threes in the advertising, even though they were being outsold 9 to 1 by the A65 in the sales room.

The fact was the BSA Group had made a huge investment in the model and it was too big an investment to fail. The tooling for the A65 on the other hand had been bought and paid for years ago so was strangely of less interest to the company, though every machine sold added to their coffers

Defending #1

Don Emde: Was I surprised when it all ended after the 1971 season? That would be an understatement. At the Ontario Speedway where we were at for the last race of the 1971 season, the garage area was built so that teams could have just one room, or the rooms could be opened for multi rooms. BSA and Triumph had us eight American riders, plus John Cooper there and we took up a long block of those rooms. After the race that Cooper had won, there

Don Emde running a steel Firebird road tank on a rare late outing on his A70

was the commotion going on at the other end about the U.S. rider who had filed a claim to buy that motorcycle, a story for the triples fans. But me, Aldana and Don Castro were all just cooling off, sharing some stories from the race when team manager Danny Macias came over and basically said that he thought we all had a great year and they were planning the same team for 1972. That all sounded fine to me as I thought at the time I would be racing for BSA for a long time. Danny ended by saying a contract would get mailed to us, to sign and return and he'd see us at the season opener at Houston.

So this was in October and there wasn't much going on except my dad was building an all-new A70 flat track bike in a Red Line frame, as otherwise we were just getting ready for the new season. Then in late-November we celebrate the Thanksgiving holiday on a Thursday. So the next day I was out in front of my parent's house where I lived, loading my trail bike and gear into my van to go out to the desert for the rest of the weekend. A mail man showed up in a van and he had a Special Delivery letter for me, which I expected was my contract. Surprise, surprise, instead it was a letter from Pete Colman advising me that the plans had changed and there would be no factory program after all that included me, Aldana or Rice, or three of the four Triumph riders. Only Dick Mann was kept on for BSA and Gene Romero for Triumph. As Pete explained: *"We were free to explore other opportunities"*.

The A70

The A70 was nobody's baby. Although Peter Brown had a long-stroke 750 in Engine Development as early as 1967, no one within the factory was much interested. The Trident/Rocket Three series engine was nearing production and the twins, both Triumph and BSA, were seen as yesterday's news. With the AMA's sudden rule changes in the late 1960s however this all changed and while the triples were tried on American ovals this was never going to end happily. In truth all the main protagonists - Harley-Davidson, BSA and Triumph - were caught napping in developing a full 750cc OHV machine, though Triumph got there first. As previously mentioned, their American wing simply bolted on an aftermarket kit to increase the Bonneville's capacity by 100cc. Harley-Davidson were working on a whole new race engine, the XR-750, which left BSA somewhat in the lurch.

Given that factory employees were racing engines up to 840cc by this stage and 750cc, in both long and short-stroke formats, the obvious move would have been to sit everyone around a table and mine the rich in-house expertise which sat their on a plate. Instead both Comp Shop and Engine Development staff were bypassed, as was the normal development process for a new road bike at the time. This was then being managed by the BSA-Triumph Group's research establishment, at Umberslade Hall. Instead, the A70 progressed as a bit of a maverick development, under Development Engineer Clive Bennett. Who evidently worked on what he assumed was the best way forward, the earlier long-stroke development of which he would have been aware. As a result Les Mason's offer to test his short-stroke engine was rejected and a sub-optimal design was progressed. Like much of the development on the A65/50 series engine the A70 was designed *despite* experience, rather than with it, as a short-stroke 750 would have been both cheaper and quicker to build, to produce a better performing engine.

As it was the engine was too little developed to offer a real advantage over the BSA team's existing A65s and was too late by September 1971, even if it had been. Jim Rice remembers hand carrying a 750 crankshaft, flywheel and pistons back from the UK following the Easter '71 Match Races but the AMA were stricter than the ACU on counting numbers for homologation purposes, which slowed down getting the bikes on to the track yet further.

Don Emde: Mid-season in 1971, we were all still running the A65 twins, then BSA came up with the new 750cc A70 motors. I forget exactly how it all worked, I think we were told that there would be a date where it was legal to start using them and looking back I believe BSA sent my dad a brand new A70 street production engine. Back home between races he built a race motor out of it and on our next trip east we took one A65 and in the other frame the new A70, ready for when it was legal. But one funny thing happened with this. In those years Gary Nixon and his dear wife Mary had turned their house in Cockeysville, Maryland, near Baltimore, into an unofficial east coast boarding house for all of us BSA and Triumph riders from California At any given time over the summers there might be me, Aldana, Castro, Eddie Mulder and a number of other non-factory BSA or Triumph riders staying at his house on couches, spare bedrooms, some even out in their vans.

So it was one of those times when one day I got a call at Gary's house from BSA/Triumph Vice President Pete Colman and he said the official count of A70s was taking place that day at the Triumph east coast warehouse in Timonium, not far from Gary's house and the A70 engines they had sent to Aldana and me were needed for the count. I told him they were already mounted in our race bikes. Pete was not sympathetic at all and just said something like: *"I don't care, I just need you and David to get right over to the Timonium warehouse and stick those engines in two A65 street bikes that will be waiting for you."* And he added that the AMA officials would be there that afternoon.

Luckily David was involved, because he was a pretty good mechanic, as back then all I knew was how to change the oil and spark-plugs, clean the air filters and change the sprockets. So we drove to the warehouse and someone showed us the two A65s that needed the motor swap, and with David coaching, we unloaded the bikes from our vans, pulled the A70 motors out of the race bikes and then installed them in the street bikes. Mission accomplished.

I don't remember exactly, but I think we came back the next day to get our A70 motors back, though it turned out that the A70s did not work out at all. Once the A70 was approved, I just treated the new engine as the primary motor, the A65 as the backup. I expected everything to work the same, just be a little faster, but I soon encountered a lot of wet sumping and the motor wouldn't run clean. I went race to race for a while trying little fixes BSA gave us. We finally got it running okay, but I found it real hard to make the Main events at the National races that year and it didn't help that I had a big crash one night late in the summer, at the race in Princeton, Indiana. I shouldn't have even ridden there, but I was hungry to gain some extra confidence that would carry over to the National races. My dad said I was out for about 3-4 hours, I was out of racing for about 3 weeks, and when I got going I wasn't quite right for the rest of the season.

Views on the A70 were mixed. As Dick Mann recounted, that for him once they had it: *"It was like cheating"* but as ever, with the development left down to individual riders, performance was always going to vary. By the time riders had A70s it was largely academic anyway, as BSA's Comp Shop was gone, with the company soon to follow.

Dick Mann tries to get his A70 in front of Dave Hansen's Triumph at the Astrodome, while Kenny Roberts lurks in the background, both literally and metaphorically. Roberts got 3rd, Hansen 6th and Mann 7th

With BSA heading towards the buffers, Dick Mann returned to defend his AMA title with a lot less support and as sole works rider. Emde, Rice and Aldana were gone from the line-up and while Emde rode his A70 for the last time at the first dirt track National race of 1972, at Colorado Springs, Rice and to a lesser extent Aldana would persevere with their A65/A70s as privateers.

The advertising had American race fans believing BSA and Triumph were on the up even as their works machines disappeared from the tracks

Dave Aldana: When BSAs gave us our bikes '72, when they went out of business, I wasn't getting any more money so I wasn't going to spend any more on development. 'Cos we did our own remember. BSA had promised a new dirt twin and I did get an A70 in the end and it did have a little bit more torque than the A65, but I never really developed it, as I saw the writing was on the wall for BSA. And when we were going for No.1 there were so many good riders didn't even make the main event. There was so much more competition then, in the early '70s than now. There were guys, privateers, would come out of the woodwork and give the experts like Kenny Roberts and what not a run for their money. Privateers who just raced once a year, or just did their local track. They couldn't afford to pay for a hotel, gas money, like we could. They had a regular job they had to go back to, but they were capable of making a National when it was really difficult. That's how competitive it was. So I stayed home mainly and raced the old bike at Ascot. It paid better than travelling to the Nationals. I could easily make $1,200 every weekend, with only 30 miles of travelling so rode the BSA that one year. You could buy a Harley off the show room floor which was as competitive as anything out there. Competitive right off the bat, so I stopped travelling around the country, rode locally and sold my BSAs. I got them for nothing so I almost gave them away for nothing too, which of course I regret now.

Aldana got a 5th at Ascot, 10th at the San Jose mile 5th at the July Castle Rock meeting, but travelled and scored less subsequently and was never in the points hunt. Signing off his A65 career with an 11th at the Ascot ½-mile in September. There would be plenty more stellar performances from Aldana over the years, starting on a works Norton in '73, but for ex-team mate Rice 1972 was pretty much it. He kicked things off with a fantastic win at the Colorado mile early in the season then consecutive ½-mile second places at San Jose and Salem in July. He subsequently missed four races due to injury and others due to mechanical issues, but placed 7th overall by the season's end, not least due to a standout final victory at the San Jose mile in May.

Jim Rice: At San Jose the stands would not only be full but there'd be people up to the chain link fences on the outsides on the bends and that day started off unusual because I remember there was some sort of freak rain and the track was a bit different in the beginning of practice. The 3rd and 4th turns had the groove next to the pole, the 1st turn if I remember correctly you had more leeway and you could ride further off the pole area. But as the day went on it got drier and drier and to cut a long story short the National that day was one of the best races of my entire life.

Kenny Roberts, boy what a talented guy he was, fast out of the gate, he had a good Yamaha too and he would pass me every time and go through the 1st and 2nd turn. I

Jim Rice was back as a privateer in 1972, though he won more races than he did in 1971

could not beat him through the 1st and 2nd turn. But the 3rd and 4th I was doing better than he was and we kept swapping places like this. He'd get the 1st and 2nd turn I'd get the 3rd and 4th. The inside fence it had 4x4 posts with square boards between them and they'd always stick out a bit further than you thought. You don't realise some-times and I was trying to keep as close to the post as possible, as the groove you had to keep in was only 18 inches wide. I'd always try to stay on the inside of that grove and my shoulder was getting close. I happened to be leading and just then my left shoulder hit the two points at 85mph and took both my hands off the bars, as oddly you're riding quite relaxed not all tense. I couldn't lift my left arm very well. I got it up but didn't really have any strength but kept

going round as I knew on the last lap Kenny was going to try to pull something out, coming or going into the 3rd of 4th turn and he you know, got a little more of a lead coming out of the 2nd turn than normal, 'cos he just banzied the 1st and 2nd and I was just trying my best to get around the groove as fast as I could. As I knew he'd do that. So I tucked in as tight as I could down the back straightaway and we went into the 3rd turn on the groove as deep as I could, carrying every bit of speed I could without getting out of shape. 'Cos I didn't want to lose time with having the rear tyre slip too much. At the same time I'm seeing him hauling his butt round the outside and he's getting the drive and getting set-up to head off down the final

US oval events attracted crowds more like British football crowds than those seen at its racing circuits. It was all about entertainment

25-Mile National Championship

BOB BARKHIMER ASSOCIATES & JOHN SOARES PRESENT

May 21, 1972 SAN JOSE FAIRGROUNDS $1.00

straight away and I knew it was gonna be close. I tell you I put my feet on the pegs and tucked in earlier and had the throttle on earlier and I was just fighting for control. But got a good, good, drive out of the turn coming down the straightway in front of standing room only people screaming their heads off. I just got the front tyre across the line as he went by, about 15mph faster. I ended up winning the race but I tell you to be able to race a quality guy like Kenny, and best him on a BSA, it felt good.

The No1 plate for BSA's sole official runner. It was lonely at the top in 1972, though Jim Rice also stuck out the full season on his own A70

It was a great talk through a classic mile battle but in truth it undersold it too. The race reports had the badly injured Rice doing another lap trying to work out how to stop the bike before a quick visit to victory lane en route to the medical crew. Mann took 3rd that day as sole works rider and while on paper the '72 schedule looked made for him, as the number of both the road racing and TT events in which he excelled were increased, so too had the opposition.

A 7th place at the season opening Houston Astrodome was a good start but with some irony Daytona was won by ex-team mate Don Emde on a 350 Yamaha. The triples were nowhere and there was then a run of bad luck and mechanical issues with his twins, before Mann took a landmark win at the Homewood mile in August. His A70 lapped everyone up to 4th place, including Markel, Romero and Rayborn, with Mann then winning the Peoria TT the following weekend. He passed Lawwill at the mid-point, then proceeded to pull away to lap the field up to 9th place this time, to the joy of a partisan crowd:

"Bugs was still smokin' He had lapped Gillespie, Romero and Scott. The crowd shouted him by on every lap, giving him the big number one with obvious approval. He lapped Bart Markel with five laps to go".[39]

That mile win put him into the record books as the first rider to ever complete the 'Grand Slam' of AMA events - a National level win in short track, ½-mile, mile, TT and road racing disciplines – but in 6th place overall by season's end that was it for the final BSA works team in America.

With the No. 6 Plate in 1973 Mann would be running as a privateer

From A65 to P45

There had never of course been a works team for the BSA sidecar racers. But as the best of them actually worked for BSA, with ruin approaching, there were obviously knock-on effects. Vincent had already set his sights on a GP campaign, having watched Horst Owesle's URS throughout 1971 and had now secured the same engine. That potentially left the path clear for a different British Champion, but it wasn't going to be Peter Brown.

Peter Brown on a new *kneeler* outfit. With his departure from BSA however sidecar racing had to take a back seat

Formation Hanks at the end of season, October Lydden *'Burn up'*. Norman Hanks was already British Champion by this point in 1972 and the BSAs were at the pinnacle of their development. 840cc, yet physically a fraction of the size of much larger machines

Peter Brown: When BSA packed up I was a bit of an idiot. Peter Chapman entered both Chris and I, but his relationship with Chris was pretty close, which he never had with me. He never actually supported me financially in any shape or form, consequently when BSAs closed up I had to get a job. I had a mortgage and what have you, so I went to work for Jaguars and it was just at the time when the twins were sort of getting a bit iffy and they started doing those König hydroplane engines. Bleeding marvellous engines but designed to run in water. Very expensive, but very successful for a time before the Japanese stuff started coming along and I was a bit of a twit really. As while I was in no position to get involved financially, I should have gone looking for a sponsor.

The König was in the wings and much larger car-engined machines were already competing, but the A65 was in no mind to bow out gracefully quite yet. The twin had nigh on a decade's development invested in it with one engine being typical of the handiwork then being brought to the track.

Norman Hanks: By '71-72 we'd made them reliable with the end-feeds and behind the clutch I made an aluminium plate with a bearing in that actually stopped the gears wearing out. Because, as an 840, I used to have to take the gearbox out after every meeting in the last two years I rode. Every meeting I used to count the pits in the teeth and write the number down and when it reached so many I'd think: *'OK, new gear'* as that would stop them breaking. I tried all the different oils you can imagine, STP all that sort of stuff, but they still wore out. Because, as an 840, you never used to rev it over 6,000rpm, you didn't need to, so there was then even more load on the teeth. To stop the cranks breaking, where the inspection cover was on the

(Above) Stuart Digby's version of the third main-shaft support bearing behind the clutch. The principle was exactly the same as on Hanks'. (Below) A typical crankshaft out-rigger bearing

chain case, for your strobe light, well that piece was machined out and I had a lump of aluminium in there, which had another bearing in it, which ran on a shouldered nut on the end of the crank. So now the crank had another bearing as well. The A70 crank that was ideal for us too, as we must have used up all the old A10 cranks we could get our hands on. As you couldn't run them for more than a few

O'Dell really got on-board with the A65 only as others were moving on. It proved a valuable apprenticeship however, on his way to a World Title

races before they cracked and if they broke that was the end of the cases as well. We were very lucky that Brian Marin was such an accommodating person though, as he helped us out a few times with a crank, as I'm sure the powers that be wouldn't have allowed it. And with those A70 cranks I put grooves in the crankcase, to stop the con-rods touching the cases and like that the engines they were very, very good.

Good enough to win the season's opening event at Oulton Park and at Thruxton on the 26th March too. The former over the aerofoiled 875 KGB Imp, the latter from Alan Sansum's Trident outfit. That pretty much set the pattern for the rest of the season, with Hanks, Rust and O'Dell the chief A65 protagonists, since Brown would only make periodic appearances. They fended off in particular the advances of the Imps of Biggs and Williams, the Saab of Dale Ward and the König of the Boret brothers. As the season progressed it was Hanks at Brands, Rust at Croft and Hanks again, over Ward's Saab at Mallory. O'Dell then won at Crystal Place on Sunday 2nd April, where Sansum's Trident holed a crankcase and Boret's

While the A65 was still regarded by many as the engine to have in sidecar racing competitors were now looking for an edge. Bryan Rust was one of the first to experiment with an aerofoil

König had problems too – a common feature of the fast but fickle two-strokes at the time. Hanks then beat Rust at Cadwell, with Rust in turn beating O'Dell at Lydden after a photo finish on the line. O'Dell was now very clearly on form having obtained a 750cc 'Birmingham' engine. It cost £70 from a West Bromwich pub car park late one night and combined with his ex-Sheridan chassis was good enough to get him on even terms with the Hanks brothers soon after.

Mick Boddice and Clive Pocklington at Thruxton. Boddice always had one of the best turned out machines and was always looking at innovation. By mid-1972 that resulted in him abandoning the A65 in favour initially of a Kawasaki two-stroke triple

George O'Dell: It was the engine to have at the time. It would pull well out of corners without any wheel-spin and it had so much low-down punch. With its short stroke and big bore it would pull top gear all the way round somewhere like Gerards at Mallory. It was the first big meeting in which I had managed a good result. Norman Hanks won it and we had a dice with his brother Roy for third spot. When they asked me about the engine, I said it was a bog standard one I had taken out of a wrecked outfit. The midlands racers would never explain the good performance of their BSA motors. So I followed the same line. I said: *"It's exactly the same as the ones you run."* It always remained a secret where it had come from. They knew it had come from their way and they wanted to find out who was selling them outside the Birmingham market.[40]

There was a bit of mythology behind '*Birmingham*' engines, but it proved its worth again for O'Dell, providing a win at Brands on 30th April, where Boddice also got two, and possibly his last two, wins on an A65. Boddice's brother-in-law, Kawasaki works rider Dave Simmons, would facilitate a Kawasaki triple engine for him post-TT and with Vincent now on the four cylinder URS the constituent parts of the *Birmingham Mafia* were starting to go their own way. It was similar with some of the independent runners too, with one leading protagonist also signing-off with a last significant placing on an A65, after taking its development as far as he thought it could go.

Brian Mee and Colin Newbold at the TT. 13th in the 500s was a good result by 1972, as 5th BSA home. But a faster sidecar engine was needed, before Mee ultimately moved on to four wheels and a career in Formula Ford

Brian Mee: We went down to Lockheed and scrounged an old ventilated disc. Because everyone was on twin calipers and had discs warping. Well, I got this big one pot caliper as I had this theory that if I could gain a 10th of a second on a bend and there were ten bends on a circuit then I could get a one second advantage obviously. Well, this proved the case as when we went to Silverstone we won the SUNBAC Bank meeting and they couldn't understand it. They called us the demon brakers, but it was all due to this disc, as we were always looking at stuff like that, Doug and I. We all had pretty similar engines, so you had to look for other things to get an advantage, as while I enjoyed the Beezers if you could have had a proper gearbox on an Imp that was the bike to have had by then. But they were putting Norton gearboxes on to them and of course ripping the gearboxes apart. But marry that engine to a 6-speed gearbox and God you'd have some sort of machine there. But I bought a König. A Boret-type, a John Renwick thing. I took it to Clermont Ferrand when Mick Boddice took his and he had a fire and I blew mine up too and thought: 'No' and walked away. I ended up with a TZ750, but that engine cost me £5K in the 1970s and I'd seen guys who'd put everything into it, living on bare floorboards it got so expensive.

That was the story moving into the early 1970s, but more teams were investing in new types of engine and to prove the point while Norman Hanks then won at Cadwell, John Biggs' Imp in turn beat him at Mallory Park, with O'Dell trailing in 5th behind Dale Ward's Saab. The face of British sidecar racing was changing and as a result the programme notes for the big pre-TT Brands Hatch International picked out Siegfried Schauzu and Rudi Kurth as the class of the field, even if O'Dell ran away with the two sidecar victories.

(Left) John Barker and Alex Macfadzean (3rd) lead John Brandon's 750 Honda (4th) over the TT start line. It wasn't as close a finish as it looked since on corrected time Barker had a comfortable lead of well over a minute. (right) John Barker with Dave Jose this time in the chair

Schauzu did the double at the TT though, where Roy Hanks showed his increasing prowess with 6th in both races. The standout result was John Barker's 3rd in the 750 race however, as it was the last time a BSA would appear on the TT podium, when the TT was still a World Championship event.

Les Mason: That third place TT finish was the year he should have won it. What happened was John came to me with his engine and asked if I'd prepare it for him, for the TT. But he didn't bring the transmission, he just brought the engine and gearbox. So I couldn't set-up the clutch and everything else. But we did the roller bearing conversion, converted it to 750cc and all that stuff, so when he came to pick it up I said: *"Did you bring the clutch?"* He said: *"No, but I can put that on"*. *"Fine, but make sure you put the correct components on for the four-spring clutch, because if you don't the cups will bottom out, as the thing wears and you will burn it out."* You see you had to put a thick packing plate in at the back, about an 8th of an inch thick, it was a combination of those sorts of bits and pieces that you picked up over time, which made all the difference. But anyway, getting back to the race, he's leading, climbing the mountain for the last time and the bloody thing started to slip and the boys overhauled him. He still managed to finish third, but he would have won the damn thing if he'd done up he four spring clutch properly.

Following the TT a pattern then emerged in the Nationals of BSAs trading places with the newer type machines. With Norman Hanks winning on an A65 at Mallory and Cadwell, then O'Dell at Crystal Palace. On the other side it was Biggs' Imp winning at Aintree, Vincent's URS at Snetterton, Weslake's development engineer Currie at Oulton and the Boret brothers' König over Norman Hanks at Mallory Park on September 16th.

Neston Lewis and George Aldred go out for the heats at the Thruxton National on March 26th. They were a typical pair of A65 privateers, but didn't feature in the final won by Norman Hanks that day

Hanks then won at the same circuit the next day, came second to Vincent at Cadwell on the 24th and came away with the same Vincent-Hanks result at the final round of the MCN Superbike Championship on 8th October. Before season end that just left the final round of the British Championship, at Snetterton, on Sunday 18th and while Norman Hanks had already done enough to win the British sidecar title by now, he went out anyway and won after an epic battle against Dale Ward's Becket Saab. He followed it all the way around until the last lap, when he broke the lap record on his un-faired outfit, to out drag a theoretically far more powerful and rapid machine to the line.

Those National results were a good snapshot of how varied the machines of the main protagonists now were. People were looking at alternatives to the venerable A65 which meant some of the best BSA twins started to find their way down to club level. As such Clyde Gough's 3rd and 5th at Cadwell Park on 24th September were enough to secure his 840cc Devimead machine the Nottingham & District's sidecar title for 1972. The same day the Hardy brothers took the Darley Moor title on their Hillman Imp-powered machine however and John Biggs and Peter Williams had similar machines also running well. As mentioned previously Dale Ward had a Saab, as did Terry Rudd with the greatest threat from these engines coming not through their greater sophistication but through their sheer size. As the flat trackers had found in America, sizes matters, though if that went with increased bulk the A65 still had an advantage. As such the BSA twins still delivered a prodigious number of victories with Tony Stark perhaps top of the heap in 1971. He won an unbelievable 31 races

Stark and Pole on their way to another club level victory on their all conquering Devimead machine

on the first officially Devimead backed machine since Pat Sheridan's death, to take the Derby Phoenix, Grantham Pegasus and Skegness Club Championships. Those sorts of wins would continue into 1973 as while the Imps and König showed the direction in which National runners were moving Club grids were increasingly packed with well sorted A65s.

If a picture could tell a story. Ken Vogl's expenses from 1972. Income £60, outgoings £281.99½. Many racers kept such Micawber-esque accounts, but as the 1960s moved into the 1970s both solo racers and sidecar crews alike found that outgoings rose exponentially. As a result the frugal A65 remained very popular

"Look out, Japs!"

It was a similar situation in the solos, as while Triumph Bonnevilles had been replaced by Commandos and Trident as the A65s prime adversary previously, these were now being supplemented in turn by Kawasaki triples, Honda fours and the ubiquitous Yamaha and Suzuki two-stroke twins. One of the best of which appeared at Aintree early in '72.

> **Frank Hodgson:** Our kid came up to us before my first go out that day in April and says: *"There's a bloke in this race, Stan Woods, who's won all the other ones"* but I remember getting off to a decent start and I liked Aintree, actually hardly lost and just hung on. That BSA was fabulous, I just felt so confident with it, so it was no problem to beat 'em and I won.

Hodgson had done the double at Croft on 8th April and the same at Cadwell on 22nd. But that win at Aintree the following weekend was a real stand out performance. Stan Wood's would soon ink a works contract with Suzuki and was on the Crooks T500 Suzuki that he would shortly ride to victory in the Isle of Man Production TT. Hodgson lapped quicker than the winners in every class that day however and it was similar the following weekend at Snetterton, where the whole set of results underlined what a competitive bike the A65 could still be.

As expected Hodgson took his customary production class win, but it was over more formidable opposition than he'd faced in previous seasons. This was evidenced by the result, which read: 1st Frank Hodgson (BSA A65); 2nd Ron Bailey (Honda 750/4); 3rd Alan Walsh (Triumph Trident); 4th 'Mac' McMillan (Triumph Trident); 5th Pete Lovell (Norton Commando) and; 6th Mick Hemmings (Norton Commando). That was a quality field by anyone's standards, but this was just the warm up. Neil Tuxworth had won the 125, 350 and 500 class races on three different capacities of Yamaha twin. He actually won six races in total, but wheeling his TR2 350 Yamaha out for the three 1,000cc events, he was in for a bit of a surprise. In the first race Hodgson took his production A65 to the win ahead of Mick Pepper's TR2 Yamaha. In the second Dave Mason mixed it up, to beat Tuxworth into second place on his Rickman framed A65, meaning only in the third and last race was Tuxworth able to salvage his dignity, by pushing Hodgson's road legal Spitfire into second place. It still

meant three A65 victories in the day however, two over 350cc, Grand Prix calibre Yamaha machinery. A bike like the A65 simply wasn't supposed to be capable of that, especially at a super-fast circuit like Norfolk's Snetterton.

Dave Mason with the tinware and celebratory burger. His Rickman A65 could still hold its own with the two-strokes in 1972 but Mason would soon be on to Hondas for a TT podium and 2nd place in the Formula Two World Championship

Hodgson on the ex-works A65 in September 1971. By 1972 he'd moved on to a jet helmet but the motorcycle remained the same. It should really have been outclassed by this point but a hat-full of victories proved otherwise

All those results came in just one breathless month and while there were no more A65 wins in April there were some good places and new names too. Dave Abrahams, Tom Pickering, Dave Ashton, Andrew Holme, Bill Stoddart and Malcolm Stanley were among them, though by mid-season A65 stalwart Clive Wall was on a Commando and Hugh Evans a Honda 750/4 or a Kawasaki Mach III. The latter on which he would lead that year's production TT. Evans would still appear on his A65 periodically, but for most of the season it was Reg Hardy - who had been stripped of his first win in 1971 - along with Hodgson reeling off the BSA twin's best results.

While he rode a Kawasaki in the production race Evans took his A65 for one last TT ride, in the F750 in 1972. The DNF was unfortunate given the A50's years of reliable service

Hodgson leads Phil Haslam, and Phil Gurner, at a murky Cadwell Park. Both his adversaries were tipped for stardom but died too young to reach their potential. In 1972 Hodgson got the better of them both

The magnitude of Hodgson's performances in particular were demonstrated towards the end of the season, with a win on Sunday 8th October at Cadwell Park. Here, immediately behind at the flag, was a Kawasaki H1 triple, two 750 Honda fours and a Yamaha 350 twin. Though by this point Hodgson had no qualms declaring his *'Production'* A65 as displacing 735cc.

Frank Hodgson: It started as our kid says: *"There's a bike over there like yours, an A65, but with different barrels on it."* It must have been Dave Mason's bike, as I seem to remember Les coming over to see me, probably as he knew mine was a works bike, saying he'd got it homologated. So we said: *"Let's go for it!"* And it gave a big boost in power, while it still rev-ed like the clappers. But then we started getting a few sort of protests: *"It's not legal that. You're running an 850 engine."* or *"You're running it on methanol."* I couldn't believe it, as I was open and put it down as a 750 on the entry forms and in the programme. Then one race Ray Knight came over to see me and says: *"If you win the race today we're making a complaint against you, but you won't, as Tony Smith's here."*

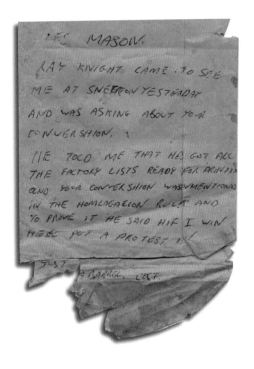

When back of an envelope meant it. Hodgson's communique to Les Mason re: the legality of his 750 barrels

In the race Tony crashed but my foot was slipping too, there was oil on my boot, and I thought: *"Oh shit the base gaskets gone."* I tootled round to the pits and my mechanic, and my brother says: *"You can't carry on, it's pouring out."* It had actually cracked the barrel, so I didn't finish either, but according to my mates me and Tony were swapping places back and forward and there was nought in it. And Ray Knight never complained either, as I didn't finish the race. Though in truth it wasn't so much that he was protesting against me, as much as he hadn't seen any supporting documentation. And it was my fault I cracked the barrel too, as I knew I rev-ed it too high and a con-rod, according to my brother, stretched and came into contact with the head. Les had said don't skim the head, to get a better squish, as when the piston came to the top there was a lip on the head, from where the engine went from 650 to 750. We left that there, but of course when it got to near 8,000 revs it must have been tapping. Les Mason smashed it open with a hammer actually, as he said he'd had a batch of faulty ones, but then said: *"Oh actually that looks OK!"* But to his credit he replaced it.

The weekend after Hodgson's Cadwell win was the Stars at Darley Moor meeting where it was traditional for the big names to come and show the circuit specialist how to do it. They did in the majority of events, Alan Barnett winning the big 'Stars' race, Steve Manship the 250cc, Phil Haslam the 350cc and John Williams the big bike race. Reg Hardy failed to read the script in the production class however and took his usual win to wrap up the Championship and add his name to Bob Heath's and Graham Sanders', as previous holders on an A65. He was challenging in the 'Stars' race too, though he wasn't yet aware this would also be his sign-off race.

Reg Hardy (10) goes up the inside of Keith Litte's Bonneville, on 24th September 1972. Hardy won

Staying within the rules. Spot the difference? Reg Hardy (top) with megaphone exhausts fitted to compete in open class races, such as the *'Stars of Darley Moor'* race. Road legal silencers in place (bottom) for his production racing, to avoid the disqualification of the the previous year

Reg Hardy: I won the production race but, well, in the *Stars* the woodruff key sheered and the clutch fell off. But before that I was out-braking guys on 350 Yamahas, with discs on and I thought: *"I'll have to get a disc brake next year"* but got married and couldn't afford it. Before then if you couldn't afford a Matchless or Manx there were loads of production races and I could make a lot of stuff myself, all my modifications. The two-strokes were just coming in then though and it just killed it for everybody really, those 350 Yams. But I was a silly boy really, I was just getting somewhere but I said I'd get married if I won the Championship, and I did. So, I should have thrown the last couple of races really! I was 24, not long off 25 when I got married, so still not very old.

That Championship win would have been a good season sign-off too, but there was an unexpected cherry on the top, at Snetterton, the same day. Martin Sharpe was a rising star and had dropped out while leading the 250 National race earlier that day. But as *MCN*'s John Brown reported the following Wednesday:

"Sharpe got his just rewards in the 750-race. Out for only the third time in the big class he romped to an easy victory on one of Les Mason's Devimead 750 BSAs. The Brackley rider was content to stay behind Roger Corbett on a Dunstall for the first two laps but then with an outside line, as he rounded Coram for the third time, he took the lead and headed off on his own."[41]

Sharpe on the Devimead-Daytona. A sister machine to that being ridden by Bob Heath in 1972

While Brian Steenson's victory at Cadwell Park in March 1970, marked the last victory at National level for a works A65, Sharpe's result was the final win by any A65 solo, at a British National Championship round. It was on an interesting machine too, since it was a sister machine to Heath's works Daytona, built by Les Mason around a spare, unused 1968 frame. It would be wheeled out again in 1973, as a test-bed for Devimead components, since with BSA itself gone there was a clamour for performance parts. This was not only at home but abroad too, with Devimead barrels going to the States, on one occasion as 'spares' when the aforementioned Martin Sharpe was racing at Daytona. These found their way onto flat track machines but oval racers were not the only solos being campaigned in North America. Canada had its own scene as experienced by one expatriate *Brit* who would later go on to frame building fame.

Curtis frames would become very popular in America. It all started with an A65 however and an A70 flat tracker for Randy Skiver was one of their earliest successes

Denis Curtis: I came to Toronto in early 1971 but had friends in Vancouver, so found myself there by late summer and took a job with the Fred Deeley organization. At their retail store at 606 East Broadway, run by Trevor Deeley. I was involved in the service and parts department and shortly after joining I found a tough looking BSA Spitfire Mk II in one of the back rooms. It turned out to be a bike that Trevor had purchased in the Isle of Man in 1968 or 69 and I was told it was a works BSA 650 Twin Production TT racer. It certainly was trick and I asked Trevor if I could rebuild the bike to race in local events. It started out with original BSA brakes but to compete with the 500 Suzuki two-strokes I converted it to use Yamaha TZ 350 wheels and brakes, front and rear. The Fred Deeley Retail store had a paint shop, and 'Joe the painter' always came up with fancy paint jobs for the bikes and helmets.

Trevor Deeley allowed me to race the BSA twin at some western USA tracks too. Seattle in Washington and Portland Oregon, and as far east as Edmonton and it was really quite competitive.

Times were changing however. Curtis would soon be on to a Norton and in '73 it would be a whole new challenge for everyone, when the two-strokes were fully on song.

Chapter 11

Last wave of the flag - 1973

BSA were going down but for BSA racers Devimead filled the breach. With complete CR gear cluster sets at £15 and 750cc barrel and piston assemblies at £75 a go they did brisk business among the sidecar racing fraternity in particular. Only BSA's inability to supply complete engines thwarted a plan for Egli-type framed production bikes

From 1973 onward it was always going to be tough for anyone racing a BSA twin. Machines with more cylinders, gears, capacity and speed were competing in every class. However, to quote the weeklies on the Mallory Park season opener: *"Sidecar-wise the British season started where last season left off…with the Hanks brothers on top."* Reigning Champion Norman Hanks won the National race, with it being Norman in the invitation race too, from brother Roy. It looked similar at Club level at Cadwell Park the same day, as while Dave Muxlow's 810cc Norton outfit won the first race, it did so only after Dave and Barry Porter's Windrick BSA had spun in sight of the winning flag and another A65 convert had selected neutral at the start on a brand-new engine. Properly engaged the unit showed its worth in the second race by taking the man who would win the TT in '78 and come second in the World Championships a year later, to a win by a staggering 11.2 seconds.

Dick Greasley: In 1971, I started racing with my brother-in-law, Stewart Atkinson, with a Triumph motor. We got through our first season with steady progress and felt that we had earned a better outfit. Mike Fiddaman was a builder/racer at that time and we decided to purchase a chassis from him, to take a BSA A65 motor. We built the BSA motor with a Devimead bottom-end conversion, an A10 crank and a jumbo top end, to make it 830cc. Twin spark coils had just been brought out and we fitted some Honda items to better the ignition. Maximum revs were only about 5,200rpm but in club races that year, no-one beat us off the line. Somewhere like Mallory you could be halfway round Gerards and others would still be pushing off the line. We won loads of club events and spares were cheap. The A65 motor, once sorted, was absolutely brilliant and we only changed to a Honda K4 later in the season, as we got sponsored by Cyril Chell.

Dave Smith: we bought that BSA off Dick to replace the Rickman/Triumph engines we had and it's funny Dick should mention Mallory. We were on the BSA for the first time I think and Dick was there with the new Honda. Start of the race and the BSA fired up so quick I remember looking back and seeing a line of outfits behind us as we went into Gerards! I don't know who did the engine for Dick but it certainly was a very good one.

Vince Winstanley and Dave Clark at Aintree with the Dick Greasley motor installed

It clearly was as the Greasley engine went on to help Vince Winstanley and Dave Smith pick up a 7th at the Ulster GP among other good results. These continued at National level at Cadwell Park again, on Sunday 11th, with Norman Hanks winning from younger brother Roy and the consistent Bryan Rust. At this point continental sidecar crews still came over to Britain, but there was an increasing flow the other way too. So, on 1st April, a large British contingent was off to France for the big pay-out Rouen International. The big 'races' were actually decided over two legs with a best of 2nd for Norman Hanks and a 3rd apiece for Roy Hanks and George O'Dell, who were all lucky to reach the finals at all.

Norman Hanks: We went to Chimay and Rouen and both were a bit of an eye opener for us. George O'Dell was there and me and Roy had been riding hard, but we didn't have fairings on then. We were parked together, with this British contingent, and George said: *"I'm really good down the mountain."* From my memory you went down the sort of side of a mountainside with Armco on one side and then went round at a convergence of two roads at the bottom, with a little link road, which was cobbled. As the track actually went across the cobbles. Me and Roy thought we were pretty good on left-handers and so George is here saying: *"You'll have to follow me down. Get in my slipstream and not too far behind, so I don't pull away from you."* So, we arranged ourselves at the top of the circuit going across the start-finish, going hell for leather. I'm right behind George and Roy's right behind me with George with the fairing making the hole in the air for us. We'd been going flatout round these left-handers and coming up to the first one he puts his brakes on and changes down! Neither of us crashed, as we went either-side of him, it must have looked like a star burst, but when we got back to the pits boy did we give him some stick: *"Didn't you see how fast we were going? That's how fast you're meant to go!"* But he was good was George.

There were similarly two 29 lap races aggregated for the £2,000 solo prize, which Ron Chandler won on his Rob North triple. In the same race Martin Sharpe finished a highly credible 8th however on the Devimead A65 twin he'd won on the previous October. He was ahead of a host of exotica including Kawasaki 750 triples, GP regular Bo Granath's 500 Husqvarna, Jack Findlay's 750 Suzuki triple and Tony Smith on the ex-Renzo Pasolini Harley-Davidson XR750.

Martin Sharpe's early performances in 1973 on Les Mason's twin were outstanding. It was only the lure of faster Yamahas that cut the partnership with Devimead before it could really flourish

Martin Sharpe in action on April 15th, in a classic case of being in the right place at the wrong time. The Devimead Daytona was the unofficial sister bike to Bob Heath's, but had the misfortune to come on song just as big four-strokes were being replaced by two-strokes

As in the sidecars the result could have been much, much, better however, as incredibly Sharpe stopped with a dead engine in the first leg and it was only when namesake Graham Sharpe, who had broken down in exactly the same spot, traced the fault to a broken electrical wire that he got going again. Without the stop he would have been easily among the leaders, as he was in the second race. It had been an auspicious start to the season all round but the pace of change was exponential. This was highlighted at Thruxton, on Sunday April 14th, where the capacity class winners - Steve Machin (125) Alan Barnett (250) Charlie Williams (350) and Paul Cott (750) – were all on Yamaha twins, and in taking 4th place in the headline Commonwealth Trophy race, the returning Martin Sharpe's Devimead 750 was the only *'diesel'* among five Japanese two-strokes in the top six. Indeed, it was the only four-stroke, in any solo class, in the top 6 in any race that day.

That same dynamic was evident even at club level. But while the Yamaha of future Grand Prix regular John Newbold won the Darley Moor opener, so too did an A65 production racer. After a final corner tussle with the man who'd eventually win the championship.

Dave Abrahams and the ex-Bob Heath Lightning. This time 29th July, when a 7th was the best he could manage

Dave Abrahams: I remember that one as Norman Overend came past me on the last lap into the final corner, but left his braking too late and went wide. I braked at my usual spot and was able to peel off behind him and come out of the corner ahead. To take the flag. It probably looked more impressive than it really was, as I just took the corner as I had on every other lap. But that was on the ex-Bob Heath bike as the Spitfire I'd originally bought wasn't too successful to begin with. The bike didn't steer too well and I think it was actually bent. But I bought Bob's off Mel Cranmer and that was much, much, better. I remember I bought it the week after we'd both competed at Aintree and Melvin was having a few problems with it. When I got it home I realised he'd wired the coils up incorrectly. He'd got the coils in series instead of in parallel, so there was only half the voltage going across them. After I'd got that sorted it was much better than my old Spitfire.

It handled properly, which was the main thing, and started better, as it had Monobloc carbs on it, instead of the Spitfire's GPs. Which was important then as it was dead engine starts which could be an absolute pain at some circuits. I remember at Anglesey, Mona, which was probably the Wirral 100 club, they'd inadvertently set the start slightly up-hill, so you can imagine people were gasping with exhaustion before they'd even got the damn things going. But I rode that bike on most of the northern circuits and I did better than I expected, and converted it to a 500cc, twice, to do the Manx Grand Prix.

The Manx was of course in August, but during the first two months of the season there were multiple wins at Cadwell for the metronomically reliable Frank Hodgson, at Cadwell again by Norman Hanks over Rust, by O'Dell at the Mallory Transatlantic meeting and Hodgson again at Aintree. Where the sidecar results read Hardy (Imp) Vogl (BSA) Kruse (Weslake) and Greasley (BSA). It was a more mixed bag of results the following weekend, for solo and sidecar alike, as another two newcomers appeared. The second on the top step of the podium, but the other in the hay bales.

Alistair Frame: My first meeting was at Staverton where I borrowed a helmet and wore a hat underneath it as it didn't fit. You'd never get away with it now but that's how it was back then. I did three meetings that first year. Staverton, Cadwell and Mallory and finished with the grand sum of £17. 'Cos back then you won perhaps a pound here, two pounds there, even in the heats. Then it was on to Dave Mason's old bike. There's this little street in Tamworth called Kings Street and up the side street is where I wheeled my first proper race bike out. At what we called Zackies, the Motor Cycle Shop Tamworth. So that's why that name was always on the bike. Soon after I remember doing the Bill Ivy

Alistair Frame on the ex-Dave Mason Rickman Métisse as bought, still adorned with the Motor Cycle Shop stickers and running its oil-in-frame

meeting, Snetterton, with the Racing 50 Club, Sunday April 29th it was and while that circuit's been vastly changed now, you used to be able to sit on the garage and watch them coming down the long Norwich straight and that was where I lost my brake. The caliper actually cracked, so I had to drop the bike and slide. I went to Lockheed's and they couldn't do enough for me after that, giving me brakes and pads and stuff, as it was a dangerous failure I guess. There was a hairline crack and it was only the beginning of the season. But the bike was actually really good and soon after I was leading at Mallory Park when the engine oil got so hot I couldn't sit on the bike, as it had the oil in the frame. I had to settle for 3rd and they literally lifted me off the bike I was so blistered. Blistered to hell, but I made the news as there was a bloke called Brian Lodwick of the Birmingham Evening Standard there, who put a story in under the headline *"Alistair's a scorcher."* So obviously, after that, it was a trip down to RGM, to have an oil tank made and by the end of that season my records say I'd won three trophies and quite a bit in prize money would you believe!

That prize money would come later as at the same meeting the money on offer for the sidecars – £50, just over £500 in 2021 values - went to the Nottingham pairing of Derek Wood and Tony Price. Who powered their 840 BSA from 26th on the grid to the front by the second lap, to win by over 50 yards, even after having to ease off before the line. The victory was significant not least since the experience gained with the A65 engine would be important to the passenger later on.

Wood and Price flying at Snetterton 15th October 1972. At this point the bike was in 734cc form. Once they got an A70 crank, they went 840cc and really started getting the results

Tony Price: Absolutely right. I learned what I knew from the sidecars. We started off on a Triumph about '69, me and Derek. He wanted to go racing so I said: *"Go on. I'll go in the chair."* We were sort of mid-pack, Croft, Mallory, Snett', and Cadwell so we decided to have a Bill Cooper chassis and we did well on that, as we went on to a Beeza engine at the same time. We were friends with the Birmingham crew and got an engine out the back door dead cheap. '72 engine, brand new, a Firebird. It had carbs on, cables, everything, as the frame had just been cut away at the head stock and everything behind of that was there. It cost us £100 and that was a good price, it really was. We ran it like that, standard for a bit, then increased it to 750 with the Devimead barrels, 734cc. BSA made everything on that engine round. Even the barrels were round, horrible things, but when Devimead came out with the big-bore barrels, which were more squarish, it looked great. And later on still we got an A70 crank and we put that in. The word was, when we had the 734, that A70 cranks were very hard to get. But Derek in his wisdom went to a small BSA agent at Long Eaton and simply ordered one, not thinking we would have a hope.

Derek Wood: The local Triumph bloke, Alf Butler, also did BSA spares, so I asked him to get his parts books out, we found the A70 crank part number and I said: *"Alfie can you order me one?"* Well he did and the guys over there in the spares department in Birmingham they just got the parts and sent them out of course. Well a fortnight later he had a telephone call from Birmingham saying: *"Can you please send it back because they're not meant to have got out!"* But he just said he didn't know the guy who had ordered it, he'd just come in, picked it up and left. But with the A70 crank that made it 840cc and that was the engine to have. We got to know one or two guys, a few of the Birmingham guys who did the club racing too and they could get old bits which the top guys had used, but had since sort of upgraded from, and passed down. As they all used to work at BSA.

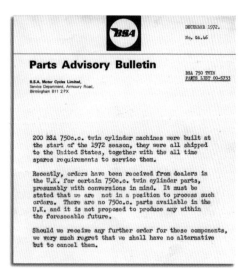

The factory said you couldn't get 'em. Wood's endeavours proved you could. A70 cranks would ultimately prove relatively common-place when it became obvious no more than the original 200 road versions were going to be manufactured

I used to do the bottom ends and the rockers, I'd lighten them, then Tony would do the heads. And that bike was quick. Dead quick. But you still had to know how to get the best out of them. Torque that's where the A65 engines won out. You'd go into Gerards at Mallory say, and if you had a good run in, down the straight, all you'd have to do was ease it off a bit then wind it back on, accelerate all the way round, and not change gear at all again until the Esses.

An engine like that meant that the results on May 6th, at Cadwell Park for the third round of the British championships, read Norman Hanks (BSA), Hardy (Imp), Roy Hanks (BSA), Bryan Rust (BSA), George O'Dell (BSA) and Ken Vogl (BSA). It was the sort of result which had been the norm four or five years previously, but couldn't quite be matched at an event filled meeting at Mallory Park on the 27th. John Newbold broke Mike Hailwood's 350 lap record in the solos but the story for the press and 12,000 fans in attendance was the lap record set by Wood's 840 BSA. In trying to hunt down George O'Dell and the fast 970cc Mini-engined Komnik of Chris Nickels.

Derek Wood: I'd beaten George in the heat and then during the break, between qualifying and the main race, old Georgy O'Dell came and sat talking to us. He sat on the front of our outfit, near the nose cone. That's where the battery was, and we've been suspicious of this ever since. Anyway, the main race came and what we used to do was just put one of the leads back onto the battery, where we'd taken it off before, and go out. Well, we were leading the race, hurtling up to the hairpin, and the engine cuts out. By the time we'd got 'round the hairpin and had rolled towards the Devil's Elbow, everybody had come by. But Tony noticed then that the *other* lead had come off, not the one we'd normally detach. So put it on, dropped the clutch and we were away again. It was working our way up, that's when the fastest lap came in, trying to catch them, as I can tell you I wasn't in a good mood by then! We always suspected George had loosened that lead as he was a bugger you know! As all the seasons we raced that was the only time it ever happened, and there he was sitting on that nose cone.

Wood and Price negotiating Mallory Park's Devil's Elbow at speed

Who knew? O'Dell was fiercely competitive and ambitious though, as demonstrated by a fine 7th as first British machine home in the 500 class TT. It was only overshadowed by the magnificent 5th place of Bill Crook in the 750 race, just one place behind the Kawasaki triple of Mick Boddice. Demonstrating that moving on from an A65 didn't always equate to moving up.

However, if there was a watershed in the sidecar racing season it was perhaps the subsequent Mallory Rothmans Post-TT International,

Bill Crook was partnered by Stu Collins in 1974 and 1975 with 5th (750cc) and 6th (500cc) places finishes in 1974 being standout performances

on June 10th. This had provided rich pickings for A65 crews in previous years' but in 1973 Bill Currie's Weslake took the victory over the Hardy brothers' Imp. It was reported that there was nothing Norman Hanks could do about it in 3rd place, with the same true of Martin Sharpe in the solos. He came 10th in the *MCN* Superbike Championship race, where the fastest lap was set by Suzuki's Barry Sheene and team mate Stan Woods took the win, on his identical liquid cooled, three cylinder, two-stroke, TR750. That was stiff opposition for any push-rod parallel twin, as was also experienced by Frank Hodgson. He did the double at Cadwell Park on April 2nd and then again on 12th May but as there was no production class at the same circuit on 8th July he took his Spitfire out in the open race instead. The Seeley Suzuki 500 he beat was typical of the machines now appearing, even at club level, and ultimately trying to compete with them saw an end to the career of this particular, highly successful, ex-works A65 twin.

Frank Hodgson: Things were changing. I knew Peter Darvill, when the Hondas came into it and the three-cylinder Kawasakis and other things too. Though luckily to begin with they didn't handle. I remember one time this bike passing me on a straight, a Kawasaki, but as soon as it got to the corner it was all over the place. So I still won the race in the end. But the Yamahas were really good. I knew Neil Tuxworth when he started. He used to come with his father and the thing was then there was money coming in to it. And we didn't have any.

Hodgson on the second incarnation of the ex-Cooper Spitfire. When JOJ 219E lost any pretence at being a production bike and became a full open class racer

Now whether the Tuxworth family were reasonably well off or not I don't know, but they finished bringing two or three bikes rather than one. They started in 125s, but then they finished off bringing a 250 and 350 Yamaha, with these big brakes and my brother says: *"We can't compete with that."* And it was riders like Steve Machin, Derek Chatterton and the Haslams on them too. But that bike, the A65, the engine was brilliant, absolutely brilliant. It was just that we didn't seem to be able to stop quick enough and the bike was too heavy by then. So my brother made a new frame and put discs on it, Seeley disc brakes on the front. But the trouble was the yokes we had on the bike were too narrow and we were getting a few tank slappers while we also made it a bit too low. So while I raced it like that in to '75, I crashed it, and it ended up getting stored in the end.

The A65 was showing its age and the two subsequent Cadwell Meetings, where Gerry Millward took a 5th on 15th July and Dick Herzberg a 2nd on 5th August, were the swan song for these two A65s also.

Herzberg about to swing left into the foot of the Mountain on the ex-Daytona, ex-Tony Smith, ex-Bob Heath A65

Dick Herzberg: I admired Bob Heath as a rider and I watched what he did at Oulton Park, '72. looked at that bike after too, but never thought I would own it. But it came up for sale in *Motor Cycle News,* I phoned, and bought it straight away, with all the bits and pieces for I think about 450-quid. It was a 750 then, with a top fin added on, and came with extra dowels and another fin, to do another barrel. 1973 it would have been, as I rode for Bennetts after.

The photo that killed-off the ex-factory A65. Herzberg's career went off in a whole new direction with the North Trident and the factory A65 was put out to pasture in 1974

Bob put 18" wheels on it and had actually cut a bit of the frame away, at the bottom, put a chamfer on it, as he was catching it on the ground. But I just couldn't get on with it like that. I actually hung off like him, but I was scraping it too, so put a 19" back on the front. I also had problems with rings breaking until Bob told me to stick to factory ones, and I thought he'd told me to only rev it to six thousand revs. But it was then he said: *"No. It was seven!"* and once I started using that I was passing all sorts. The ex-Tony Jefferies triple, Don Morton on his newly built Rob North triple. It was fast. And I had a couple of good years on it. I won the Formula Five Club production and 1,000cc championships on it, as well as the overall Club championship on points. It was primarily at Cadwell I raced but I had some good results at Darley Moor and took it about quite a bit really. To Mallory and Oulton, but it was a photo in the press from that Cadwell Park win, at the bottom of the Mountain, which got me the sponsorship from Bennetts. Brian Bennett saw that photo, wrote me a letter and said: *"Contact me if you want some sponsorship."* I couldn't wait to rush off to find a phone box, as that's how it was back then, and it was all Triples after that. As they gave me a Rob North three to ride.

By the time of Herzberg's victory Martin Sharpe had also left the ranks of A65 solo racers. As while he'd taken three wins at Wroughton, on June 24th, these had been won on Yamahas. Sharpe was a young racer moving forward - he went on to race in GPs and at Daytona - and he had made the right decision in putting the Devimead A65 to one side. It was eventually sold on to and raced by Gary Allen but as the season progressed it meant it was left largely to the chairs to provide the wins. As exemplified by one taken by one of the nearly men of the A65 racing story, at the final round of Aintree's Waterloo & District Championship.

Final incarnation of the Devimead Daytona-framed A65, as ridden by Gary Allen

246

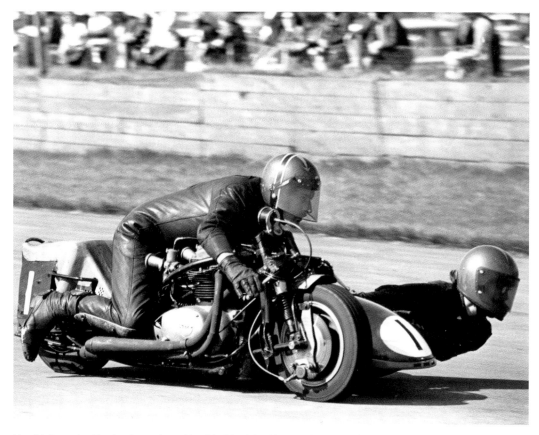

He didn't get the Trophy, but at least Ken Vogl had the Aintree No1. Plate for 1974. His last year of racing. Note the railway sleeper *'run-off'* Like at Crystal Palace, you needed some bottle at Aintree

Ken Vogl: With the Waterloo & District Club the ones to beat were the Hardy brothers, who were then on an Imp, and Dave Kruse. They'd normally be us three at the front. The Hardy's Imp would slowly pull away, but Dave's Weslake, though it was quicker down the back straight, I could lose it round the bends and lead onto the back straight, before he'd come past again. He'd get two lengths clear on the straight so I thought: *"This is no good. I'll have to slow up. Let them past when I want, then tuck in behind"*. This way I'd be 6" behind sort of thing by the end of the straight. There were just three races that year going towards the Aintree Championship and in the first the Hardys were off and won. But on the last lap, after the right-hander, I whipped out and went around Dave's Weslake and beat him for second place. It was much the same at the second meeting.

Coming to the last meeting Chris Vincent had done the engine for me. The first time he'd ever done the top-end, with different bits and bobs of his on it. I didn't know him that well till sort of then, as it was a job to get to know Chris, as it was difficult to get him talking. Oddly, I just think he was very shy. The reason he helped out was that one of my helpers, Fred Connelly, used to supply Chris with the rubbers and 'O' rings he needed. Without them he would have been stuck as Chris used to have to rebuild his URS every race. Anyway, before we started this last meeting Bill Applegate I think it was, another guy with an Imp, was talking to the Hardy brothers saying: *"Mine's quicker than yours"* and all this, so it was clear they were all set for a ding-dong when they got out in front, leaving me battling for 3rd. Then, about the 3rd lap, I saw the Hardys' Imp go straight on - their distributor drive had actually broken - and Applegate's in the field, half way round the next corner. So, I was now in 2nd and passed Dave Kruse again on the last lap as before, after the right-hander. Dave's passenger, Dave Rawlinson, kept looking back at us, but whatever side he was on I'd go the other. It didn't bother me, left or right, provided we were close enough, he'd gotta brake and I'd just be able to carry on. We'd beat them every time on the last corner. And that's what I did to take the win and the Championship, but that's when the Club did the dirty on us. We were ever so disappointed, but it was a bit comical too. Mirabel Topham, who owned the famous horse and Grand Prix car circuit, used to come and present the overall Trophy. A massive silver lion. It was worth thousands this thing. I was reading the regulations actually, and they said: *"The Silver Lion Trophy to be held for 11 months by the riders breaking or equalling or nearest to class record, whichever is the best, by the Mellano Trophy principal."* Which was us. But then, on the night of the presentation there was something going on, we never did find out what, but they came over and said; *"You've won but we want to give it to one of the solo riders!"* It should have gone to us, but there we go. Racing's full of ifs and maybes.

Les Hurst on the sort of outfit which was working its way down to Club runners, as *Birmingham Mafia* members moved on to other machines. The engine was believed to be ex-Pat Sheridan, with the remote points/Daytona cases certainly pointing to something special. Daughters Trudy and Sadie's outfit was undoubtedly a case of parental influence, with Sadie going on to passenger John Childs in British Championship F2 and TT racing

As the season wore on it was ifs and maybes for the twins too, on 12th August at Silverstone. As Bill Crook's 5th place was the best an A65 could do behind a leading trio of Boret (680 König), Vincent (750 URS) and Hardy (Imp), with Vincent and Boret sharing the fastest lap of 97.57mph. Those speeds were really outside of the A65s league and threatened the winners at Oulton Park later in month too, where the headlines read: *"Chairman Wood tops at Oulton scorcher."*

A worried glance from Price to Wood? There was no need at Oulton, though like others they had the misfortune to get their A65 sorted just as the Birmingham twin's star was on the wane

Derek Wood: Yeah, we won the ACU Championship at Oulton Park '73, really at the left-hander, going into Island bend. As it was always a question of line there and I drifted right and Dick Greasley was behind, but closer in. It showed if you could ride them, if you were willing to push them, the A65 was still competitive. Competitive for quite a while, as what we'd done with our outfit was fit twin discs at the front, with one linked to the sidecar wheel and the rear. With a Mini equalising system. So, you never really touched the front brake lever. We must have been one of the very first like that and you could leave your braking really late. But it still got that you couldn't stay with things like the Imps. You couldn't cope with them. I remember we had a really good day at Cadwell Park, but there was a guy there came from Birmingham way, with an Imp. He was the bee's knees in those days, and we pushed him to a 1minute 17second lap record to beat us. But afterwards Tony said that going down Park Straight he was actually pushing Tony's feet, which were hanging over the back, with the nose of his outfit! At the time that Imp was about the quickest one going, but once people started getting all exotic you couldn't afford it anymore. Once you got on to the wide wheels it was 70 quid for a back tyre, and you could ruin that in one race. I know 'cos later we had a TZ and oh God it was expensive. Unbelievable. Every so many miles it was change this. So many miles, change that. Change everything. You had to keep a complete record of all the mileage you did and I just couldn't get on with them. I'd grown up on Gold Stars and then the A65, where all we ever used to do was run it for half the season, strip it, put new shells in, bearings, etc. put it back together again and that would last the whole year. I mean the rev counters you used to use in those days you'd take them up to 7 thousand revs, but you could be doing nearer to 8 the rev counters were so crap! But they'd still hang together as other than one chipped gear tooth and that electrical wire at Mallory Park, that was it in terms of problems over the whole time we ran an A65. They were bullet proof.

In this case it's Roy Hanks attempting to negotiate Dick Greasley's Honda 750 four. The Honda wasn't the ideal power plant but in 1973/4 everyone was looking for the next big thing. It would be the TZ700. But no one knew it yet and until they did the A65 could still give a good account of itself

The TZ hadn't quite arrived in the sidecars in 1973 but that story of increasing speed and increasing expenses played out at the Snetterton International too, on Sunday 26th August. Where George O'Dell's BSA was reported as simply not fast enough to catch the leading Langridge/Evans Imp, irrespective of some stylish riding.

Laurie Evans: Over the winter of 1969/70 Les built a new frame for our Triumph which handled impeccably and we knocked up 14 wins out of 22 starts. In the Race of the South we recorded an identical lap time to Siegfried Schauzu on his Rennsport BMW, which cost about half a red-bricked semi in Brighton in those days, compared to our home-built £300 Triumph. As a result, Ron Gardner approached with a proposition. He had fitted four of his carburetors to a Hillman Imp powered outfit and Les and I were introduced to the development team of Rhombus Imp racing.

O'Dell/Bollidson (2) lead Langridge/Evans (15) at the Race of Aces. But not for long.

It was a handful to start with, having raced an outfit that handled you couldn't describe how badly this thing compared. From the sublime to the ridiculous. Really scary in fact. It needed stabilisers! But the power of the Imp engine was tremendous and we were made an offer there and then to race it. And we agreed. We were young and foolhardy and being part of the Rhombus team we were fully sponsored. We didn't even have to arrange our own race entries. We would be given a schedule of meetings throughout the year, turn up and race and leave the entire spanner tweaking to their two mechanics. We were attracting start money and retained any prize money. 1972 was very much a development year and 1973 didn't start on a good note either. Duckhams announced that they would only provide us with their ordinary mineral oil and consequently we suffered numerous major engine failures during the first part of the season. Eventually they agreed to join us at a National meeting at Cadwell Park during which the engine let go big time. Connecting rods broke and exited through the block, along with the pistons, so they agreed there was a problem! They re-instated our supply of Duckhams R and then at Snetterton we scored that first International win, beating George O'Dell. But '74 we had trouble, the only race we finished was the TT and at the British Grand Prix at Silverstone we were holding a good position and mixing it with the best when *'pop,'* or should I say *'bang'* went the engine. A valve-head had broken off and wrecked the engine and unfortunately, that was a bridge too far. We'd had no end of engine failures and tempers were getting frayed, so we all went our own ways after that as it wouldn't have been worth it to have continued. As the costs got absolutely ridiculous from the early '70s onward.

Sign of the times. The Vincent BSA now in the hands of John Wright-Bailey at the Brands round of the Transatlantic series

In the National championship others were willing to swallow those costs, so while it had been all A65s at the start of the season the results now started to drop off. August Bank holiday O'Dell had a 4th at the Oulton *MCN* Superbike meeting, while Ken Vogl had a 5th at Scarborough. On 16th September Norman Hanks got a 2nd at the Mallory Park Race of the Year, where even Bryan Rust was now out on an Imp. Over the weekend of 23rd/24th Barry Sheene was the star of the show at Cadwell Park, breaking Agostini's lap record on his 500 Suzuki, but a degree of normality prevailed in the sidecars, as Roy

Hanks took the win over brother Norman. Mick Boddice could only finish second in the B race that day, on his new König an engine he reported as completing just two final finishes all season, indicating the costs and work which could be involved in the newer type of engines. The better results continued for the A65s though with a win for O'Dell over Norman Hanks at Lydden on 30th September, before the season's final round.

George O'Dell's A65 in pursuit of Vincent's new URS at the Rothmans Race of the Year

On Saturday October 27th Norman Hanks lead for three laps at Brands Hatch, but first Vincent's URS passed him round Druids, then Gerry Boret in turn went passed Vincent on his König. The race ultimately ended Boret, Hardy, Hanks and the following day everyone stayed over for the Brands Hatch MCN Superbike meeting. This saw two wins for Phil Read and one for Agostini on their MVs, in what was a last hurrah for the Italian fire engines. For the A65 however that hurrah had already come. In the first race the Hanks brothers could make only 5th and 6th and in the second race there wasn't a single BSA in the top six. Chris Vincent won both races on his URS, but behind him it was various combinations of 1,000cc Imps, big bore Weslakes and König two-strokes.

It pretty much summed up the 1973 British national season which had started where 1972 had left off but over just a few months had seen the whole landscape in British racing change. The two-stroke - and largely Yamaha two-stroke - domination of the smaller solo classes had spread all the way up to Unlimited level with the omnipresent '351' twins. While in the chairs, bigger engines, more cylinders and a greater number of gears had finally outstripped the previous advantages of the A65 power unit. Torque and flexibility. The 1973 British Sidecar title went to Gerry Boret and his 680cc, four-cylinder, two-stroke, König.

From this to this. While many A65 racers went on to a variety of machines in the search for *the next big thing* Mac Hobson went straight from his A65 to a TZ700 for 1974. The TZ would become the definitive item as the 1970s wore on, for those with deep enough pockets

Norman Hanks: I won in '72 and was third in '73 but had been mechanic-ing on the BSA works motocross team, for Jeff Smith at the time, and Smithy went to work for Bombardier, who formed Can-Am. By then Can-Am had offered me an engine to do the World Championships, so I started building another outfit to house it. They gave me the drawings for their engine, which was made by Rotax, as Bombardier owned Rotax too. Which was a 6-speed, laid-down, water-cooled, twin cylinder, two-stroke, 500cc, with a disc valve on the top. I thought *"Wow this couldn't be better"*. Essentially half a unit construction Konig. I made a wooden mock up engine and a bike with hub centre steering and wishbone suspension. Everything more modern than we'd been racing so far, nearly slipping into a LCR type. I knew I'd have to have a year off, so '74 I was building the bike, then it was: *"No, it's going to be another year"*. By '76 they still had problems getting it through emissions, then realised to pass in Canada and America it was never going to happen. So, it was: *"No. Big two-strokes are dead."* To start again then it would have been massive. I borrowed Roy's bike, but I'd got straight off a BSA A65 and onto a TZ 700 and was like a flag in the wind. You might as well have had a switch on the handlebar. Because it was either on or off. Nothing in between. And coming from a BSA I couldn't change gear quick enough. I had 3 or 4 meetings with Donnie Williams in the chair and while my head knew what to do the bike was too much for me.

It was a neat summary of what had happened technologically in the space of a couple of seasons and mirrored what had happened on the other side of the pond too. The AMA Grand National Championship road races were dominated by Japanese two strokes, while on the ovals it was all Yamaha and Harley-Davidson XR750 four-stroke twins. Dick Mann was on a Triumph for a 10th place overall and an A65 qualified for just one final all season, in the hands of Teddy Newton. Jim Rice did win the Colombus ½ Mile, but it was achieved on a Harley-Davidson and it would prove to be his last.

Jim Rice: The Harley XR750s were starting to dominate. You basically had to have one of those bikes to compete. It wasn't set in stone, but they got those XRs going so well that I finally had to go and buy one. Though as Dick O'Brien at Harley really supported the factory riders it was pretty hard to be competitive if you weren't one of those guys. And I wasn't really. I was a guy who came off a good run with BSA and was sort of an outsider, trying to fit in, and I retired for a combination of a couple of things. The technology was getting to the point where you really had to have everything perfect and guys were flowing their heads, taking them down to Axtell, getting special engine work done and I thought: *"This is the end of the racing I really love."* Where guys were working on their own bikes, even at the highest level. Can you imagine it was just turning up with all your buddies, it's all basically grass roots, guys are trying out multi-cylinder two-strokes and the AMA were letting them and then it all changed when the XR750s came in. And that took out a lot of the fun.

I remember talking to another racer about this very situation. I'd started out working on my own bike, learning race by race, and there was almost as much satisfaction, if not an equal balance in that, with how you rode. But once it got too technical, when you need someone else to work on your bikes, where was the satisfaction in that?

The A65 was yesterday's news at National level on both sides of the pond but the scene Rice described still existed at Club level, where the virtues of simplicity and robustness ensured the A65 remained a popular choice. 1973 had seen privateer flat trackers, road racers and sidecar racers picking up tried and tested units at a song and a winner on August 5th, still racing today, was typical of that group.

Eddie Wright: Yeah early on at Cadwell Park, it might have been the Skegness Club? Goughy was on the Devimead bike and it was probably my first win. I got started on an outfit I bought off a guy call John Watson, who'd just won the Southern 100 on a BSA A65.

Eddie Wright and Robert Hartell, Hangar Bend, Siloth 1972

He had an old Triumph outfit, so I played round with that for a bit before I bought a Windrick BSA from a chap called Dave Mallon, who lived in Morpeth. And once I got that, with the A65 engine in, that's when I started to go well.

When I was a teenager the Hanks were already well established. Norman and his dad Fred. I used to watch them at Oliver's Mount, as I lived near there, and used to go down to the Mallory Race of the Year too where Vincent was fantastic. My teenage years were spent peering over the fences watching Brown and Vincent, those sorts of people, but they were racing special A65s as most of the people who started with the A65, they all came from the Birmingham area and had factory connections. They could get their hands on things and had the know-how to bore and stroke them, but when these guys moved on to other bikes, their old ones got handed on, so those BSAs came down the line to people like me.

And what you could do was get an A65 out to a ridiculous capacity. Something like 840cc, by stroking it with one of Les Mason's cylinders on it. And as long as you didn't rev the balls off them they'd hang together and pull really, really well. And because they were a unit motor - a lot of the Triumph's used were pre-unit - they were stiff in the chassis, so you got no flexing round the gearbox and transmission. I did OK with them and got mine going reasonably well in the end, but whilst they were a great sidecar engine the drivers pushed them beyond their limits and I was no exception. I remember I was at the Southern 100 and a guy on a Saab called Steve Rowe won the race, but I was in contention to win it until the last couple of laps. When a flywheel bolt broke what with the crank flexing, and it fired straight out through the crankcases! It still kept going, but there was oil mist everywhere, on the tyre and that, so I had to slow down a bit and actually that was it for me, '74. I went to a Weslake, then an Imp, after which it was a TZ Yamaha. But I thought the BSA engine was lovely, for the torque and that, and it was certainly as quick as a Triumph, quicker, and nicer to ride.

It was a ringing endorsement by a racer representative of the sort of privateer who continued to campaign the A65 in British sidecar racing and American flat track in particular. By the end of 1973 wins at National level looked increasingly unlikely but in the A65 story it was always a case of never say never.

Going down fighting - 1974 and beyond

An A65 leading a Honda-4 and Stan Woods Suzuki TR750? Indeed, but only in practice. However, Kevin Fletcher scored a 3rd place in the 1300cc qualifier and flirted with the top ten in the final at the Stars of Darley Moor meeting on 18th July 1976, on what should have been a hopelessly outclassed machine

Poverty and obstinacy explained why some persevered with the A65 as the 1970s progressed. Familiarity, reliability and spares availability also played their part. The 1970s were littered with world beaters which became wallet busters, so many racers kept to their twins until it was clear any trade up really was to *'the next big thing.'*

Alistair Frame: '74 I was on to the *'Appendix Special.'* 830cc. The one which fell off the bench! Les and Dave Mason didn't see eye to eye in the workshop and this engine, which Dave had just built, fell on the floor and cracked. Well Rob Peabody who worked at Devimead, he was a fantastic welder and he stitched it back up. It was scarred all the way from the barrel neck down to the sump. So, it needed a big stitch. But it was a flying machine, it really was. And of course, Les started to get involved then at times and lent me a special head. A head

Frame works on his Métisse in the paddock. Such al fresco arrangements were normal for even the most well-heeled teams

The Devimead stickers came with a degree of official support

done by Al Gunter, a US tuner. As before that, when I'd started out, I was buying my bits of course, though things were so cheap then. Here we are, from my notebook: *"Constant mesh sleeve pinion, chain case gasket, rubber O-rings, seal for back plate behind clutch. £4.85."* That was from Fred Hanks. £5 odd. *"Les Mason. One set of close ratio gears £8.75 plus VAT. 88p. A total of £9.63."* That's crazy ain't it? Fantastic! And by the end of the season I'd had seven wins, won ten trophies and taken some money.

It was around then at Cadwell that I borrowed a mate's bike, as I had a problem with mine for some reason. It was Roger Appleby's, a Yamsel, and it was my first try on a two-stroke. I was so impressed. It was fantastic. My A65 could beat it on the corners, but this thing would have come by on the straight and I thought: *"Right, this is the end. That's it now. It's all over for the BSA"* because I'll always remember the first water cooled Yamaha to come to Cadwell Park round then too. It just cleaned up. Water-cooled. Wow! Everyone was round it, looking at it. And that was the killing really. 'Cos if you had the money, well, you could blitz the opposition. Anyone could with something like that so, 28th September 1975, Mallory, that was my last race on the Métisse. As by then Beebee Brothers Racing had picked me up after a good race at Mallory, where I'd been leading Ian Martin, Guy's dad. It was Malcolm Lucas that put it to Mike Hoskison that he should try me, so I owe Malcolm a lot. As after that I was on the ex-works Rocket Three triples and had a lot of success. 52 race wins and three championships, three years running, which wasn't bad. So the Rickman went on to Mick Ward.

Around the same time as Frame's last A65 ride Dave Abrahams took his own over the water to the Isle of Man for the Manx Grand Prix. To achieve a result which only those accusing him of an over-size engine were aware of.

The ex-Dave Mason, ex-Alistair Frame Rickman Métisse in its final form with Mick Ward. By 1974 British twins such as the A65 were not the competitive machines they had once been but still dominated the paddock

Dave Abrahams with his machine in normal 654cc Production specification

Dave Abrahams: The first time I took it over I had an ex-Chris Vincent top-end on it from Dave Ashton. But of course I wasn't thinking about it too much when I put it on and the balance factor was all wrong. The vibration was out of this world really and in practice I stopped at Ginger Hall thinking I had a puncture the handling was that bad. When I had a closer look the only thing holding the front and back wheels together was the top tube. I couldn't believe it. All the other frame tubes had snapped through it was so badly out of balance. The alternator exploded too. The magnets actually migrated out and seized in the rotor. I had a hell of a job getting that apart, but the Lucas bloke gave me a racing version, with the welded in magnets and I finished OK both years. I was told I was the fastest BSA there, I could have been the only BSA there, but someone actually complained that I was racing a 650, not a 500 and they said they wanted the scrutineers to strip it and measure it. But the scrutineers said they weren't bothered, if it had won the race, perhaps.

Dave Abrahams at the Manx Grand Prix, 1975. His race speed of 87.14mph was the fastest ever achieved by a genuine A50 round the Isle of Man circuit

By 1975 Abrahams was competing against Yamaha 350 and Suzuki 500 two-strokes in the Manx Senior, but the protest came in as he was first British twin home, with his average race speed of 87.14mph being the fastest ever recorded by an A50 round the Isle of Man. It was actually the second fastest time recorded by any 500 BSA round the Mountain course and only bettered by Clive Brown's 87.79mph on the ex-works B50 in 1973, when he came 4th in the Production TT. The speed was helped no doubt by the cylinder head, which came through the hands of an A65 racer who had even better results in 1975.

Dave Ashton: When I bought that 500 head off Chris Vincent he said: *"Whatever you do don't mess around with it. Cos that head is one on its own. We tried and tried but we just couldn't get the same figures off any other head."* It seems it was just luck of the draw and Graham Sanders said the same with the 650cc cylinder head on the production racer. The head produced a step in power. It had such a step that you could hear it, you still can now, and Graham said that they tried to replicate that head exactly too, but they never could. It was staggering. I was on that A65 1974 and it was all A65s in 1975 too. My sponsor wanted to buy me a TZ750 and I said, stupidly: *"Don't do that. It's a lot of money and we might not like it. Buy something that we know."* So bought Ray Knight's production Trident, to go with my open class Trident I had at the time, but it was a disaster. The Trident only did one race or so, before it broke the crank, and you were up against it by then in the production class, as it was all Kawasaki 900s and Laverdas by '75.

At Darley Moor on 20th July 1975, Ron Haslam won the big 'Stars' title on the Pharaoh TZ750 Yamaha but a gaggle of top machinery lined up for the production race too. They included at least one Laverda Jota and several Kawasaki Z900s but Dave Ashton's A65 took the victory, with Pete Bennett (No 73) best of the Kawasakis, in 3rd

Dave Ashton towards the end of the season, 28th September 1975. 4th place in production race was good enough to take the Darley Moor title. The last time by a BSA A65

Dave Ashton still had wins at Snetterton, Cadwell, the now forgotten Longridge and Silverstone that season. But again, it was at Darley Moor - the A65's banker circuit – where he scored its best results. Ashton had five race wins among ten top four placings, to take the A65's final title. The Darley Moor Production Bike Championship, 1975. Ashton was no mean rider – he had a Manx Grand Prix victory and second place, while taking over John Newbold's TZ750 ride when Newbold got works RG500 Suzukis - but the ex-Graham Sanders machine was no mean performer either. Even if it still suffered from most of the A65s long standing shortcomings.

> **Dave Ashton:** Best thing to happen to an A65 was when plastic gasket came out 'cos you could fasten all the wires on, so they didn't fall off. They'd vibrate so much they'd crack the frames. I remember going round Cadwell Park I think it was when the back end started going all over the place, as the swinging arm spindle was coming out. The end plate on it had broken off due to vibration, so I just kicked it back in. With the sidecars, with more tubing, the small wheels and less suspension, that probably damped it all down, but those engines on the solos vibrated. And the braking was a bit of an issue too. You had to do a bit of planning with it! But it worked and I had some right good rides. I remember Roger Winterburn came up one time on that Laverda, as it was some sort of championship round, and he rocked up with all the tables and chairs outside, the brolly girls and the big van and that. As Roger Winterburn was winning everything up and down the country in production racing back then.

(Left) Leading 1974 champion Norman Overend and (right) un-faired at Silverstone. He still took a win there in 1975 with his machine a match for any other, at a circuit known for speed

Anyway, about the fourth or fifth lap we were coming down in to Paddock Corner and he thought he'd look round, as he was so well ahead. Well he thought he was. 'Cos he had to look around again and lost his brake, as I guess he was a bit surprised that this old BSA was up his backside? Fortunately, he wasn't hurt, but it was good to beat that lot as that bike was still as fast as anything. At Silverstone it was just as fast as Mick Hemming's 920cc Commando, a fantastic engine, but by '76 I'd only ride the production bike as a sort of fill in ride, as I'd bought a Suzuki by then and it was all Japanese stuff after that.

As such those wins and that 1975 title could have been the bike's parting shot. Similar machines were also starting to be put under the dust covers, as newer types took over. The machine finishing fourth in the 1300cc event the same day Ashton wrapped up the Darley Moor Championship being a case in point.

Kevin Fletcher: My brother Mick started with an Eddie Dow TLS back plate on it, then put a 220 or 230mm Fontana on and it just progressed bit by bit after that. I picked up a TD Yam brake for it, but then you could run a disc, so I went to that too. I never missed a race when Mick ran it and the very first day I raced it we'd had the barrel off with a problem. So we had to put the 650 kit back on it instead of the Devimead

Fletcher at speed. The proximity of parked cars, posts and other trackside furniture were accepted and part and parcel of racing in the 1970s

261

stuff. Anyway, I didn't quite make the A final, but led the bloody B right until the last straight when a T150 came past me. At the time it had straight tubes under the seat, with all the ignition under, and the oil tank in the back of the tank, as I altered the frame, so it was a bit more like the Daytona bikes. It had the Devimead stickers as we had all their bits and pieces off them, everyone did, the end-feed conversion, the line contact rockers and that. I remember I got knocked off while lying second one time and had some cracking rides, but I don't think I ever got a win on that bike? As it was Dave Ashton winning everything in the production bikes back then and we went to TZs in the Open class by the end. It was a shame about that, but I went to a Z1 in the Proddy bikes and a TZ in the other classes as you needed to, to keep competitive by then.

Kevin Fletcher 10th October 1976, followed by a Métisse and a Kawasaki triple

It was similar for Malcolm Stanley, but while he too toyed with many other machines his A65 was wheeled out even later than Fletcher's after benefiting from the same sort of period improvements and updates on a disc-braked, but still production legal, machine.

Malcolm Stanley: 'Start of '72 I was 16 and couldn't even drive, so my first meeting I rode there and took a mate on the back. I had to wait until I passed my test in May before I could get an old van and drive myself. I was very green, not knowing much about it, but had started as an apprentice mechanic at the time, so was soaking it all up and everything was cross referenced to the bike. The bike had high level pipes and short A10 silencers with their ends cut off. You used to weld a circular plate back in the end, with holes in it, no baffles, then put it all back together again. There used to be a thing called Metalloid filler and you'd smear that over the weld, then spray it black, so when they put a broom handle up the silencer, to see it had baffles or not for production racing it would just hit this metal plate and they'd think it did!

Mine was an original Spitfire MkII and the brake when it was set up right by Ferodo, with AM4 linings, it worked really well. My friend Andy Cooper he'd got a Triumph Bonneville with the TLS at the time and I could easily brake with him, with the 190mm. While Les Mason did the porting on my head. He said; *"You only want it out to 30mm, as while you might lose a little bit of speed you'll have that bit more torque."* So, I had the standard 1¾" Devimead carb-spacers, but I had 32mm Amal MkIs, so I just tapered the carb-spacers down from 32mm down to 30mm to match. And while Andy had a new Morgo 750 kit on his Triumph we both ended up at the same meeting and my 650 with this Les Mason head, with the reverse rockers and that, it actually matched his increase in speed.

On the (legally) disc-braked A65. July 1977. By August Stanley was out on a Suzuki GT750 *'Kettle'*. Typical period accessories include Bill Cooper end-feed conversion visible below the rev-counter drive and hair visible below the Kangol helmet. **Malcolm Stanley:** Usual long hair trailing!! Would be black flagged for it these days!

Stanley tried a Rickman A65 too, but like others found it too rigid and lacking feedback after a standard A65

1975 I had a TD3 Yamaha, but I couldn't get on with it. At Mallory the front end would go, then the back and I lost confidence. I preferred a big Production bike anyway and eventually got the *'Production'* bike up to 840cc. I got the A70 crank out of Bill Cooper's sidecar outfit, but I'd got used to reving it to 7,200 and with the 840 kit it was more like 6,500. There was more torque but there was more vibration too and I just didn't get on with it. But I was racing against Andy Cooper still at the time and Andy had been loaned a Z900 and I overtook him down the straight. It was the first time racing I'd ever heard the crowd cheering and it was great, as to match a machine like that on top speed was tremendous even if later on, desperate to keep in front, it lost power down the straight as it had blown a hole in the wall of the cylinder!

But the interesting thing was that after 1973 BSA-Triumph approved a disc brake for production racing. The production rules meant you could use parts which were six years newer or six years older than your bike which also meant my '66 bike could have the later forks. So, after a bad crash when I went over the bars breaking an arm, I went down to Bermondsey in London and got this thing with a bracket round the fork leg to hold the calliper in place and a heavy cast iron disc, from Pagehiln. And once I put those later type forks in it was just so much easier. When I used to go through the Gooseneck at Cadwell a quick direction change, at the speeds I was going, it was a real problem. But once I changed the front end it was like a different bike. So, I kept the A65 even as I went through other production bikes - an R90 BMW, a Guzzi, H1 Kawasaki, GT750 – and I ended up racing it again in 1979/80. They had a twins and triples race at Donington, which was quite unusual at the time, and as I'd got rid of the 840 I put a 650 engine in, from a Firebird I had as a temporary measure. Wileman's had their ex-works Trident there and I beat it and the best thing was I was only going to the meeting to pick up points on my big proddy bike, the GS1000 or 900 Honda, I can't remember which? I came 5th I think on the A65 that day and have kept the bike ever since.

These were typical *'last wave of the flag'* stories from the solo racers as the 1970s rolled towards the '80s. But with the outfits the wheels continued to roll. In the British Sidecar title chase Roy Hanks was the last to seriously stick it out on an A65 however, as by 1974 even George O'Dell, a late convert, had come to the end of the road:

George O'Dell: Some people were beginning to talk about two strokes. I was among those who laughed at the idea of seeing them race successfully. As well as regarding them as not being good enough I hated them for the noise they made as much as anything. It just showed how wrong you can be. The end was in sight for the Beezer. I was used to having good results in 1972 and 1973 and I realised there was no point in having a wasteful year as I did in 1971. I had started to feel I was beginning to do a good job and to get noticed. There were three choices open to me: Spend a lot of money on a two-stroke I was not enthusiastic about and doubted my mechanical ability to look after, buy a Hillman Imp outfit, which also seemed a bit involved, or get a Weslake. All I bought it turned out was a load of rubbish. But I think being involved in such a bad deal proved to be a turning point in my attitude toward racing and those involved. I wasn't going to be so green in future. There was so much vibration it made your hands tingle. That was just in the pits. I may have been no great engineer at the time but that rattling and shaking just wasn't expected. Weslake engineer Bill Currie was in the paddock and he explained it was the normal behaviour of the 700cc Weslake. It was unbearable to ride. I was so depressed I thought I would like to get my BSA back. I was in a desperate position. There was certainly no future for me with the Weslake.[42]

There wasn't, he would soon be on a König then Yamaha and off to the World Championship,. But for many the TT was still the ultimate barometer and the BSAs could still spring a few surprises. In 1974 while Mac Hobson arrived on one of the impossibly exotic TZ Yamahas, over a third of the finishers in the 750cc sidecar class were A65 mounted. With Bill Crook's 6th place on a 500 and 5th place on a 750 overshadowed only by John Barker's 4th in the bigger class. How good were those results? Well Crook was just 25 seconds and two places behind Mac Hobsons TZ500. The Yamahas were the coming breed however. Hobson would win on one in 1976 and Dick Greasley and Roger Dutton were also aboard them by 1975. By which time an increase in maximum sidecar capacity allowed machines up to 1000cc. Ex-BSA employee and future TT winner Nigel Rollason was still able to manage 10th though, a result he was to repeat in 1976. Both times there were König and TZ750/700s in his wake but subsequently the push to get more power out of the BSA in 1977 and '78 proved too much for the ageing twin.

By the mid-1970s anyone racing an A65 was pushing it the limit to try to match the performance of newer rival machines.

Passenger Alan Joyce pleads innocence while his driver and brother Mick looks on, seemingly unimpressed after a shunt at Croft.

By the mid-1970s a major appeal of the BSA twins in sidecar racing was the abundance and availability of affordable spares and the user-friendliness of the engine unit. Anyone with a modicum of mechanical knowledge could carryout all the work required to keep an A65 running which was not always the case with other machines

Sign of the times. Rollason and Pete Shiner alongside George O'Dell and Alan Gosling's hub-centred steered Renwich König at Mallory Park in 1975. By the mid-1970s the conventional A65 outfit was beginning to look antiquated, but was still capable of front row qualifications. And just look at the crowds

Nigel Rollason: For that Les Mason supported me and we built a couple of very special engines. The biggest baddest engines ever built. The barrels looked like an A65 or A70 but they were cast extra high, so they didn't need a head gasket. We just had cast iron onto aluminium, that was it. So, you could never blow a head gasket. We also had two oil returns out of the engine, so it never wet sump-ed, which gave at least another 5hp. With these 860s we had over 90 brake horse power, through a 3 bearing crankshaft, and a 3 bearing gearbox main-shaft. Where the alternator goes we had a solid block and outrigger bearing and the crankshaft was located from the outrigger, not from the timing side. With shims it meant the primary chain stayed absolutely in line all the time so primary chains gave no problems at all. The engines still used to eat sleeve gears though.

With sleeve gear pinions we pretty much put a fresh one in every meeting. Just used to eat 'em. But me and Mick Coomber lapped at over 93 mph with one of these engines, but I blew up each engine on the last lap, of each race, darn it!

1977, Nigel Rollason and Mick Coomber on the Island. Like many of his generation competing on the Isle of Man was everything for Nigel Rollason, who remains only one of two people to have won there on both two and three wheels

Having won the Manx GP in 1971 and the F.I.M. Coupe d'Endurance in 1972, with Clive Brown on the Mead and Tomkinson BSA B50, he then decided to take up sidecar racing. Logically, as an ex-BSA employee, on an A65

Rollason was subsequently off to experiment with a British Barton two-stroke, which he eventually took to TT victory in 1986, but as ever, this was not the end of the story for the racing A65. No longer a top line National level machine BSA twins continued to score wins in the hands of up and coming stars of the future, serving their apprenticeships on third or fourth-hand machines.

Around the same time that O'Dell and Greasley moved on from their BSAs - O'Dell to win the Sidecar World Championship in 1977 and Greasley to take second place in 1979 - 1980 World Champion Jock Taylor started a flirtation with an ex-Mac Hobson Windrick (Terry Windle/John Crick) chassis powered by an A65 engine bought by passenger Lewis Ward. The purchase involved a train journey from Scotland to London, then car journey to Newmarket, which saw Taylor riding Alex Harper's A70 outfit round a housing estate for testing. Then stripping the engine and exhausts out for £230, to transfer via the train's guard's van back to Scotland. So equipped, they came second first time out at Silloth, after which the victories started to mount.

Mixing long-stroke 750cc and short-stroke 650cc units, depending on the circuit, a string of successes convinced Taylor to invest in a more modern engine. A move which was made easier since a major blow up of his A65 on the last day of the season, at East Fortune, rendered his BSA little more than scrap. It was in truth the fate of many a BSA outfit at the time, when hard pressed engines were passed on to heavy handed newcomers. Another to learn his craft with an A65 was the 2002 World Champion whose first ever race was at Cadwell Park, on 6th March 1977 and resulted in a 5th place.

Steve Abbott. I was 21 and just dipping my toe in the water. This BSA came up in Nottingham, a 750 Devimead in pieces, with a Bill Cooper chassis. So, I put the engine back together and we went racing, me and Sean Smith. At that time there were no real racing engines you could get hold of, or which were affordable anyway, so it was the best thing you could have. People used them instead of Triumphs as they were a stronger engine. A nice strong unit construction engine, which was better than the Weslake and other stuff around and ours was one of the last, though very reliable. There were a lot of people with Imps and some with Königs. Stewart Pearson had a Yamaha TZ and I don't know if we were riding well or what, but we sure got among them. The A65 wasn't at all bad, but in truth pretty soon we were outriding it.

As a result it was sold in 1978 to Mick Hollingsworth, in Abbott's search for a machine which could win at National level. In the UK the A65 was now a stepping-stone machine for younger competitors on their way up, or those looking for a cheap way of entry into the sport. There was no serious chance of another National win, which was ironic. As that was what A65 was just about to deliver on the other side of the Atlantic.

Rogues gallery: Many stars of the 1970s and 1980s started out their careers on an A65. From top to bottom drivers Jock Taylor, Terry Haslam, Steve Abbott and in the chair Roger Marshal. Though Marshal too piloted a chair before going on to a hugely successful solo career

The Jorgys Motorcycle's A65 airborne at the Houston Astrodome. Harley-Davidson and Yamaha tried to contest it but in TT events the British twins continued to be competitive long after retirement age. Through a combination of power, engine flexibility and weight . Celebrations begin (below) with long time Camel Promo girl Lynn Griffis

The last big one

Following the demise of the BSA factory team in 1972 the A65/70 disappeared rapidly from the American AMA series. While still run by myriad Amateurs Randy Skiver's 3rd at the Castle Rock TT was the only time one appeared on the leader board subsequently. That was until a youngster called Alex Jorgensen matched that placing, both at Houston and Ascot in 1977. To prove it was no fluke while Harley and Yamaha won 25 of the 28 events which made up the title schedule in 1978 Jorgensen ground out one last win for BSA, at the Ascot TT on 15th July. It was a great send off, but two years later it came close to being so much better.

Taking on Kenny Roberts

On February 8th 1980 a huge crowd was on hand at the iconic Houston Astrodome to see returning hero and two times World 500cc Champion Kenny Roberts on his Yamaha try to put it over Harley-Davidson's three times AMA champion Jay Springsteen. Jorgensen was known by now as a bit of a West Coast TT specialist, with real form at Ascot in particular, but no one expected an antique, home built BSA, to feature. Particularly as it was a huge field in which half the entrants didn't even get through to the heats. Bruce Hanlon's works Yamaha won the first heat and Scott Pearson won the second from which reigning AMA No.1 plate man Steve Eklund couldn't even qualify. As expected, Roberts and Springsteen won the other two heats and as the tapes went up the solitary BSA which had made the final wasn't expected to get in the way of the favourites. It didn't. Since it left them in its wake. Incredibly Jorgensen got the hole-shot and led Roberts and Springsteen through the turns and over the jumps, with the rest of the pack in pursuit. Springsteen was the first to falter, dropping the Harley in an attempt to keep up and as such it was a head to head between Kenny Roberts and Jorgensen as the end of the race approached. There were fans in both camps and the *Cycle World* report caught the facts and sentiments of the day to perfection:

"..........to mixed expressions of despair and delight Roberts passed Jorgensen for the lead and the win, which KR celebrated with the traditional wheelie to the flag. .... As they lined up for the trophies and prizes, Jorgy's crew noticed something. The righthand carb hose on the BSA was broken and the carb was dangling. Did it lose power? "Well, Yeah" Jorgy said. But he wasn't going to offer any excuses, not even in the press box later. Everyone went home winners. The crowd saw great racing. Roberts returned to the USA in convincing style. Jorgensen and BSA gave heart to the traditionalists."[43]

Alex Jorgensen: Yeah, that year at the Houston Astrodome when I ended up second, I had a good lead and what happened, the last lap when I went over the jump, I hit really hard and the manifold split. The carburetor manifold split and the carburetor fell off. I was able to limp it around you know, for second place, but I came so close to winning, even with that carb dangling! My dad built that bike, a 750. Remember the BSA Hornet? That's what it was originally but I was running one of a kind, a Cycle Factory frame, which came from Sacramento California, as while they had built some for Triumphs I think I was the only one with one built for a BSA.

Without a front brake for flat track racing. Jorgensen moved onto a Norton on the ovals but kept to his A65 for TT events, in which it's engine characteristics excelled

He was and whichever way you looked at it, it was a sensational result. Jorgenson held off Bruce Hanlon on a second Yamaha in 3rd, a remounted Jay Spingsteen on the fire-breathing Harley in 4th and some kid called Freddie Spencer on the works Honda in 5th. An A65 beat Freddie Spencer? Yes, that's right and all a good decade after the A65 had peaked as a serious piece of competition machinery. It was also a privately entered machine in a period when, as pointed out by Jim Rice, factory support was pretty much mandatory.

Alex Jorgensen: Back in the day my dad was always a Triumph guy but there was a dealership that sold Triumph around the corner, so we became BSA dealer instead. That was the big reason we started with the BSA as the bike was my dad's deal really. I helped him with it at the shop, but he was the builder. You remember Al Gunter, the racer and tuner? He did the head on that BSA, the porting, but everything else my dad did himself. 'Cors, he had good rods and things like that. Hi-Vo clutch and things in the motor, but it was always a battery ignition it ran and that's why if you ever see any pictures there's a box kind of behind the motor, below the swinging arm. Down really low, to keep the weight down low and we never had a problem with that.

Ascot again with a different incarnation of the A65, which was campaigned for pretty much a decade

I tried high pipes with megaphones on it too. I gave that a try on the little bit faster tracks. I don't know if it helped me that much but I did that as it used to bend those low-level TT pipes. Smashed those TT pipes quite a bit over the jumps, so we always had a wedge, so we could open them back up! We got a couple of seconds, had the win at Ascot and results at Castle Rock too. It was tough, a challenge, but that was what was really neat still about the dirt track racing that we did. I mean we could build bikes in our garage and compete against the best in the world and never once did I think I couldn't win. It was a really special time and it was the same as for all us privateers. You didn't have a pay cheque, you were just lucky enough to have a once in a while win, for the prize money. But the BSA it was a good motorcycle. It really worked good and you know one year at the Astrodome, I tried to run one gear the whole race. Just second gear and run it around the whole track. I gave that a go - I didn't do it all night long. Only in practice and the heat race - but like that all I had to do was gas it and stop, gas it and stop! A great bike and we were just so lucky to be the last in history to win on a BSA.

Jorgensen was, at National level on a solo, with 13 years between his win and Tony Smith's first at Brands Hatch on 21st March 1965. In the sidecars however a remarkable 22 years spanned the period between Chris Vincent's first victory on 22nd March 1964 and the A65s last win in 'modern' racing in 1986. The win being taken by a pair of Scotts, who like Jorgensen, created headaches for the Yamahas.

A front exit A65 among the rear exit TZs. A 6" front wheel and extended sidecar platform kept the BSA competitive well into the 1980s .It made the Hogg BSA ineligible for the Classic Racing, but they weren't interested in that

Billy Hogg: It was impressive when we saw Mac Hobson at Silloth. The solos were processional, but the sidecars were explosive, so we got an A65 and that was the year when both us and Jock Taylor were on BSAs. Though I was always thinking of his: *"How is that still going?"* As we were just trying to keep ours in crankshafts back then.

Gordon Hogg: It wasn't a good bike at all but it was a chap Rod Vardy who convinced us to stick with the BSA. We were watching one time and suddenly appeared this bike without a fairing or anything, making this incredible noise. It was really spine tingling and it was a BSA in the lead of all these Yamahas and what have you and I thought: *"A BSA can do that?"* Later in the year his engine came up for sale, it was a lot of money, but a two-year old Windle chassis came up at the same time in Barnsley, so it was the perfect marriage and that was the start of it really.

We put good tyres on when everyone else was sticking with Mini Green Spots, and we got Terry Windle to do a new front-end, so we had 6" wheels all round, and extend the sidecar 4" wider, which was the modern style. It was 840cc, then eventually 900cc and actually a Peter Brown bottom-end I was told when I bought it. It had an A70 crank and was certainly a well sorted bike. The crank eventually broke though so we got another, that broke, so we went to A10s. Tuftrided A10s were pretty good but they broke too, so we got a Weslake crank and got that and machined it to fit, the journals ground down and that. But when that broke too we wrote to Dave Nourish and asked him to beef it up on the drive side. He did that and that was a great engine.

No1 plate at Cadwell. Sleek and well presented, only the open face helmet and front exit chassis gave away the fact that something more dated might lurk underneath

As neat an outfit as you would see on track in the 1980s

It was and delivered results not just in the twins and F2 categories, but open events too. 1982 saw them win the Hepolite twin-cylinder four-stroke championship, while in 1983 they won the Formula 5 twins class and were 2nd in the open class too. Which was a result they replicated in 1985. And if that 1985 result doesn't sound too impressive they were beaten only by the four-cylinder, two-stroke, Armstrong/Barton Phoenix 750 of Paul Hansen, sporting an engine identical to that of Nigel Rollason's, which won the TT the following year, averaging over 103mph, for over 100 miles.

Billy Hogg: If you told people today they wouldn't believe you. It was the same once I remember at Cadwell. The twin cylinders were started behind the multis. They let the multi cylinders go so the F2 twins wouldn't get in the way. Well, we went right through them all, but we got a tiny wee Trophy while the second-place man got a huge big trophy, as that was the premier class! But the Formula 5 Club used to give us free entries and pay our petrol money. They were good to us - considering they were Barnsley based and it was during the miner's strike – but it was a gorgeous thing the Windle BSA as there wasn't another twin-cylinder which was even close to it by the end.

Gordon Hogg: We were the last. The last fast one anyway and probably the last front exit machine of any sort in modern racing. But then the barrels started breaking and of course Devimead were phasing out and SRM hadn't opened up, so we couldn't get the spares. The last one we had to just bore out A65 barrels to take T140 pistons, but it was too slow like that and we decided it was time to give up. F2 was going to the fours, as Mick Boddice and Honda I think pushed for the 600 four-strokes and that's what sidecars all is now. But F2 when it first started it was hugely popular, before it was all subsumed by the 600s and 1987 the *'Worms'* were coming in too. The LCRs. That was the end of sidecar racing as far as I was concerned. So, 1986 was the last year we won an open class race on an A65. The engine was never stripped down after its last race and it's probably all clogged up with Castrol R now, but it's still there, as you never think at the time: *"That's the last time it'll ever race."*

Passenger Billy and driver Gordon Hogg on a rare excursion to Lancashire's Three Sisters circuit

Becoming a *'Classic'*

It was exactly that sentiment which saw Classic Racing start six years previously in the UK, when dust covers were taken off dormant machines nationwide. A wealth of primarily

1980. Malcolm Stanley on the disc-braked A65, racing in a modern production race. The fact was that by 1980 - care of the CRMC – his machine was now eligible for a completely different category, since the A65 was now officially a *'Classic'*

British machinery lay redundant and as a result the birth of the Classic Racing Motorcycle Club (CRMC) saw a trickle of interest rapidly grow into a torrent. The CRMC had 540 members by the time of its first meeting, on August 17th 1980, even as Mick Stanley and the Hogg brothers were still competing in modern events. As before A65s were numerous in the sidecars, less so as solos. But achieved the same disproportionate success rate as in their heyday, with two competitors from the 1960s really standing out.

Tony Price at Mallory Park's Devil's Elbow. 1986, in beautifully raucous, pre-silencer days

Tony Price: I went onto my solo '83. I put a BSA engine in the Featherbed because I knew the engines and knew they were strong, from my sidecar racing days. I thought: *"We'll have a go"* and the bike just got better and better.

I used to go to TMS in Nottingham, as they had lots of heads on the shelf, to pick the best. As the valve inserts were hardly ever in the middle of the casting, hardly ever in line with the valve guide centre. Getting a good one I could then get the largest inlet valves in, which were out of a BSA B50. The original A65 type valve was more tulip shaped, while the B50 was a penny-on-a-stick type. Now whether BSA got it wrong or not I don't know, but the B50 valve really worked. I used to only have my seats about 1mm wide, and used to get as much compression as I could, as it was all about that really. I think I got about 11.5:1 and I was always on ordinary petrol, no additives. I also avoided breaking through on the inlet tract, where the springs sat as usually happens, as I used to make my inlet ports oval in that area, but it still worked. It worked bloody well actually, and I used to

1989. Snetterton. The CRMC Race of The Year. Leading the Triples of top guns Steve Veasey (257) Trevor Osbourne (258) and Phil Davenport (157). In many ways the 1980s were like the 60s all over again. Lots of Triumphs, a lone A65

spend a lot of time on the crank balance too. I started with a factor at about 68%, ran it and it was: *"Oh no. 'Vibrating about 7K. That's no good."* So, 'balanced it at 69 then 70, 71, 72, etc. And it took hours stripping engines down and rebuilding. I took it to about 74% and then it was dead smooth at about seven thousand revs, but the trouble was at about 5½ it was bad. So, I think I ended up at around 72% as that was pretty good (his notes say 72.2%!).

Showing quadruple World Champion Hugh Anderson a clean set of heels at Snetterton in 1988. **Tony Price:** I remember at Corams he cut me off. The Beezer didn't quite have the go out of the Bomb Hole, so he came up the inside of me. I thought *"I'm not having that"* so went on and beat him

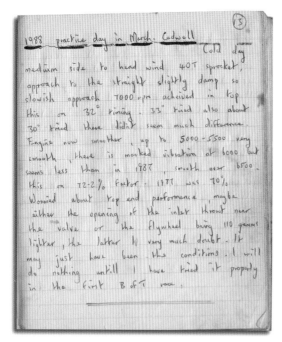

Practice at Cadwell Park in 1985 along with the accompanying notes. As was the case for A65 solo racers in preceding decades there we no off the peg parts nor tuning notes available, so Price relied on meticulous and exhaustive trial and error testing

It was still a very torquey engine though and I used to run mine in top quite a lot. Every year I replaced the crank, rods, proper pistons, valves, etc. I replaced quite a lot, but back then you could buy a brand-new crank for not a lot of money, which you couldn't do now of course. I never dyno-ed it, but there were loads who couldn't believe the power and claimed it was a big engine. But it was only ever 734cc. I just got it right. I got the valves right and I got the ignition right as I was always testing the ignition: *"36°? No, not quite right. 37°? May be. 38°? That's about right."* And that was what I ran it at.

I won the CRMC championship, the Fair Spares 750 championship. The Norman Hyde I think I nearly won that but not quite? But I won quite a few and I was right quick round Mallory, Snetterton on a good day too I was doing about 140mph on the long straight. Which is bloody good, as it was always naked my bike. No fairing.

At Snetterton when I was up against the triples I could easily move with the 750s and I had lots of races with the 8-valve Triumphs too. I had lots of dices with Alan Bennallick's. His engine was the equal to mine up to sort of 90-95mph but once you reached 100mph, I went on. That was the big advantage with the BSA engine, it just ran on. He'd be *"What is in that bloody engine of yours"* and Mick Hemmings used to moan about me with a big engine. It wasn't and when someone did formally complain, at Snetterton – as no one could believe the speed of it – it got measured on the stroke and of course it was dead standard. But those triples they were spending thousands on them and like in the sidecars in the early '70s the engines people were using just got bigger and bigger. Those triples were 900cc and above by the end and while I could easily live with them on the corners, once I got on to the straights it was hopeless. It was bloody fast for a twin though.

For anyone who saw it in action, that was an understatement and the same went for the engines powering the sidecars of two of those early 70s racers. Stuart Digby and Pete Krukowski exemplified the type of competitor who charged as hard as they had a decade earlier, with Krukowski in particular dominating the early days of Classic Racing with an engine under constant development.

> **Pete Krukowski:** I tried various combinations of valve size but eventually decided that the standard valves were perfectly OK, even in the final big 894cc engine fitted with a Norton Commando crank and Devimead barrel. Technically using a Norton crank in an A65 is not a good thing - as the bore centres on a Commando are closer together than those on an A65 – but the engine didn't seem to mind and there was no need to use more than 6,000rpm, as it generated tremendous bottom end power. All the bearings were standard and I never tried needle rollers in the timing gears and camshaft. When the clutch and gearbox had a little attention they never needed it again and none of the engine failures I suffered between 1968-74 and 1982-89 were as a result of original BSA parts. The A65 was very reliable, even when using the plain timing side bearing and none of my engines had a crankshaft bearing failure on them.

Reliable and fast the machines of Price and Krukowski were incredibly dominant with the 1986 CRMC season being a case in point. Neither Price nor Krukowski were ever out of the top three in any race they finished, with Krukowski taking 16 wins alone, though not running a full season. They weren't unbeatable, but it was close and interestingly around the

Polish Eagle on display, Krukowski and McGahan on their all conquering jumbo A65

same time a shark toothed A65 outfit appeared piloted by Steve McFarlane. Which was good news for BSA runners all round. This outfit wrapped its tubing around an A65 engine reputed to rev to 9,000rpm and McFarlane saw the opportunity in Devimead's winding down – they were by this point a major Honda dealer - to secure a deal in 1987 to buy up the BSA side of the business. SRM (Steve Ronald McFarlane) engineering was born, offering their own end-feed conversions and rapidly expanded into a comprehensive spares service.

These may not have benefited Price, as he withdrew gracefully from Classic Racing as engines grew in size, but perhaps they did Frank Hodgson, who similarly couldn't quite retire. A local speedway rider had offered to resurrect his defunct machine and when Hodgson had expressed the opinion he wasn't racing it to its maximum had been challenged to do better. Which he promptly did, winning the Forgotten Era Championships in 1991 and 1992 before broken ribs saw the bike laid up again.

As in their heyday, the real stumbling block to greater success in Classic Racing was simply the paucity of solo A65/ 50s in the paddock. They were as thin on the ground in the States as the UK, but as with Tony Price and Frank Hodgson around the British circuits, the Americans had a standard bearer for the twins too, this time the smaller A50.

Frank Hodgson: The Kushitani leathers I got from GP racer Alan Carter. I had a cobblers shop and he was always coming in for things. One time he'd run in saying: *"I've got a sponsor coming up. Can you put their name of me arms?"* or what not. He needed something fast and I said: *"I can't do it"*. I was busy, but he said: *"What do you want?"* So, I said: *"Give us some leathers."* So, he did. Two hours work for the equivalent of £1000. That's not bad

Bill Lindsay negotiating Loudon's Turn 6 in 1986. The frame at this point was a Trackmaster

Bill Lindsay: 'Interesting that you mentioned Tony Price. I corresponded with him for many years back in the day. He sold me a Devimead 750 kit which I used on the 180 degree works engine that I road raced in the ED256 frame for a couple of years in the early '90s. I ran it in the 750 class. It also had a 4-plug head. A very interesting engine. But for me it all started at Bryar Motorsport Park, which was an hour and half from my home in Boston. I would spend weekends at the race track and eventually, I prepared an A50 Wasp, placed third in my first race and was bitten. I was the only guy racing a BSA twin in the East at the time. A few guys in the Midwest and West Coast were racing A65s but I was the only one on an A50 and in 1984 I acquired Don Vesco's 1966 ex-factory racer. It seems it was passed around between racers on the West Coast, but I picked up the rolling chassis from Jim Hunter's shop in California.

In 1985 I was actually campaigning a modified T3 Moto Guzzi in the AMA Battle of the Twins. I raced in the lightweight modified class, which was open to 750cc OHC twins and up to 1000cc push-rod twin production bikes. A lot of bikes qualified for this class and I had crashed my T3 the weekend before at Pocono trying to win practice - not the greatest move! - so, I said: *"Well, I have my BSA A50. It's a twin and qualifies for the class. Why not?"* As we gridded up for the race I realised I was on the smallest and oldest bike in the field. *"This does not look good. I may finish last?"* Bryar Motorsport Park at the time was a 1.6-mile circuit, with 10 turns, and elevation changes. Speed is not a big factor, it was my home track and knew it well. So, as the flag dropped I got a decent start, in the top ten, and proceeded to pick away at the field, one by one, using the BSA's handling and my track knowledge. On the penultimate lap I got by a Guzzi LeMans, using my cornering speed to pass him on the outside of Carousel turn 6 and lead the entire field to the flag. I just put my race face on and went for it. The last BSA twin to win an AMA race.

I raced that bike for 16 years and was lucky enough to place third at Daytona in the 1994 vintage races. It proved to be very potent and was clocked at 135mph at Pocono International Speedway coming off the banking. A triple killer as well, as at one of our tighter circuits I bumped up a class to get some more track time. My mate, Frank Smith pointed to a Triumph T150 racer and class champion Jessie Morris and said: *"You want to get in front of that guy."* But I got the hole shot and never looked back. We had a great duel. On the banking he would go high and I would stay low. I knew my bike was 100lbs lighter than his, so coming off the banking into the 1st turn I would wait for him to brake, then I would after. This continued for 15-laps and he was never able to overtake me. After the race Jessie wouldn't talk to me and insisted there was no way my bike was a 500!

Capacity issues ultimately killed off A65/50 solos in much of classic racing as a plethora of changing rules, dates and wallets, saw the very principles established to resurrect classic machines altered to undermine them. In the sidecars the situation has been similar with bigger engines and smaller wheels recreating the factors which ended the golden age of drift. Irrespective, as this book goes to print in July 2021 Shaun Motson and Lizzie Quinlan have just taken their first CRMC class win of the season, so the A65s racing story goes on.

Mid-Ohio 1993, and Bill Lindsay back racing the machine with the ex-works frame. ED256, the machine originally earmarked for Dan Haaby way back in 1966

Epitaph

The A65 and A50 twins will never be remembered as great racing machines. In the United States their reign at the top was too brief. While their domination of British sidecar racing, while complete, is now too distant a memory in a class which no longer comands the same mass appeal it ounce did.

The mystery remains however as to why an engine which proved so dominant in British sidecar racing and American flat track was never picked up on with greater enthusiasm as a solo racer on the track. As highlighted, those which were campaigned scored prodigiously, particularly given the weight of opposition they were up against. The reason probably lies with the fact that the road machines never had the same cachet as their contemporaries, while the parent company had a long standing ambivalence towards road racing. Had BSA built on the early, high profile wins of Hailwood and Cooper the story could have been very different, but unfortunately they did not. It remains the case however that there hasn't been a season since 1962 when at A65 hasn't competed somewhere around the globe, pretty often winning. Which isn't bad for an engine never designed for competition from a company which famously didn't go racing.

References

[1] Page 5 - The 2nd part of unpublished Roland Pike autobiography.

[2] Page 6 - The 2nd part of unpublished Roland Pike autobiography.

[3] Page 16 - *Motor Cycle News*. 23rd September 1964

[4] Page 18 - *Motor Cycle News*. 10th February 1965

[5] Page 18 - BSA Dispatch records (C/O VMCC)

[6] Page 23 - *Motor Cycle News*. 19th May 1965

[7] Page 25 - *Motor Cycle News*. 28th April 1965

[8] Page 25 - *Motor Cycle News*. 21st July 1965

[9] Page 28 - *Motor Cyclist Illustrated*. Alan Peck interview notes, March 1970

[10] Page 37 - *Motor Cycle News*. 23rd February 1966

[11] Page 49 - *Motor Cycling*. 20th August 1966

[12] Page 50 - *Motor Cycle News*. 2nd November 1966

[13] Page 52 - *Motor Cyclist Illustrated*. April 1967

[14] Page 55 - *Sidecar Championship*: George O'Dell. Hamlyn ISBN 0 600 38304 0

[15] Page 59 - *Motor Cyclist Illustrated*. Ray Knight PR Notes April 1967

[16] Page 62 - *Motorcycle*, P574. 4th May 1967

[17] Page 63 - *Cycle Racing* - Annual Review 1967

[18] Page 72 - *Motor Cycle News*. 9th August 1967

[19] Page 75 - *Motor Cycle News*. 22nd November 1967

[20] Page 75 - *Motor Cycle News*. 22nd November 1967

[21] Page 75 - *Motor Cycle News*. 13th December 1967

[22] Page 86 - *Motor Cycle News*. 13th March 1968

[23] Page 95 - *The Complete Grand National Championship* Volume I: Greg Pearson. Page 538

[24] Page 96 - *Motor Cycle News*. 28th August 1968

[25] Page 107 - *Motor Cycle*. 5th March 1969

[26] Page 108 - *Motor Cycling*. April 1969

[27] Page 108 - *Motor Cycle News*. 7th May 1969

[28] Page 118 - *Motor Cycle News*. 9th July 1969

[29] Page 120 - *Motor Cycle*. 30th July 1969

[30] Page 133 - *Motor Cycle News*. 4th March 1970

[31] Page 141 - *Motor Cycle News*. 22nd April 1970

[32] Page 146 - *Motor Cycle News*. 12th August 1970

[33] Page 147 - *Motor Cycle News*. 2nd September 1970

[34] Page 148 - *Motor Cycle News*. 2nd September 1970

[35] Page 159 - *Motor Cyclist Illustrated*. August 1970

[36] Page 174 - *Motor Cycle News*. 2nd June 1971

[37] Page 175 - *Motor Cycle*. 9th June 1971

[38] Page 209 - *Cycle World*. June 1976

[39] Page 219 - *Cycle News*. August 1972

[40] Page 223 - *Sidecar Championship*: George O'Dell. Hamlyn ISBN 0 600 38304 0

[41] Page 233 - *Motor Cycle News*. 18th October 1972

[42] Page 265 - *Sidecar Championship*: George O'Dell. Hamlyn ISBN 0 600 38304 0

[43] Page 270 - *Cycle World*. January 1980. Page 167

Index